J. Fred Weston

University of California, Los Angeles

Eugene F. Brigham

University of Florida

Study Guide for Essentials of Managerial Finance and Managerial Finance

THE DRYDEN PRESS
Hinsdale, Illinois

Preface

While the purpose and general nature of this revised edition of the *Study Guide* are unchanged from the third edition, our experience in using the earlier versions has enabled us to make important improvements. Since this book is designed mainly as an aid to students, we class-tested both the third *Study Guide* and the manuscript for this edition extensively, asking students for advice on how to make it most helpful to them. This trial-by-fire process has helped us improve the organization and coverage of the material. In addition, this fourth edition of the *Study Guide* incorporates new developments in financial market theory that increase our understanding of financial decision-making.

Managerial Finance and *Essentials of Managerial Finance* are decision-oriented textbooks. Their contents reflect the present-day emphasis on decisions affecting the value of the firm. This approach has been found to be more useful than a descriptive or institutional approach. The main purpose of this *Study Guide* is to focus on the central ideas that provide the conceptual framework of *Managerial Finance* and *Essentials of Managerial Finance*. The *Study Guide* seeks to carry out this objective by providing two kinds of assistance.

First, an outline of the subject matter of each topic is set forth. This presents the material in a stream-lined perspective. The outline should be examined prior to reading the chapter to obtain an overview of the material contained in the chapter, then also should be used later for review purposes. After having studied the chapter, the student can go over the outline, recalling relatively quickly the major points that were covered.

The second major feature of the *Study Guide* is the set of problems and solutions it provides. Many instructors emphasize the problems found at the end of each chapter. Ideally, the students should be able to work the problems without an exorbitant expenditure of time, and the majority of the class should be able to reach a correct solution. This reduces the necessity of devoting much classroom time to the mechanics of the problem and permits more time for discussing the basic ideas the problem illustrates. If the student spends too much time reaching the solution, then he has an insufficient amount of time left to think through the principles the problem is designed to illustrate. If a substantial number of students are unable to reach the correct solution, then the instructor must devote an inordinate amount of time to explaining the mechanics of the problem.

We have attempted to forestall these pitfalls by providing a sample set of problems and solutions in the *Study Guide*. The end-of-chapter problems give examples of most of the important points covered in the text. The problems and solutions provided in the *Study Guide* illustrate most of the end-of-chapter problems. Therefore, if a student conscientiously works through the *Study Guide* problems, he should be able to complete most of the assigned end-of-chapter problems without difficulty.

In summary, this *Study Guide* is designed to enable the student to use his time more effectively and to get more from a finance course. The subject outline can be used to show what to look for in a chapter, as well as to facilitate study when reviewing for examinations. The problems and solutions can be used to help the student understand the mechanics of the various arithmetic operations as well as the analytics involved. He can refer to the solutions to check his own work, and he can look over the solution when he is unable to solve an assigned problem relatively quickly. This enables him to determine the correct approach without an excessive amount of "spinning his wheels." He then has time to reflect on the general methodology presented for arriving at solutions to the key decision-areas of managerial finance. Hence the *Study Guide* can serve as a useful supplement for use with other books and reading materials for the study of finance. This edition of the *Study Guide* is therefore relatively more self-contained than its predecessors, including a complete set of financial tables in the Appendix to facilitate verification of the problem-solutions set forth.

Basically, our aim has been to provide an outline of the subject matter of *Managerial Finance* oriented to decision-making. The problems and their solutions seek to demonstrate how the analytic tools and concepts can be used to make financial decisions. Thus the *Study Guide* can serve as a useful learning instrument.

January 1977

J. Fred Weston
Los Angeles, California

Eugene F. Brigham
Gainesville, Florida

Contents

Introduction

Part One

Introduction: The Scope and Nature of Managerial Finance

THEME

This chapter is concerned with a general overview of financial management as it is presented in this book.

I. The *role of finance* within the firm has shifted through time.
   A. Prior to the 1950s finance emphasized *obtaining* funds.
   B. In the early 1950s emphasis shifted to *use* of funds, with a focus on flows of funds and the internal management of the firm.
   C. By the early 1960s the scope of finance was extended to policies and decisions which affect the *value* of the firm. The valuation of the business enterprise is determined largely by two factors:
      1. Its expected stream of future earnings.
      2. The riskiness of this earnings stream.
II. These shifting emphases in the study of finance can be attributed to major developments in the world economies and in the internal operations of business firms.
   A. These developments include the following:
      1. Rise of large-scale business units.
      2. Extensive product and market diversification.
      3. Growth of research and development expenditures.
      4. Increased emphasis on growth of the economy.
      5. Social awareness.
      6. Narrowing profit margins and intense competition.
      7. Continued inflation.

        8. Accelerated progress in transportation and communication.

    B. Some impacts of these developments on the firm include:

        1. Large-scale, decentralized operations have become commonplace.

        2. The development of new techniques of financial management is taking place.

        3. Firms need to finance a high rate of growth.

        4. International operations have expanded.

        5. Planning and control are becoming increasingly important.

           a. Overall and departmental profit goals are established.

           b. Results are measured against standards.

           c. Action is taken as a result of feedback information.

        6. There is greater use of computer-assisted managerial decision-making.

        7. More use is made of formal quantitative models in financial analysis and decisions, including linear programming, game theory, and simulation.

        8. Firms are faced with a worldwide financial capital shortage and high costs of funds.

III. Orientation of finance textbooks.

    A. They emphasize four major approaches to the financial manager's functions.

        1. Financial analysis, planning, and control.

        2. Management of working capital.

        3. Long-term *investment* decisions.

        4. Long-term *financial* decisions.

    B. *Insider versus outsider view.* The internal view receives primary emphasis because of the managerial orientation of this book.

    C. *Small firm versus large firm.* Principles of managerial finance are generally applicable to both small and large firms. Some of the factual and institutional materials may differ, and the nature of the problems may differ in degree, but not in their fundamentals.

IV. The place of finance in the organization.

    A. Usually the financial manager occupies a top-level position for these reasons:

        1. The planning, analysis, and control operations for which he is responsible are of critical importance to the firm.

        2. Many financial decisions affect the survival of the firm.

        3. Significant economies may be realized through centralization of financial operations.

V. Managerial finance and related disciplines.

    A. Accounting is primarily data gathering, while finance is concerned with data analysis.

    B. Financial management deals with data and people.

        1. Quantitative analysis enables the financial manager to use data meaningfully.

        2. Behavioral science facilitates the financial manager's relations with people.

        C. Business finance is an aspect of the economic theory of the firm.

VI.   Organization of *Essentials of Managerial Finance* and *Managerial Finance.*

      A. These books deal with five closely connected areas:

        1. Financial analysis, planning, and control.

        2. Working capital management.

        3. Long-term investment decisions.

        4. Long-term financing.

        5. Valuation and financial structure.

The Tax Environment

2

THEME

Government plays an increasingly important role in business and economic life. One of the significant areas of impact is taxation. Since most business decisions are influenced by tax factors, this chapter provides a summary of the basic elements of our tax structure and shows how they relate to financial decisions.

I. *Fiscal policy* involves altering the level and composition of government receipts and expenditures to influence the level of economic activity. Three principal methods of changing tax receipts are employed presently.
    A. *Changing tax rates.*
       1. An *increase* in tax rates reduces personal disposable incomes and corporate after-tax profits. This, in turn, (a) reduces each individual's purchasing power and demand for goods, (b) lowers the profitability of new investments, and (c) reduces funds available for investment.
       2. A *decrease* in tax rates has the opposite effect, stimulating economic expansion.
       3. Tax rates change infrequently because Congress is reluctant to take such action.
    B. *Accelerated depreciation.*
       1. Depreciation charges are deductible for federal income tax purposes.
       2. If a more rapid or accelerated depreciation is allowed for tax purposes, tax payments are lower and business is encouraged.
          a. Accelerated depreciation increases corporate cash flows making more funds available for investment.
          b. Faster cash flows increase the rate of return on investments.

       3. Depreciation methods are determined by the Congress.

          a. In 1954 two accelerated depreciation methods were permitted.

            1) Sum-of-years-digits method.

            2) Double declining balance method.

          b. In 1962 and 1970, the depreciable lives of assets for tax purposes were reduced.

      C. *Investment tax credit.*

          1. Under the investment tax credit program, business firms could deduct, as a credit against their income tax bills, a specified percentage of the dollar amount of new investment in certain categories of assets.

II.   The corporate income tax structure has wide implications for business planning.

      A. For 1975, the normal tax rate is 20 percent on the first $25,000 of taxable income and 22 percent on the next $25,000. There is a 26 percent surtax on amounts over $50,000.

          1. Hence there may be some limited tax benefits of separating companies into two or more separate corporations to hold the income of each below $50,000.

          2. This indeed has been a practice of some firms in the past.

          3. The Tax Reform Act of 1969 limited the tax savings from this practice.

      B. Corporate capital gains and losses affect the decision as to whether a firm should incorporate.

          1. Capital gains and losses are profits and losses on the sale of capital assets —those assets, such as security investments, which are not bought and sold in the ordinary course of business. These receive special tax treatments under certain circumstances.

          2. Real and depreciable property used in the business is not defined as a capital asset. However, profits made on the disposal of such property may be treated as capital gains, while losses are fully deductible from ordinary income.

          3. An asset must be held at least six months to produce a long-term gain. While net short-term gains are taxed at regular corporate income tax rates, net long-term capital gains are subject to a maximum tax of 30 percent.

      C. Treatment of depreciable assets affects investment decisions.

          1. The book value of an asset is defined as the original purchase price of the asset less the accumulated depreciation taken.

          2. Sale of a depreciable asset for more than its book value may result in either a capital gain or an ordinary gain for tax purposes.

            a. That part of the gain which is less than or equal to the depreciation taken is taxed as ordinary income (recapture of depreciation).

            b. Any gain over the accumulated depreciation is taxed as a capital gain.

          3. If the sale of a depreciable asset results in a net loss (if the cost less depreciation incurred is greater than the sale price), the net loss can be deducted in full from ordinary income.

D. A net capital loss on nondepreciable assets is not deductible from ordinary income, but may be carried back three years, then forward for five years, and used to offset capital gains for that period.

E. To avoid multiple taxation of corporate income, 85 percent of dividends received by one corporation from another is exempt from taxation.

F. While *interest payments* by a corporation *are* a deductible expense to the firm, *dividends* paid by a corporation *are not* deductible by the firm.

G. Firms must estimate their taxable income and pay taxes quarterly.

H. Net operating income carry-back and carry-forward aids corporations whose income fluctuates widely by permitting income averaging of a sort.
   1. Losses may be carried back three years, then forward for five years in offsetting profits for the period.
   2. Adjustments begin with carry-back to the earliest year.

I. If a corporation retains earnings to avoid paying dividends which would be subject to personal income taxes, these retained earnings are subject to penalty rates under the *improperly accumulated income* section of the Internal Revenue Code.

III. Personal income taxes have an important effect on business decisions.

A. More than 80 percent of all firms in the U.S. are organized as individual proprietorships or as partnerships, not as corporations; the income of these firms is taxed as personal income to the owners or partners.

B. The personal income tax rate structure is lower than the corporate tax rate at lower incomes, but at higher incomes the corporate rate is lower. This influences business decisions as to whether to be taxed as corporations or as proprietorships or partnerships.
   1. Personal income tax rates for both individuals and married persons filing jointly are progressive.
   2. Personal income tax rates start at 14 percent of taxable income and rise to a maximum of either 50 percent for earned income or 70 percent for other sources; corporate income tax rates range from 20 percent to 48 percent.
   3. See Table 2-1 for the schedule of returns for individuals and Table 2-2 for joint returns.

C. Individual capital gains and losses, like those of corporations, are separated as to short term and long term by the six-month holding period.
   1. Net short-term gains are taxed at regular rates.
   2. Net long-term gains of up to $50,000 are taxed at the lower rate of 25 percent or the ordinary rate on one-half the net long-term gains. One half of all capital gains over $50,000 are taxed as ordinary income.
   3. One half of an individual's net long-term capital losses and the full amount for short-term capital losses in any year may be deducted from ordinary income up to a limit of $1,000 a year. Excess amounts of capital losses may be carried forward indefinitely until used up.

D. The first $1,000 of dividend income received by an individual stockholder

Table 2-1 Individual Income Tax Table, 1975 Table 2-2 Table for Joint Returns, 1975

Taxable Income (A)	Regular Tax on Amount in (A) (B)	Amount of Taxable Income in Excess of (A) but not in Excess of (C) is taxed at rate shown in (D)		Taxable Income (A)	Regular Tax on Amount in (A) (B)	Amount of Taxable Income in Excess of (A) but not in Excess of (C) is taxed at rate shown in (D)	
		(C)	(D)			(C)	(D)
$ 0	$ 0	$ 500	14%	$ 0	$ 0	$ 1,000	14%
500	70	1,000	15%	1,000	140	2,000	15%
1,000	145	1,500	16%	2,000	290	3,000	16%
1,500	225	2,000	17%	3,000	450	4,000	17%
2,000	310	4,000	19%	4,000	620	8,000	19%
4,000	690	6,000	21%	8,000	1,380	12,000	22%
6,000	1,110	8,000	24%	12,000	2,260	16,000	25%
8,000	1,590	10,000	25%	16,000	3,260	20,000	28%
10,000	2,090	12,000	27%	20,000	4,380	24,000	32%
12,000	2,630	14,000	29%	24,000	5,660	28,000	36%
14,000	3,210	16,000	31%	28,000	7,100	32,000	39%
16,000	3,830	18,000	34%	32,000	8,660	36,000	42%
18,000	4,510	20,000	36%	36,000	10,340	40,000	45%
20,000	5,230	22,000	38%	40,000	12,140	44,000	48%
22,000	5,990	26,000	40%	44,000	14,060	52,000	50%
26,000	7,590	32,000	45%	52,000	18,060	64,000	53%
32,000	10,290	38,000	50%	64,000	24,420	76,000	55%
38,000	13,290	44,000	55%	76,000	31,020	88,000	58%
44,000	16,590	50,000	60%	88,000	37,980	100,000	60%
50,000	20,190	60,000	62%	100,000	45,180	120,000	62%
60,000	26,390	70,000	64%	120,000	57,580	140,000	64%
70,000	32,790	80,000	66%	140,000	70,380	160,000	66%
80,000	39,390	90,000	68%	160,000	83,580	180,000	68%
90,000	46,190	100,000	69%	180,000	97,180	200,000	69%
100,000	53,090	———	70%	200,000	110,980	———	70%

is excluded from taxable income. The exclusion is $200 if the stock is jointly owned by a married couple.

E. A $750 deduction is allowed for the taxpayer and each of his dependents. This is doubled on the taxpayer who is over 65 years old or is blind.† There is, in addition, a $30 deduction allowed on the tax due for each personal exemption for 1975.

F. Certain other items are also tax deductible if the taxpayer chooses to itemize such deductions. The alternative is to take the standard deduction computed as the lower of $2,000 or 15 percent of gross taxable income.

PROBLEMS

2-1. The Long Corporation has taxable income of $75,000 in 1975.
    a. What is the tax bill?
    b. What is the marginal tax rate?

†While the deduction of $30 for each personal exemption from the tentative amount of taxes owed is for 1975 only, we have incorporated it in the discussion because of the possibility that it will be continued beyond 1975.

Solution:

a. 20% x $25,000 = $ 5,000
   22% x   25,000 =   5,500
   48% x   25,000 = 12,000

   $75,000 $22,500

b. The marginal tax rate is 48 percent.

2-2. The Alexander Corporation has income (before interest, dividends, and taxes) of $200,000 in 1975. Interest expense is $10,000 and preferred dividend payments are $30,000. What is the tax bill?

Solution:

Operating income	$200,000
Less: Interest expense	−10,000
Taxable income	$190,000

Tax payable
$ 25,000 x 20% = $ 5,000
   25,000 x 22% =   5,500
  140,000 x 48% = 67,200
$190,000 $77,700

2-3. In 1975, the Brown Corporation has ordinary income of $150,000 and receives in addition corporate dividend income of $50,000. What is the tax bill?

Solution:

Dividend income	$ 50,000
Less: dividend exclusion:	
.85 x $50,000	42,500
Taxable dividends	7,500
Plus: ordinary income	150,000
Total taxable income	$157,500

Tax payable
$ 25,000 x 20% = $ 5,000
   25,000 x 22% =   5,500
  107,500 x 48% = 51,600
$157,500 $62,100

2-4. A corporation had a $27,500 tax bill this year. What were its taxable earnings?

Solution:

Step 1:	Total tax bill		$27,500
	Less: 20% of first $25,000 =	$ 5,000	
	22% of next $25,000 =	5,500	10,500
	48% of earnings in excess of $50,000		$17,000
Step 2:	Taxable income at 48% = $17,000/0.48 =		$35,417
	20% = 5,000/0.20 =		25,000
	22% = 5,500/0.22 =		25,000
			$85,417

2.5 A mirror manufacturer had ordinary income of $150,000 this year. During the year, the firm sold off capital assets (acquired three months earlier) for a net capital gain of $100,000. Other capital assets (acquired two years earlier) were sold off to net a gain of $200,000. What is the firm's tax bill?

Solution:

Ordinary income $150,000:	$ 25,000 x 20% = $ 5,000
	$ 25,000 x 22% = 5,500
	$100,000 x 48% = 48,000
	$ 58,600
Short-term capital gain:	$100,000 x 48% = $ 48,000
Long-term capital gain:	$200,000 x 30% = $ 60,000
	Tax bill $166,500

2-6. George Foster is a single man without dependents whose 1975 earned income was $15,000. His deductions for 1975 total $3,400. This includes a deduction of $750 for his personal exemption. Determine his taxable income for the year and his tax bill.

Solution:

a. $15,000 gross income
   −3,400 deductions
   $11,600 taxable income

b. Tax bill: Use Table 2-1, single individuals.

Tax on first $10,000	$2,090
+Tax on additional $1,600 @ 27%	432
Tax due	$2,522
−$30 tax credit for 1975	30
Tax bill	$2,492

2-7. Tom Copeland has ordinary income of $80,000 after deductions and long-term capital gains of $15,000. If his average tax rate is 35 percent on the $80,000 and his marginal tax rate is 45 percent, his lowest possible tax will be _____.

Solution:

Option 1 (ordinary tax rate on one-half capital gain)

$80,000 (.035)	=	$28,000
½ ($15,000) (0.45)	=	+3,375
		$31,375

Option 2 (25 percent rate on entire capital gain)

$80,000 (0.35)	=	$28,000
15,000 (0.25)	=	+3,750
		$31,750

Note: Option 1 is always preferable to option 2 if the individual is in a marginal tax bracket less than 50 percent.

2-8. Joe Carter is a married man with two children. His gross income for 1975 is $13,500, which includes $4,450 of corporate dividends received by his wife. He takes the standard deduction. What is his taxable income for the year, a and what is his tax bill?

Solution:

a. $13,500 gross income
   −100 dividend exclusion on wife's stock
   $13,400

b. $13,400
   −2,000 standard deduction (the lesser of $2,000 or 15% of $13,400)
   $11,400

c. $11,400
   −3,000 four exemptions at $750 each
   $ 8,400 taxable income

d. Tax:†
Tax on $8,000	$1,380.00
Tax on additional income:	
(22% of $400)	$ 88.00
Tax due	$1,468.00
—Four $30 tax credit	120.00
Tax bill	$1,348.00

2-9. The taxable income of Elly Corporation, formed in 1970, is as follows (losses in parentheses).

1972	$(450,000)
1973	200,000
1974	325,000
1975	350,000
1976	(200,000)

What is Elly's tax payment each year after carry-forwards and carry-backs are accounted for?

Solution:

					Tax on				Tax refund resulting from carry-back
Year	Income	Carry-forward	Carry-back	Income before tax	Up to $25,000 (20%)	$25,000 to $50,000 (22%)	Over $50,000 (48%)	Total tax	
1972	$(450,000)								
1973	200,000	450,000							
1974	325,000	250,000		75,000	5,000	5,500	12,000	22,500	
1975	350,000			350,000	5,000	5,500	144,000	154,500	
1976	(200,000)		(200,000)						82,500†

†Calculation of 1976 tax refund:
$75,000 carried back to 1974 for refund of entire $22,500 taxes paid
$125,000 carry-back to 1975 for refund of $60,000 ($125,000 x 0.48)
  $22,500
  +60,000
  $82,500 total tax refund.

2-10. This year Company A expects taxable income of $300,000. Company B forecasts a $60,000 loss for the year. If the two firms merge before the end of the year, how much will be generated in tax savings?

†See Table 2-2, joint returns.

Solution:

a. Separately:

	Company A	Company B
Taxable income	$300,000	$(60,000)
Tax payable:		
$ 25,000 @ 20% =	5,000	
$ 25,000 @ 22% =	5,500	
$250;000 @ 48% =	120,000	
Tax bill	$130,500	— 0 —

b. Merged:

Taxable income of A company	$300,000
Taxable income of B company	(60,000)
New taxable income	$240,000

$ 25,000 @ 20% =	$ 5,000
$ 25,000 @ 22% =	$ 5,500
$190,000 @ 48% =	91,200
Tax bill	$101,700

c.

Separate tax bill	$130,500
Less: Merged tax bill	−101,700
Tax saving due to merger	$ 28,800

Financial Analysis, Planning, and Control

Part Two

Ratio Analysis

3

THEME

Ratio analysis is basic to understanding and evaluating the results of business operations. It provides a framework on which the financial manager can plan his future financial requirements. Because ratio analysis employs financial data taken from the firm's balance sheet and income statement, these reports and their interrelation must be mastered to fully understand the significance of the various financial ratios.

I. The basic financial statements include:
   A. The *balance sheet*, which shows the firm's financial position at a point in time.
   B. The *income statement*, which reports on operations during a period of time.
   C. The *statement of retained earnings*, which shows the amount of profits that are reinvested in the business.
   D. It is important to recognize the following points:
      1. The balance sheet item "retained earnings" represents funds reinvested in the business down through the years.
      2. Retained earnings *are not* typically held as cash, and they are not generally "available" for anything. They have already been invested in physical assets.

II. Financial ratios may be classified into four fundamental types:
   A. *Liquidity ratios* measure the firm's ability to meet its maturing short-term obligations.
      1. The *current ratio* (current assets divided by current liabilities) is a generally accepted measure of short-term solvency.

      a. Current assets include cash, marketable securities, accounts receivable, and inventories.

      b. Current liabilities consist of accounts payable, short-term notes payable, current maturities of long-term debt, accrued income taxes, and other accrued expenses.

  2. The *quick ratio*, or acid test, is calculated by deducting inventories from current assets and dividing the remainder by current liabilities. This ratio measures short-term solvency, but removes inventories from the calculation because inventories are the least liquid of a firm's current assets and their liquidation frequently results in losses.

B. *Leverage ratios* measure the extent to which the firm has been financed by debt. Creditors look to the equity to provide a margin of safety, but by raising funds through debt, owners gain the benefits of maintaining control of the firm with a limited investment. If a firm earns more on borrowed funds than it pays in interest, the return to the owners is magnified.

  1. The *debt-to-total-assets ratio* measures the percentage of total funds that have been provided by creditors.

      a. The lower the ratio, the greater the protection against creditors' losses in the event of liquidation.

      b. Owners may seek high leverage either to magnify earnings or because raising new equity means giving up some degree of control.

  2. The *times-interest-earned ratio* (net income before interest and taxes divided by interest charges) measures the extent to which earnings can decline without resultant financial embarrassment to the firm because of inability to meet annual interest costs.

  3. *Fixed charge coverage* (net income available for fixed charges) generalizes the preceding ratio by adding fixed charges such as long-term lease payments to interest payments for calculating the fixed obligations of the company.

C. *Activity ratios* measure how effectively a firm is using its resources.

  1. *Inventory turnover* (sales or costs of goods sold divided by average inventory) measures the efficiency of inventory utilization.

      a. A high inventory turnover demonstrates that a company does not hold excessive stocks of inventory.

      b. The average figure should be adjusted if the firm's business is highly seasonal or if there has been a strong upward or downward sales trend during the year.

  2. The *average collection period* (receivables divided by sales per day) is compared to the terms on which the firm sells its goods. This measures efficiency in collection of accounts receivable.

      a. Sales per day equals annual sales divided by 360 days.

      b. The average collection period should be supplemented with the aging schedule. This groups accounts receivable according to how long they have been outstanding.

3. *Fixed asset turnover* (sales divided by fixed assets) measures the turnover of capital assets or the efficiency of fixed assets; a low ratio indicates idle capacity of assets.

4. *Total assets turnover* (sales divided by total assets) measures the overall utilization of assets. A low ratio indicates that the company is not generating a sufficient volume of business for the size of its asset investment.

D. *Profitability ratios* measure management's overall effectiveness as shown by the returns generated on sales and investment.

1. *The profit margin* (net profit after taxes divided by sales) gives the profit per dollar of sales. A profit margin somewhat below the industry average indicates that the firm's sales prices are relatively low or that its costs are relatively high, or both.

2. *Net profit to total assets* measures the return on the firm's total investment, or the ROI as it is frequently called.

   a. Sometimes interest costs are added to net profits after taxes to form the numerator of the ratio because assets are financed by both stockholders and creditors.

   b. A low ratio can result from a low profit margin on sales, or from a low turnover of total assets, or both.

3. The *net-profit-after-taxes-to-net-worth* ratio indicates the rate of return on the stockholders' investment.

III. *Trend analysis* involves computing the ratios of a particular firm for several years and comparing the ratios over time to see whether the firm is improving or deteriorating. *Comparative analysis* is comparing the key ratios of the firm with those of other similar firms in the industry, or with an industry average.

IV. The *du Pont system of financial analysis* reveals the manner in which activity ratios and profit margins on sales interact to determine the profitability of assets.

A. The modified du Pont control chart pictured in Figure 3-1 encompasses many factors. The chart illustrates, among other things, that profits and return on investment depend upon control of costs and investment. If costs are too high, profit margins on sales fall. If investment is not controlled, the turnover (sales to net operating assets) declines.

B. Profit planning depends to a great extent upon control of costs and turnover of investment.

1. Cost control requires detailed study of the operations of the individual business firm.

2. The importance of turnover for determining return on total investment is shown by the following relationship.

$$\frac{sales}{investment} \times \frac{profit}{sales} = ROI$$

3. The turnover concept can be extended to show how leverage affects the return on net worth. This is shown by the relationships in Table 3-1.

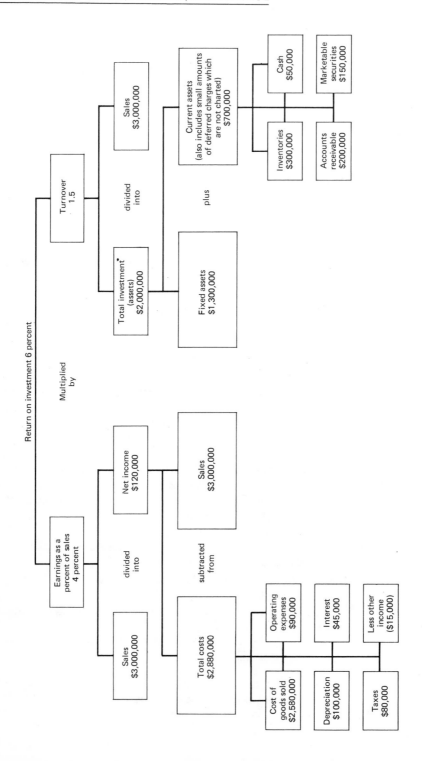

Figure 3-1. Modified du Pont System of Financial Control

Table 3—1   Turnover, profit margins, and returns on net worth, 1974

	Sales to total assets	x	Profit to sales	÷	Net worth to total assets	=	Profit to net worth
1. All manufacturing firms	1.40		5.45%		53.1%		14.4%
2. $10m—$25m	1.84		3.6%		51.7%		12.7%
3. $100m—$250m	1.48		4.2%		49.3%		12.5%
4. Dow Chemical	0.97		11.3%		38.6%		28.3%
5. Alcoa	0.85		6.4%		48.4%		11.2%
6. Clark Equipment	1.36		3.7%		38.1%		13.1%
7. International Harvester	1.49		2.50%		41.0%		9.1%
8. Safeway	5.49		0.97%		46.5%		11.4%

Note that the smaller firms ($10 million to $25 million in total assets) have a somewhat lower profit-to-sales ratio than do the larger firms ($100 million to $250 million), but with a higher sales to total asset turnover achieve a higher return on net worth, despite somewhat lower leverage. Safeway because of a much higher turnover and somewhat greater leverage achieved a higher return on net worth than Alcoa despite a return on sales of less than 1 percent compared with Alcoa's return on sales of 6.4 percent.

Source: Federal Trade Commission, Quarterly Financial Reports for 1974 and Moody's Industrials, 1975.

    C. There are critical checkpoints in the du Pont system.
        1. The system is applied to divisions, products, or other profit centers.
        2. Profit center performance is used to allocate additional resources. Naturally, resources are funneled into the profit centers that are contributing the highest return on investment.
        3. The use of the du Pont system for control purposes is discussed in more detail in Chapter 6 in *Essentials of Managerial Finance*.
    D. The du Pont system can be extended to include leverage.
        1. The following formula shows how financial leverage can be used to increase the rate of return on net worth.

$$\text{Percentage return on net worth} = \frac{\text{(turnover) times (profit margin on sales)}}{\text{percent of assets financed by net worth}}$$

        2. Limitations to the use of leverage are twofold:
            a. Creditors refuse to supply funds when high leverage ratios are reached.
            b. High leverage ratios increase the risk of bankruptcy to the firm.
V.   Financial ratios are useful in credit analysis.
    A. It may be necessary to calculate many ratios or only a few to provide a picture of the state of the firm.
    B. Among the qualitative factors considered by the credit manager are the economic position of the customer firm and its managerial qualities, as well as his own firm's profit margin.

C. Abbreviated analysis is used in credit decisions involving a large number of customers per day.
1. The current ratio is calculated to determine the degree of pressing burdens of short-term debt.
2. The total debt-to-assets ratio is calculated to determine the extent of debt financing.
3. Inadequate equity often results in a current ratio that is too low.
4. Excessive debt usually results in slow payments.
5. The decision to grant credit to a marginal credit risk rests heavily on whether the profitability ratio is high enough to bring the customer to a current payment position in the foreseeable future.

VI. Financial ratios are useful in security analysis.
A. The principal emphasis is on the long-run profit potential of the firm.
B. The focus is, therefore, on activity and profitability ratios.

PROBLEMS

3-1. The financial statements of the Sundown Company for 1975, 1976, and 1977 follow. The norms of the financial ratios given below for the household appliance industry are from Dun & Bradstreet.
   a. Fill in the blanks to show Sundown's financial ratios.
   b. What management problems are reflected in these financial data during each of the following years: 1975? 1976? 1977?

The Sundown Company—Comparative Balance Sheets for Years 1975-1977

Assets	1975	1976	1977
Cash	$ 5,000	$ 4,000	$10,000
Receivables, net	25,000	15,000	15,000
Inventories	22,000	34,000	25,000
Total current assets	$52,000	$53,000	$50,000
Net property	25,000	25,000	26,000
Other assets	2,000	2,000	2,000
Total assets	$79,000	$80,000	$78,000
Liabilities and Capital			
Accounts payable	$10,000	$12,000	$12,000
Notes payable (5%)	7,000	7,000	7,000
Other current liabilities	3,000	1,000	2,000
Total current liabilities	$20,000	$20,000	$21,000
Long-term debt (6%)	15,000	15,000	15,000
Net worth	44,000	45,000	42,000
Total claims on assets	$79,000	$80,000	$78,000

The Sundown Company—Comparative Income Statements for Years 1975-1977

	1975		1976		1977	
Sales		$120,000		$110,000		$130,000
Material	$45,000		$39,000		$47,000	
Labor	40,500		37,000		43,000	
Heat, light, and power	9,000		9,000		9,000	
Depreciation (10%)	1,500	96,000	1,500	86,500	1,500	100,500
Gross profit		24,000		23,500		29,500
Selling expenses	10,000		10,000		10,000	
General and administrative expenses	9,500	19,500	9,250	19,250	8,750	18,750
Operating profit		4,500		4,250		10,750
Less: Interest expenses		1,250		1,250		1,250
Net profit before taxes		3,250		3,000		9,500
Federal income taxes		1,625		1,500		4,750
Net income		$ 1,625		$ 1,500		$ 4,750

The Sundown Company—Financial Ratios

	1975		1976		1977	
	Company Ratio	Average Ratio	Company Ratio	Average Ratio	Company Ratio	Average Ratio
1. Current assets / Current liabilities		2.5 times		2.6 times		2.7 times
2. Sales / Inventory (at book)		4.6 times		4.8 times		5.0 times
3. Receivables / Sales per day		53.0 days		51.0 days		48.0 days
4. Net profit / Sales		3.4%		3.5%		3.7%
5. Net profit / Net worth		10.0%		10.2%		10.5%
6. Net profit / Total assets		4.3%		4.9%		5.7%

Solution:

a.

The Sundown Company—Financial Ratios

	1975	Norm	1976	Norm	1977	Norm
1. Current ratios	2.6	2.5 times	2.7	2.6 times	2.4	2.7 times
2. Inventory turnover	5.5	4.6 times	3.2	4.8 times	5.2	5.0 times
3. Collection period	75.0	53.0 days	49.0	51.0 days	42.0	48.0 days
4. Net profit to sales	1.4	3.4%	1.4	3.5%	3.7	3.7%
5. Net profit to net worth	3.7	10.0 %	3.3	10.2%	11.3	10.5%
6. Net profit to total assets	2.1	4.3%	1.9	4.9%	6.1	5.7%

b. During 1975 the Sundown Company had a poor collection policy. This was evident in that the average collection period was about one and one-half times the norm for the industry. Because of the poor collection policy, the profit ratios were also low. By 1976 although the collection policy had been remedied, the inventory policies were poor. This is evident in the inventory ratio. The turnover is much less than the norm for the industry. The statement for 1977 shows that the company has overcome most of the major difficulties and compares reasonably well with the norms for the household appliance industry.

3-2. Determine the sales of the Stone Company with the financial data given below.

Current ratio   2.5
Quick ratio   2.0
Current liabilities $600,000
Inventory turnover   4 times

Solution:

a. $\dfrac{\text{current assets}}{\$600,000} = 2.5$

current assets $= \$1,500,000.$

b. $\dfrac{\text{current assets} - \text{inventory}}{\$600,000} = 2.0$

current assets $-$ inventory $= \$1,200,000$
inventory $= \$\ \ 300,000.$

c. $\dfrac{\text{sales}}{\text{inventory}} = $ inventory turnover

$\dfrac{\text{sales}}{\$300,000} = 4$

sales $= \underline{\$1,200,000.}$

3-3. Complete the balance sheet and sales data (fill in the blanks) of the Brown Company using the following financial data for 1977:

Debt/net worth	60 percent
Acid test ratio	1.2/1.0
Asset turnover	1.5 times
Days sales outstanding in accounts receivable	40 days
Gross profit margin	30 percent
Inventory turnover (at cost)	6 times

Balance Sheet, Brown Company, December 31, 1977

Cash	_____	Accounts payable	_____
Accounts receivable	_____	Common stock	$15,000
Inventories	_____	Retained earnings	$22,000
Plant and equipment	_____		
		Total liabilities	
Total assets	══════════	and capital	══════════
Sales	_____		
Cost of goods sold	_____		

Solution:

a. $\dfrac{\text{debt}}{\text{net worth}} = \dfrac{\text{debt}}{37{,}000} = 60\%$; debt = $22,200.

b. $37,000
  +22,200
  ─────────
  $59,200 total assets

c. acid test = $1.2 = \dfrac{\text{cash} + \text{A/R}}{\text{current liabilities}} = \dfrac{\text{cash} + \text{A/R}}{22{,}200}$

   cash + A/R = $26,640.

d. asset turnover = $1.5 = \dfrac{\text{sales}}{\text{assets}} = \dfrac{\text{sales}}{59{,}200}$

   sales = $88,000.

e. days sales outstanding = 40, 40/360 x 88,800
   in accounts receivable = 9,876 accounts receivable.

f. cash = cash + A/R − A/R = $26,640
  $\underline{-9{,}876}$
  $$$16,773 cash

g. gross profit margin = 30 percent
   cost of goods sold = 70 percent x sales
   $88,800
   $\underline{\text{x}0.70}$
   $62,160 cost of goods sold

h. inventory turnover (at cost) = 6

   $\dfrac{\text{sales}}{\text{inventories}} = \dfrac{\$88{,}800}{\text{inventories}} = 6$

   inventories = $14,800.

i.   cash $16,773
    A/R   9,867
    inventories   <u>14,800</u>
                       $41,440

    total assets   59,200
                      <u>−41,440</u>
                      $17,760 plant and equipment

Profit Planning

4

THEME

In addition to the ratios described in the preceding chapter, the financial manager has other tools available to aid in profit planning and control: break-even analysis, analysis of operating leverage, and sources and uses of funds statements.

I. *Break-even analysis* is an important tool for profit planning.
   A. It provides information on the volume of sales at which total revenues begin to cover total costs fully.
   B. The practical significance is that break-even analysis guides the manager in the comparison of prices, expected volume, and the required volume to cover total costs.
   C. Figure 4-1 illustrates break-even analysis, as do the tables and related materials that follow it.
      1. Relations among units produced, total variable costs, fixed costs, total costs, and total income:

Units Sold	Total Variable Costs	Fixed Costs	Total Costs	Total Sales	Net Profit (Loss)
20,000	$ 24,000	$40,000	$ 64,000	$ 40,000	$(24,000)
40,000	48,000	40,000	88,000	80,000	(8,000)
50,000	60,000	40,000	100,000	100,000	—
60,000	72,000	40,000	112,000	120,000	8,000
80,000	96,000	40,000	136,000	160,000	24,000
100,000	120,000	40,000	160,000	200,000	40,000
120,000	144,000	40,000	184,000	240,000	56,000
140,000	168,000	40,000	208,000	280,000	72,000

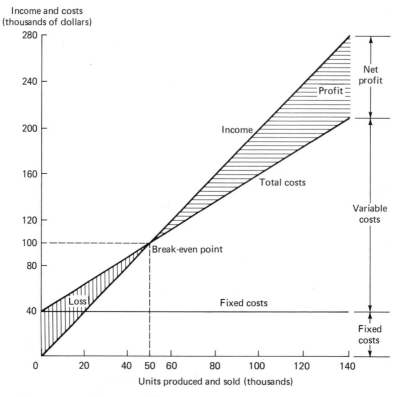

Figure 4-1. Break-even Chart

2. Formula using totals:

a.
$$\frac{\text{total fixed costs}}{1 - \dfrac{\text{total variable costs}}{\text{total sales volume}}} = \text{break-even point}$$

b. Illustration in table above.

1. For lowest sales volume shown in table:

$$\frac{\$40{,}000}{1 - \dfrac{24{,}000}{40{,}000}} = \frac{\$40{,}000}{1 - .6} = \$100{,}000$$

2. For highest volume shown in table:

$$\frac{\$40{,}000}{1 - \dfrac{168{,}000}{280{,}000}} = \frac{\$40{,}000}{1 - .6} = \$100{,}000$$

3. Algebraic solution to break-even volume:

a. The break-even quantity is defined as that volume of output at which revenue is just equal to total costs (fixed costs plus variable costs).

b. Let:

P = sales price per unit

Q = quantity produced and sold

F = fixed costs

V = variable costs per unit.

c. Then: $P \times Q = F + V \times Q$

$P \times Q - V \times Q = F$

$Q(P - V) = F$

$Q = \dfrac{F}{P - V}$ at break-even Q

d. Illustration:

$$Q = \frac{\$40,000}{\$2.00 - \$1.20}$$

= 50,000 units.

II. Among specific uses of break-even analysis are the following:

A. In assessing a modernization or automation program, break-even analysis indicates the degree to which a firm may profitably utilize operating leverage.

B. To study the effects of a general expansion on the level of operations, break-even points are calculated on the basis of total sales (in dollar amounts rather than in units of output) and total costs.

C. In new product decisions, break-even analysis will indicate how large a sales volume the new product must attain in order to realize a profit.

III. *Operating leverage* is defined as the extent to which fixed costs are used in operations. High fixed costs arise from employing larger amounts of capital, thus permitting the firm to operate with reduced labor and smaller variable costs.

A. The degree of operating leverage (OL) is defined as the percentage change in operating income that results from a percentage change in units sold.

$$OL = \frac{\text{percentage change in operating income}}{\text{percentage change in sales}}$$

B. This can also be expressed in a formula developed for calculating the degree of operating leverage at any level of output Q.

Degree of operating leverage = $OL = \dfrac{S - VC}{S - VC - FC} = \dfrac{Q(P - V)}{Q(P - V) - F}$

where

S = Sales

VC = Variable Costs

FC = Fixed Costs

C. Figure 4.2 illustrates the effects of variations in operating leverage.

D. Calculations for the degree of operating leverage involve the following steps:

1. Operating leverage is measured by the ratio of the percentage change in profit to the percentage change in output (quantity sold). OL is calcu-

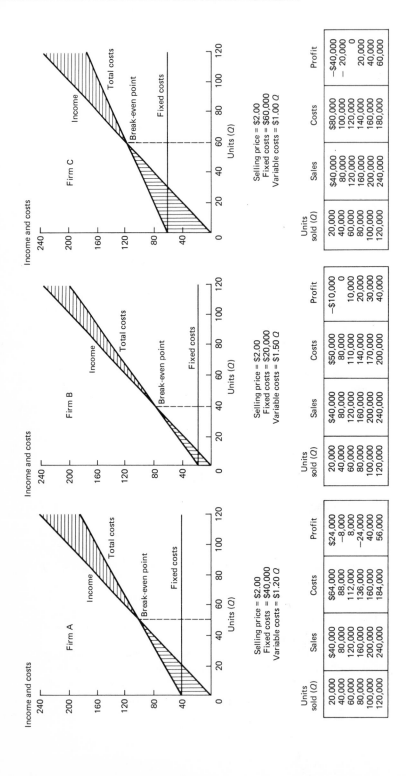

Firm A

Selling price = $2.00
Fixed costs = $40,000
Variable costs = $1.20 Q

Units sold (Q)	Sales	Costs	Profit
20,000	$40,000	$64,000	−$24,000
40,000	80,000	88,000	−8,000
60,000	120,000	112,000	8,000
80,000	160,000	136,000	24,000
100,000	200,000	160,000	40,000
120,000	240,000	184,000	56,000

Firm B

Selling price = $2.00
Fixed costs = $20,000
Variable costs = $1.50 Q

Units sold (Q)	Sales	Costs	Profit
20,000	$40,000	$50,000	−$10,000
40,000	80,000	80,000	0
60,000	120,000	110,000	10,000
80,000	160,000	140,000	20,000
100,000	200,000	170,000	30,000
120,000	240,000	200,000	40,000

Firm C

Selling price = $2.00
Fixed costs = $60,000
Variable costs = $1.00 Q

Units sold (Q)	Sales	Costs	Profit
20,000	$40,000	$80,000	−$40,000
40,000	80,000	100,000	−20,000
60,000	120,000	120,000	0
80,000	160,000	140,000	20,000
100,000	200,000	160,000	40,000
120,000	240,000	180,000	60,000

Figure 4-2. Operating Leverage

lated for the three firms shown in Figure 4-2, as units sold increase from 80,000 to 100,000 units, an increase of 25 percent.

	Firm A	Firm B	Firm C
Profit at 80,000 units	$24,000	$20,000	$20,000
Profit at 100,000 units	$40,000	$30,000	$40,000
Percent change in profit	67%	50%	100%
Percent change in output	25%	25%	25%
Operating leverage (OL)	2.7	2.0	4.0

2. Operating leverage at 80,000 units of output is measured by the OL formula.

$$OL = \frac{S - VC}{S - VC - FC}$$

Firm A

$$\frac{\$160,000 - 96,000}{\$160,000 - 96,000 - 40,000}$$

OL = 2.7

Firm B

$$\frac{\$160,000 - 120,000}{\$160,000 - 120,000 - 20,000}$$

OL = 2

Firm C

$$\frac{\$160,000 - 80,000}{\$160,000 - 80,000 - 60,000}$$

OL = 4.

3. This is significant for the following reasons:
   a. The relative influence of fixed costs in operations is affected by (1) price changes, (2) changes in variable costs, and (3) changes in the relative importance of fixed costs.
   b. The higher the degree of operating leverage, the greater the impact of a given percentage change in output on profit *in both directions.*
   c. The degree of operating leverage (OL) influences decisions on the amount of financial leverage the firm employs because financial and operating leverage jointly affect the variability of the firm's earnings. This interaction is discussed in Chapter 18.

IV. *Nonlinear break-even analysis* as illustrated in Figure 4-3 is intellectually appealing. However, for many decisions, users of break-even charts require analysis of changes only in a small "relevant range" of production. Within this range, linear functions may be useful approximations to more complex functions.

V. *Cash break-even analysis* as illustrated in Figure 4-4 can be used to analyze the firm's situation on a *cash* basis. Although the analysis does not fully represent cash flows, it is useful because it provides a picture of the flow of funds from operations.

A. For the financial manager and for considerations of solvency, the analysis of cash flows is of paramount importance.

B. Some decisions have a greater impact on cash flows than on net income.

    1. A firm may capitalize some types of expenses paid in cash. This will have a favorable effect on net income but will nevertheless represent a cash outlay.

    2. In comparing alternative forms of financing, the cash outflow requirements of different forms of financing can be substantial. (See balance sheet and sources and uses of funds on pages 33-34.)

VI. There are limitations to linear break-even analysis.

A. Some have to do with demand.

    1. Linear relationships assume that the quantity demanded is independent of price.

    2. However, price change effects can be exhibited by having a different total income line for each price.

    3. Alternatively, a curved total income line implies that prices may have to be changed to achieve a higher volume. (See Figure 4-3.)

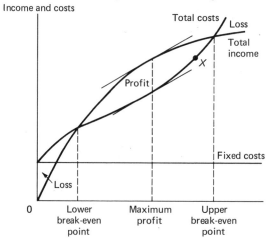

Figure 4-3. Nonlinear Break-even Analysis

Note: The angle of a line from the origin to a point on the total-income line measures price, that is, total income/units sold = price, and a line from the origin to the total-cost curve measures cost per unit. It can be seen that the angle of the line to the revenue curve declines as we move toward higher sales, which means the price is falling. Unit costs (Total cost/Units produced) declines to point *X*, the tangency point of a line from the origin to the total-cost curve, then begins to rise. The slopes of the total-cost and total-income lines measure marginal cost (*MC*) and marginal revenue (*MR*) respectively. At the point where the slopes of the two total curves are equal, *MR = MC*, and profits are at a maximum.

B. Other limitations relate to costs.
1. Some costs are semifixed and, hence, also semivariable.
2. As the scale of plant is changed, a step type of cost function results.
3. At larger scales of operation, further economies and higher returns from both the fixed and variable factors may be achieved, but later on capacity is strained, so that the total cost curve first increases at a decreasing rate, then increases at an increasing rate. Figure 4-3 illustrates such a cost curve.

VII. The sources and uses of funds statement indicates on an historical basis where cash came from and how it was used.
A. The sources and uses of funds analysis is an important planning tool. With it the firm is able to respond to the question raised by prospective lenders: "How has the firm used the funds it received in the past?"
B. Sources and uses analysis on a *pro forma* basis is essential for planning, as it provides both a plan for the use of funds and, later on, a check to see if the funds were used according to plan.

Comparative Balance Sheets and Sources and Uses of Funds
(in millions of dollars)

	12/31/76	Estimated 12/31/77	Sources	Uses
Cash	$ 10	$200	$ 5	
Marketable securities	25	15	10	
Net receivables	15	20		$ 5
Inventories	25	30		5
Gross fixed assets	150	180		30
Less: Allowance for depreciation†	(40)	(50)	10	
Net fixed assets	110	130		
Total assets	$185	$200		
Accounts payable	$ 10	$ 6		4
Notes payable	15	10		5
Other current liabilities	10	14	4	
Long-term debt	60	70	10	
Preferred stock	10	10	—	—
Common stock	50	50	—	—
Retained earnings	30	40	10	—
Total claims on assets	$185	$200	$49	$49

†The allowance for depreciation is actually a liability account, even though it appears on the left side of the balance sheet. Note that it is deducted, not added, when totaling the column.

Statement of Projected Sources and Uses of Funds, 1977
(in millions of dollars)

Uses	Amount	Percent
Gross fixed assets expansion	$30	61.2
Inventory investment	5	10.2
Increase in receivables	5	10.2
Reduction in notes payable	5	10.2
Reduction in accounts payable	4	8.2
Total use of funds	$49	100.0
Sources		
Increase in long-term debt	$10	20.4
Increase in retained earnings	10	20.4
Noncash depreciation outlay	10	20.4
Sale of marketable securities	10	20.4
Reduction in cash holdings	5	20.4
Increase in other liabilities	4	8.2
Total source of funds	$49	100.0

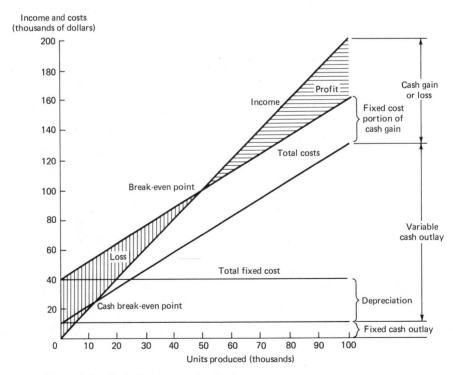

Figure 4-4. Cash Break-even Analysis

C. To construct a rough-and-ready sources and uses statement, tabulate the changes in the balance sheet items from one year to the next and classify them as follows:

1. *Uses of funds* include increases in asset items or decreases in liability items.

2. *Sources of funds* include decreases in asset items or increases in liability items.

3. *Depreciation* is a noncash outlay. Since it is deducted from revenues to determine net income, it is added back as a source of funds. A *pro forma*, or projected, sources and uses of funds statment is illustrated below.

4. A brief summary of the illustrative statement may be helpful.

   a. The main *sources* of funds are expected to come from (1) an increase in long-term debt financing, (2) a reduction in holdings of marketable securities, (3) retained earnings, and (4) the noncash depreciation charge.

   b. The major *uses* of funds are expected to be (1) investments in fixed assets, (2) inventories, (3) accounts receivables, and (4) the reduction of a portion of the notes payable.

PROBLEMS

4-1. You are planning to establish a pizza parlor off campus. A market survey of the service area indicates that you could sell 150,000 pizzas at 75 cents apiece. Pizza parlors of this type normally have a 25 percent profit margin before tax. If you require a 15 percent before-tax return on investment, how large an investment should you be willing to make?

Solution:

a. 150,000 pizzas
   x0.75
   $112,500

b. $112,500
   x0.25
   $ 28,125 profit margin before tax

c. $\dfrac{\$28,125}{0.15}$ = $187,500 maximum investment.

4-2. The Mikall Company indicates that the following statement is representative of its operations.

Net sales (1,250,000 units at $4)		$5,000,000
Less: Cost of goods sold		
Materials	$1,000,000	
Labor	1,400,000	
Overhead	1,600,000	4,000,000
Gross profit		$1,000,000
Less: Operating expenses		
Selling expenses	$ 350,000	
Administrative expenses	250,000	600,000
Profit		$ 400,000

Costs and expenses in the income statement are redistributed as follows:

	Total	Variable	Fixed
Materials	$1,000,000	$1,000,000	
Labor	1,400,000	1,400,000	
Factory overhead	1,600,000	400,000	$1,200,000
Selling expenses	350,000	150,000	200,000
Administrative expenses	250,000	50,000	200,000
	$4,600,000	$3,000,000	$1,600,000

a. From the above information, construct a break-even chart in its conventional form and designate areas and points of particular significance.
b. What is Mikall Company's degree of operating leverage at sales of 1,250,000 units?
c. Indicate the special assumptions involved in break-even analysis, as well as any limitations that may be found in such an analysis.

Solution:

a. The following two problems illustrate a typical break-even analysis. See Figure 4-5.

Break-even in terms of units:

$$V = \frac{\$3,000,000}{1,250,000 \text{ units}} = \$2.40 \text{ per unit}$$

$$Q = \frac{F}{P - V} = \frac{\$1,600,000}{\$4.00 - \$2.40} = 1,000,000 \text{ units}$$

Break-even in terms of dollar sales:

$$\text{Break-even point} = \frac{F}{1 - \dfrac{TVC}{\text{Sales}}} = \frac{\$1,600,000}{1 - \dfrac{\$3,000,000}{\$5,000,000}} = \frac{\$1,600,000}{0.4}$$

$$= \$4,000,000$$

b. Degree of operating leverage at point Q is

$$\frac{Q(P - V)}{Q(P - V) - F} = \frac{1,250,000\ (\$4.00 - \$2.40)}{1,250,000\ (\$4.00 - \$2.40) - \$1,600,000}$$

$$= \frac{\$2,000,000}{\$2,000,000 - \$1,600,000} = 5.0.$$

c. *Assumptions.*
1. Behavior of costs is reliably determined and linear over the relevant range.
2. Costs can be broken down into fixed and variable categories.
3. Fixed costs remain constant over the volume range on the break-even chart.
4. Variable costs fluctuate with volume.
5. Prices or costs do not change.
6. Efficiency and productivity remain unchanged.
7. Sales mix is constant.
8. All factors are based on a going concern.
9. Beginning and ending inventories are fairly stable.

Limitations.
1. Major limitations is the validity of the assumptions in all the above cases.
2. Break-even is a static analysis.
3. Break-even analysis disregards the relationship between price and quantity sold.

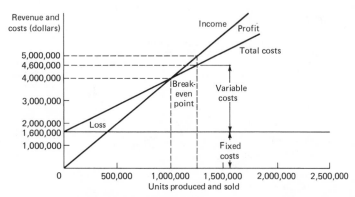

Figure 4-5. Mikall Co. Break-even Chart

4-3. Thorp Company sells finance textbooks at $8 each. The variable cost per book is $6. At current annual sales of 800,000 books, the publisher is just breaking even. It is estimated that if the authors' royalties are reduced, the variable cost per book will drop by $1. Assume that the authors' royalties are reduced and that sales remain constant; how much more money can the publisher put into advertising (a fixed cost)?

Solution:

$Q = F/(P - V)$ at break-even Q
Q = quantity produced = 800,000
F = fixed costs
P = sales price per unit = $8
V = variable costs per unit = $6

a. $800{,}000 \text{ books} = \dfrac{\text{fixed cost}}{\$8 - \$6}$; fixed cost = $1,600,000.

b. $800{,}000 \text{ books} = \dfrac{\text{fixed cost}}{\$8 - \$6}$; fixed cost = $2,400,000.

c. $2,400,000
   −1,600,000
   $ 800,000 difference

4-4. Given the following balance sheet changes, what change, if any, should appear in retained earnings?

$ 3,000 increase in cash
$11,000 increase in inventories
$ 3,000 increase in depreciation
$11,000 increase in accounts payable
$ 6,000 decrease in notes payable

Solution:

Source and Uses of Funds Statement

	Use of Funds	Source of Funds
Cash	$ 3	
Inventories	11	
Depreciation		$ 3
Accounts payable		11
Notes payable	6	
	20	14
Increase in retained earnings		66
	$20	$20

Financial Forecasting

5

THEME

In obtaining funds at the lowest interest cost and on the best possible terms, it is important to plan needs far enough in advance to allow sufficient time for effective negotiations. Financial planning makes a great contribution to the efficient performance of the financial manager's responsibilities.

I. The cash flow cycle.
   A. The logic behind financial forecasting is made clear by tracing through the firm's cash flow cycle. Firms need assets in order to make sales, and if sales increase, assets must also grow.
   B. The cash cycle, also called the working capital cycle, shows the process of turning cash into inventories, then into receivables, then back into cash.
   C. This is the sequence of steps.
      1. Original cash investment is used to pay rent and buy equipment.
      2. Raw material purchases are financed by trade credit, giving rise to accounts payable.
      3. Funds are paid to labor to begin processing the raw material.
      4. Before goods are completed, they represent work-in-process inventories. The firm's cash has declined, and current liabilities in the form of accounts payable and accrued wages payable are in existence.
      5. Goods are finished and go from in-process inventories to finished goods inventories. The firm is more liquid at this point because finished goods have salability which work-in-process inventories do not have.
      6. When goods are sold on credit, they become accounts receivable.

7. Collection of accounts receivable generates cash for the repayment of outside creditors.

8. The firm buys raw materials, and the working capital cycle, or cash cycle, is repeated.

D. Rising sales projections call for increases in assets, and funds may be needed to acquire these assets.

1. Total permanent assets increase in the form of both fixed and current assets.

2. With fluctuations in sales, total assets fluctuate.

3. Permanent assets, both current and fixed, should be financed from long-term sources.

4. Fluctuating asset requirements, or temporary increases in assets, may be financed from short-term sources. This is illustrated in Figure 5-1.

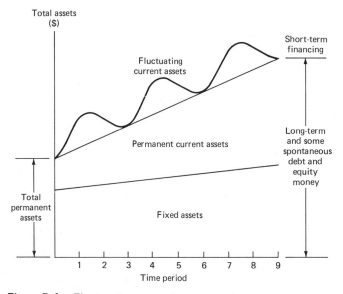

Figure 5-1. Fluctuating versus Permanent Assets

II. Forecasting methodology.

A. Basic relationships.

1. Forecasting requires the identification of a cause-and-effect relationship. Otherwise, any forecast represents a judgment or a "hunch."

2. In financial forecasting, sales is the "causal" variable: To make sales, a firm must have both inventories and the equipment used to manufacture or store inventories. When a firm makes sales on credit, these sales "cause" accounts receivables to come into existence.

B. Leads and lags necessitate planning.

1. A firm must have equipment and inventories before making sales. Thus, the need to finance inventories and equipment precedes sales.

    2. Receivables result after sales are made; thus the asset item receivables "lags" sales.

    3. The interaction of these leads and lags gives rise to financial dynamics and the need for effective efforts in both planning and control.

  C. Basic methods of forecasting.

    1. Percent-of-sales method expresses each item as a percentage of sales. For example, if sales were $1,000,000 and accounts receivable were $200,000, the percent-of-sales relation for accounts receivable would be 20 percent.

    2. The scatter diagram, or regression, method must be used if the relation is such that the proportionality factor changes with the volume of sales (explained below).

III. Percent-of-sales method.

  A. Determine those balance sheet items that vary directly with sales.

  B. Increases in assets represent financing requirements; some liabilities grow spontaneously with sales and provide a spontaneous source of funds.

  C. The difference between the required growth in assets and the spontaneously generated funds from liability increases represents the firm's total financing requirements. This is normally first met by internally generated increases in retained earnings (profit margin on total sales less dividend payout). Financing needs in excess of this must be obtained from external sources, such as through borrowing or by selling new common stock.

  D. In equation form:

$$\text{External funds needed} = \frac{A}{S}(\Delta S) \; - \; \frac{L}{S}(\Delta S) - MS_2(1 - d)$$

where A/S = assets as a percent of sales, L/S = liabilities which increase spontaneously with sales as a percent of sales, ΔS = change in sales, M = profit margin, S_2 = total projected sales for the year $(S + \Delta S)$, and d = dividend payout percentage.

  E. Table 5-1 provides an illustration.

Table 5-1. The Valian Company—Balance Sheet Items Expressed as a Percent of Sales, December 31, 1976.

Cash	2.0%	Accounts payable	10.0%
Receivables	17.0	Accrued taxes and wages	5.0
Inventories	20.0	Mortgage bonds	N.A.
Fixed Assets (net)	30.0	Common stock	N.A.
		Retained earnings	N.A.
Total	69.0%	Total	15.0%

Assets as a percent of sales	69.0%
Less: Spontaneous increase in liabilities	15.0
Percent of each additional dollar of sales that must be financed	54.0%

Suppose sales increase from $500,000 to $800,000; profit margin on sales of $800,000 is 4 percent; and dividend payout is 50 percent.

External funds needed = .69 (300,000) − .15 (300,000) − .04 (800,000) (.5)
= .54 (300,000) − .02 (800,000)
= $146,000

However, if sales increase by only $15,000 to $515,000

External funds needed = .54 (15,000) − .02 (515,000)
= ($2,200)

This means no external funds are required. The company in fact has $2,200 in excess of its requirements. This could be used to increase dividends, retire debt, or seek additional investment opportunities.

F. This example highlights two points:
  1. Higher levels of sales bring about greater needs for funds.
  2. While small levels of growth can be financed by internal sources (through retained earnings), higher levels of growth require external financing.

IV. Scatter diagram or regression method.
  A. Regression analysis develops relationships based on sales as the independent variable (plotted on the horizontal scale) and on the asset item as the dependent variable (plotted on the vertical scale).
  B. Proceed as follows:
    1. Forecast or project the sales of the firm by GNP, industry sales, or other logical business indicators.
    2. Plot the scatter diagrams for major asset, liability, and net worth categories related to sales.
    3. Fit the regression line by freehand (inspection) or by numerical calculations (least squares).
    4. Project the regression lines and determine the level of each balance sheet category for the forecast value of sales.
    5. The difference between total asset requirements and financing sources directly related to sales indicates financial requirements.

V. Comparison of forecasting techniques.
  A. For short-term forecasts, such as month-to-month, either the ratio method or the regression method may be employed.
  B. For longer term forecasts, it is best to use the regression method to avoid major errors that might result from systematic shifts in the ratios.
  C. Table 5-2 and Figure 5-2 illustrate the use of the percent-of-sales method of forecasting financial requirements compared with the regression method.

Table 5-2 Relations between Inventory and Sales

Years	Sales	Inventory	Inventory as a Percent of Sales
1971	$ 50,000	$22,000	44
1972	100,000	24,000	24
1973	150,000	26,000	17
1974	200,000	28,000	14
1975	250,000	30,000	12
1976	300,000	32,000	11
1980E	500,000		

D. The implications of the data in the table and figure can be indicated by first calculating the regression line for the data. (The following simplified procedure is applicable when the regression line is a straight line.)
1. First calculate the slope of the line by relating the change in inventory to the change in sales.
    a. When sales increased by $100,000, the increase in inventories was $4,000.
    b. The slope is, therefore,

$$\frac{\text{Change in inventories}}{\text{change in sales}} = \frac{\$4,000}{100,000} = .04 = 4 \text{ percent}$$

    c. The intercept of the regression line can be estimated by taking a point on the regression line, using the slope as calculated above, and solving for A in the following equation of a straight line.

$$Y = A + BX$$

    For sales of $250,000, the corresponding inventory value for 1975 is $30,000; we know that $B = .04$, so substituting,

$$\$30,000 = A + .04 \ (\$250,000)$$
$$\$30,000 = A + \$10,000$$
$$\$20,000 = A.$$

    d. The general relationship for the data in Table 5-2 is

    inventories = $20,000 + .04(Sales).

2. The intercept term indicates that a $20,000 base stock is held, to which additional amounts of inventories are added as sales change. Mathematically, a nonzero intercept is associated with a *changing* percentage of inventories to sales as shown in the last column of Table 5-2, indicating that the percent-of-sales method would cause faulty forecasting.

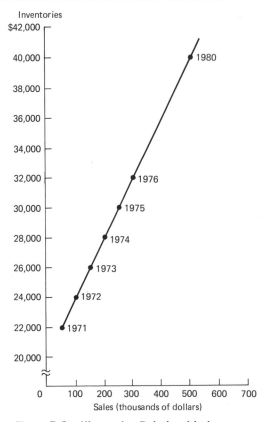

Figure 5-2. Illustrative Relationship between Sales and Inventory

E. These are some guidelines for use of the percentage method versus the regression method:
1. When the regression line has a nonzero intercept, the use of the percentage method for forecasting would involve error.
   a. Since the percentage of inventories-to-sales is declining, the use of any of the percentages in the last column of Table 5-2 for forecasting with a rising sales volume would represent lax standards for control.
   b. Using our present example, the use of the regression method would result in the following forecast of inventories for 1980 when sales are forecast to be $500,000.

$$\text{Inventories} = \$20,000 + .04(\$500,000)$$
$$= \$40,000.$$

Using the percentage for the latest year, 1976 would result in an inventory projection of .11 ($500,000) = $55,000. This represents an inventory control standard of $15,000, which is too large as compared with the amount determined by the regression method.

2. In general, the regression method is more dependable as a method for forecasting.
3. Either method provides about the same results under two circumstances:
   a. The regression line has a small intercept (close to zero).
   b. For monthly forecasts or other circumstances in which sales do not vary greatly, the percentage method will provide reasonably dependable control estimates.

PROBLEMS

5-1. The Walton Corporation's sales were $900,000 in 1976. During 1977 it expects its sales to increase by 50 percent. Total assets were $300,000 in 1976. The same percentage of assets to sales will be maintained in 1977. At the close of 1976 common stock was $150,000 and retained earnings were $80,000. Net profit after taxes is expected to be 8 percent of sales in 1977. No dividends are paid. Assuming the debt on hand as of the close of 1976 is not repaid, what amount of new financing will be needed in 1977?

Solution:

1976
total assets — (stock + retained earnings) = debt
$300,000 — ($150,000 + $80,000) = $70,000
sales = $900,000

$$\frac{\$300,000 \text{ assets}}{\$900,000 \text{ sales}} = 33.3\%.$$

1977
sales: 1.5 x $900,000 (1976 sales) = $1,350,000

$$\frac{\text{assets}}{\text{sales}} = \frac{\text{assets 1977}}{\$1,350,000} = 33.3\%$$

assets 1977 = $450,000
net profit = 8% x sales = 8% x $1,350,000
   net profit = $108,000.

$ 70,000 debt	**Note:** $ 80,000 (1976)
150,000 stock	108,000 (profits net 1977)
188,000 retained earnings	$188,000
$408,000	

$450,000 new asset level (1977)
 408,000 existing financing
$ 42,000 new financing needed in 1977

Alternative solution:

Step 1:

Total sales in 1976	$ 900,000
Add:	
Increase in sales in 1977 = 0.5 ($900,000):	450,000
Total sales in 1977	$1,350,000

Step 2:

$$\frac{\text{Total assets (1976)}}{\text{Total sales (1976)}} = \frac{\text{Total assets (1977)}}{\text{Total sales (1977)}}$$

$$\frac{\$300,000}{\$900,000} = \frac{\text{Total assets (1977)}}{\$1,350,000}$$

$$\text{Total assets 1977} = \$450,000$$

$$\frac{\text{Total assets 1977}}{\text{Total sales 1977}} = \frac{\$450,000}{\$1,350,000} = 33.3\%$$

Step 3:

Use the equation form:

$$\text{Financing needed} = \left[\begin{array}{c} \text{assets as \%} \\ \text{of sales} \end{array} - \begin{array}{c} \text{spontaneous liabilities} \\ \text{as \% of sales} \end{array} \right] \times \Delta S$$

$$- \frac{\text{profit}}{\text{margin}} \times S$$

where ΔS = increase in sales, and S = total sales during forecast year;

or in our case:

$$\text{Financing needed} = \frac{\text{assets as \%}}{\text{of sales}} \times \Delta S - [\text{profit margin}] \times S$$

$$= [33.3\%] \times \$450,000 - [8\%] \times \$1,350,000$$

$$= \underline{\$42,000}.$$

5-2. The Horrigan Company's sales were $720,000 in 1976 but it expects to double this volume to $1,440,000 during 1977. The net profit after taxes is expected to be 5 percent of sales. Each balance sheet account will have the following percent of sales tied up in it.

Cash	2%	Fixed assets	5%
Receivables	6%	Accounts payable	5%
Inventory	12%		

On December 31, 1976 the Common Stock account shows $100,000 and the Retained Earnings $44,000. No dividends are to be paid on common stock during 1977.

a. Complete two balance sheets, one as of December 31, 1976 and the other as of December 31, 1977 using "financing needed" as the balancing entry.

b. Determine "financing needed" by the formula method.

c. What is the significance of your results?

Solution:

a. Horrigan Company—Balance Sheets, December 31, 1976 and 1977

	1976	1977		1976	1977
Cash	$ 14,400	$ 28,800	Accounts		
Receivables	43,200	86,400	payable	$ 36,000	$ 72,000
Inventory	86,400	172,800	Financing		
Fixed assets	36,000	72,000	needed	–	72,000
	$180,000	$360,000	Common stock	100,000	100,000
			Retained		
			earnings	44,000	116,000
				$180,000	$360,000

Retained earnings during 1977 will equal $72,000 (5% of $1,440,000). This amount added to $44,000 gives a retained earning total of $116,000 at the end of 1977.

b. Financing needed $= \left[\begin{matrix} \text{assets as \%} \\ \text{of sales} \end{matrix} - \begin{matrix} \text{spontaneous liabilities} \\ \text{as \% of sales} \end{matrix} \right] \times \Delta S$

$$- \frac{\text{profit}}{\text{margin}} \times S$$

Assets as % of sales = 2% + 6% + 12% + 5% = 25%

Spontaneous liabilities as % of sales = 5%

Financing needed = [25% – 5%] x $720,000 – [5%] x $1,440,000
= $72,000.

c. The practical significance of this problem is that, if a firm is successful and if it grows, it faces increased financing requirements that may not be obtained from internal sources, but must be obtained from external sources.

Note: It should be noted that forecasting by the percent-of-sales method assumes that historical balance sheet and income statement relations are constant. While in fact these relations may be stable in many cases, they often are intended as simplifying assumptions (especially as the time horizon is extended) and should be applied with judgment. Note that in this problem the balance sheet items maintained a stable percentage relation to sales, as sales doubled.

Financial Planning and Control: Budgeting

THEME

An essential part of the financial manager's role is short-term budgeting, and especially cash forecasting, or cash budgeting. The entire budgeting process is examined in Chapter 6.

I.   A budget is a tool for obtaining the most productive and profitable use of the company's resources by improving the firm's internal coordination.
    A. Budgets are used for planning purposes, and also for control, by comparing plans with results.
    B. Budgets provide management with a continuous monitoring system which allows the firm to anticipate new events and react quickly to change.
    C. Budgets are an additional form of communication between top management and divisional personnel.
    D. Budgets help to clarify the relationship of the divisions to the totality of the firm.

II. The process of control is carried out in three steps:
    A. Standards of performance are established in advance of actual performance.
    B. Performance is evaluated relative to the standards.
    C. Corrective action is taken if performance is below standard.

III. Figure 6-1 illustrates budget relations.

IV. Assuming that a sales forecast has been made, the series of budgets follow logically.
    A. The production budget is developed to include the following:
        1. Beginning and ending inventory requirements.

2. The adjusted cost per unit of goods produced.

3. The number of units produced.

B. The number of units to be produced is the first input for the *materials purchases budget.* This budget derives an estimate of raw materials purchases.

C. Formulation of the *cash budget* relies on elements from previous budgets.

    1. The *production budget* provides the following:

        a. Sales data, which determine accounts receivable collections and selling expenses.

        b. Units produced, which determine direct labor expense and variable manufacturing expense.

    2. The *materials purchases budget* provides the raw materials purchases estimate, which determines the accounts payable payments.

D. The *budgeted income statement* requires the adjusted cost of goods sold figure. This figure is calculated from the following:

    a. Cost of goods produced.

    b. Inventory data in the *materials purchases budget.*

E. Finally, the *budgeted balance sheet* can be derived by the use of information from all the previous budgets.

V. The *cash budget.*

A. In a complete budget system, a cash budget performs an important planning and controlling function.

B. The methodology is quite logical.

    1. If a firm sells on credit, there is a lag between sales and cash collections.

    2. Similarly, a firm buying on credit benefits from a waiting period before having to disburse cash.

    3. In expenditures, some cash payments are made in "lumps" at uneven intervals, while expenses may be assigned on a uniform monthly basis.

    4. It is important to take into account debt service requirements, including interest and principal repayment, as outward cash flows.

    5. In general, the cash "throw-off" from operations should meet debt service requirements plus an appropriate margin of safety.

    6. Capital outlays may be covered by specific financing programs.

VI. A *flexible budget* is achieved by varying budget allowances related to sales, by establishing different budgets for different sales volumes, and by supplementing a basic budget by periodic adjustments.

A. The flexible budget utilizes the logic of the regression technique to determine the impact of the control variable (that is, the independent variable) on the item for which a budget figure is to be determined.

B. Knowledge of the firm's operations is required to discover the cause and effect relationships and to apply them in a budget system.

VII. The following are suggestions for making budget systems work.

A. Budgeting is often done implicitly in lieu of a formal budget system. *Implicit budgeting* does not bring assumptions into focus and can lead to errors.

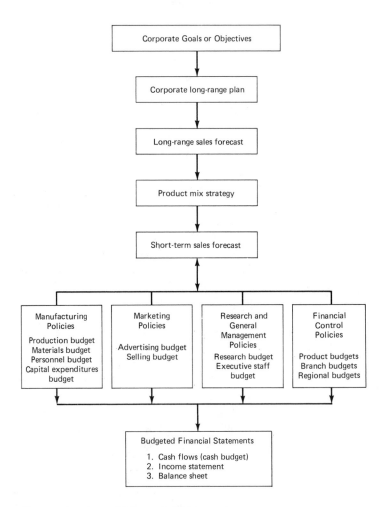

Figure 6-1. **Overall View of the Total Budgeting Process and Relations**

   B. The choice of a budget period is flexible and should fit the needs of the firm.

   C. For the budget system to be of the most value in the control process, a series of charts should be set up. In that way, trends can be most easily observed.

   D. The financial manager should avoid common pitfalls in budgeting.

      1. Budgets can become cumbersome.

      2. Budgetary goals can supersede enterprise goals.

      3. Budgets can hide inefficiencies.

      4. Budgets can cause inflexibilities.

      5. Budgets can be used as instruments of tyranny.

VIII. Financial plans and budgets are used by other departments in addition to finance.
  A. They are used for overall company planning; the personnel department uses them for hiring and training activities; and the production department uses them for planning capacity requirements.
  B. The plans are used in both long-term and short-term decisions.
    1. Long-term decisions.
      a. The regression method is used to plan needs for three to five years.
      b. The sequence and mix of retained earnings, common stock, and debt financing is planned.
    2. Short-term decisions.
      a. The percent-of-sales method is frequently used.
      b. The cash budget is emphasized, indicating how funds will be used and when they will be repaid.
      c. Such information is important in obtaining bank loans.
      d. The full integration between balance sheets, income statements, cash budgets, and other budgets is presented to provide prospective lenders with information indicating that the firm and its financial manager have a full understanding of the business and have developed effective plans, budgets, and controls. The objective is to avoid "surprises" both for management and for its financing sources—to demonstrate that the firm can effectively control its operations according to plans.

IX. An effective financial control system encompasses these areas:
  A. The controls used should be designed to measure deviations from plans. Managers should evaluate controls periodically in order to remove obsolete ones and institute new ones as needed.
  B. Controls must be related to levels of authority, because the one who carries out the control function must be responsible for the performance of the controlled activity.
  C. The cost of controls should be kept consistent with the importance of the item under control.
  D. The acceptance of controls is increased if those who operate under the standards participate in formulating them.
  E. Performance must be measured against standards. Judgment is necessary in the appraisal of performance.
  F. Deficiencies that are revealed by controls must be corrected to complete the feedback system.

X. Many organizations having decentralized operations use return on investments (ROI) as a measure of division efficiency.

PROBLEMS

6-1. You have been asked to prepare a cash budget for Crystal Stores for the period July 1 through December 31. The following data are provided:
   a. All sales are for credit. Payment for 10 percent of the sales is received during the month in which the sales are made, 60 percent in the month following, and 30 percent in the second month following.
   b. Purchases during each month equal 75 percent of the following month's sales. Payment for purchases is made in the month following the purchase.
   c. Inventory equals a base stock of $8,000 plus purchases for the following month.
   d. The firm's minimum level of cash is $5,000. Cash is $6,000 as of July 1.
   e. The firm buys no additional fixed assets during the period.
   f. Accrued wages and salaries remain unchanged at the end of the period.
   g. Borrowings are in the form of notes payable.
   h. Other current liabilities remain unchanged at the end of the period.
   i. The firm is a corporation that pays no dividends.
   j. The gross profit margin is 25 percent.
   k. Sales data and wages and salaries data are the following:

	Actual	
	Sales	Wages and Salaries
May	$20,000	$2,000
June	$20,000	$2,000

	Forecast	
	Sales	Wages and Salaries
July	$30,000	$2,500
August	50,000	3,000
September	50,000	3,000
October	60,000	3,500
November	30,000	3,000
December	20,000	2,000
January	20,000	2,000
February	20,000	2,000

   1. Rent is $500 per month, depreciation is $400 per month, and other cash expenses are 2 percent of sales.

Prepare a cash budget for the six-month period.

CRYSTAL STORES—CASH BUDGET WORK SHEET

	May	June	July	Aug.	Sept.	Oct.	Nov.	Dec.	Jan.	Feb.
Sales	$20,000	$20,000	$30,000	$50,000	$50,000	$60,000	$30,000	$20,000	$20,000	$20,000
Collections:										
10% (present month)			$ 3,000	$ 5,000	$ 5,000	$ 6,000	$ 3,000	$ 2,000	$ 2,000	$ 2,000
60% (next month)			12,000	18,000	30,000	30,000	36,000	18,000	12,000	12,000
30% (two months later than present month)			6,000	6,000	9,000	15,000	15,000	18,000	9,000	6,000
Total			$21,000	$29,000	$44,000	$51,000	$54,000	$38,000	$23,000	$20,000
Purchases of 75% of next month's sales	$15,000	$22,500	$37,500	$37,500	$45,000	$22,500	$15,000	$15,000	$15,000	
Payments		15,000	22,500	37,500	37,500	45,000	22,500	15,000	15,000	

CRYSTAL STORES—CASH BUDGET

	July	Aug.	Sept.	Oct.	Nov.	Dec.
Receipts: collections	$21,000	$29,000	$44,000	$51,000	$54,000	$38,000
Payments:						
Purchases	$22,500	$37,500	$37,500	$45,000	$22,500	$15,000
Wages and salaries	2,500	3,000	3,000	3,500	3,000	2,000
Rent	500	500	500	500	500	500
Other (2% sales)	600	1,000	1,000	1,200	600	400
Total payments	$26,100	$42,000	$42,000	$50,200	$26,600	$17,900
Net cash gain (loss) during month	($ 5,100)	($13,000)	$ 2,000	$ 800	$27,400	$20,100
Cash at start of month if no borrowing is done	6,000	900	(12,100)	(10,100)	(9,300)	18,100
Cumulative cash (= cash at start plus gain or minus loss)	(4,100)	(12,100)	(10,100)	(9,300)	18,100	38,200
Less: desired level of cash	5,000	5,000	5,000	5,000	5,000	5,000
Total loans outstanding to maintain $5,000 cash	($ 4,100)	($17,100)	($15,100)	($14,300)	-	-
Surplus cash	-	-	-	-	$13,100	$33,200

Working Capital Management

Part Three

Working Capital Policy

7

THEME

Working capital management involves a large portion of the firm's total assets, as more than half the typical firm's total investment is in current assets. This chapter focuses on principles and techniques used for effective control of overall working capital management.

I.   Working capital management is important for these reasons:
    A. A great deal of the financial manager's time is allocated to working capital management and the day-to-day operations of the firm.
    B. More than half of the total assets are typically invested in current assets.
    C. Growth of sales results in increased investment in current assets.
    D. Investment in fixed assets may be reduced by renting or leasing, but investment in inventories and receivables is unavoidable.

II. Working capital management consists of decisions relating to managing current assets and arranging the short-term credit used to finance them.
    A. Working capital management initially consisted of financing the agricultural process until the crops were sold and loans were paid off.
    B. The realization that there is a "permanent" portion of current assets led to the modern depiction of current assets as having a permanent base and some seasonal or cyclical fluctuation. See Figure 7-1.
        1. This maintains the traditional notion that permanent assets should be financed with long-term capital, while temporary assets should be financed with short-term credit.
        2. The idea is that a firm should attempt to match the maturity structure of its assets and liabilities.

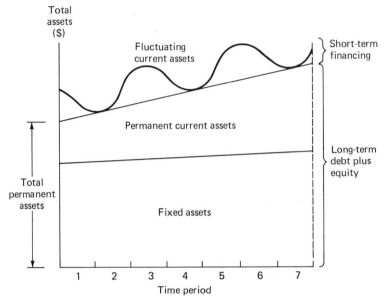

Figure 7-1. Fluctuating versus Permanent Investment

C. Some firms follow other maturity matching policies.
   1. Figure 7-2 depicts a firm financing all of its fixed assets with long-term capital but part of its permanent current assets with short-term credit. This indicates a rather aggressive working capital policy and may result in loan renewal problems.
   2. Figure 7-3 depicts a firm financing all of its permanent assets plus some of the seasonal demand with permanent capital. Such a conservative working capital policy loses, to a certain extent, the advantages of using shorter-term credit.

III. Use of short-term debt versus long-term debt.
   A. Short-term debt is used because it is often cheaper than long-term debt.
   B. Short-term debt also provides greater flexibility in meeting fluctuating financing needs.
   C. However, the possibility that it may not be renewed makes short-term debt more risky to use.
   D. Thus, the use of short-term debt involves a risk/return tradeoff.

IV. Relationship of current to fixed assets.
   A. Both current and fixed asset investment analyses require estimates of the effects of such investments on profits.
   B. Three considerations, however, must be kept in mind.
      1. Discounting plays a minor role in current asset analysis compared to capital budgeting.
      2. Increasing current assets while holding constant production and sales decreases risk, but it also decreases profits.
      3. Short-run adjustment to sales fluctuations can only be made by working

capital management.

C. A risk/return tradeoff exists in current asset holding.
   1. The minimum balance of each asset to be held must be determined.
   2. The level of safety stock required to protect the firm against forecasting error must also be established.

V. Working capital policy combines current asset and current liability management.

   A. The two aspects of working capital policy, the liability maturity structure and the current asset policy, should be coordinated.

   B. The aim of the working capital policy is to optimize the return to the stockholder through a risk/return tradeoff.

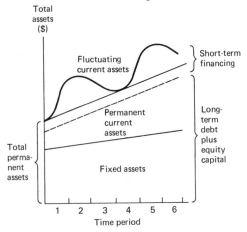

Figure 7-2. Aggressive Working Capital Policy

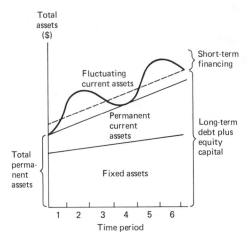

Figure 7-3. Conservative Working Capital Policy

PROBLEM

7-1. Bailey Mill Supplies Company has traditionally maintained current assets at a conservative 75 percent of sales. Mr. Bailey asked his financial manager to formulate some alternative policies based on current assets at 50, 60, and 70 percent of sales for next year. Net sales are forecast to be $2,400,000. Fixed assets total $1,000,000, and the firm's optimal capital structure has been determined to be 40 percent debt, 60 percent equity. EBIT is expected to be at a rate of 20 percent on net sales. The firm's cost of debt capital is 8 percent, and its tax rate is 50 percent.

Show the expected return on equity under each proposed policy.

Solution:

	Alternative		
Current Assets =	*50%*	*60%*	*70% of Sales*
Fixed assets =	$1,000,000	$1,000,000	$1,000,000
Current assets			
(% of Sales) X (Sales)	−1,200,000	1,440,000	1,680,000
Total assets	$2,200,000	$2,440,000	$2,680,000
Debt (40% of assets) =	880,000	976,000	1,072,000
Equity	$1,320,000	$1,464,000	$1,608,000

	Alternative		
Current Assets =	*50%*	*60%*	*70% of Sales*
EBIT (20%) X (Sales)	$ 480,000	$ 480,000	$ 480,000
Interest @ 8%	70,400	78,080	85,760
EBT	$ 409,600	401,920	394,240
Taxes (50%)	204,800	200,960	197,120
Earnings	$ 204,800	$ 200,960	$ 197,120
Return on equity	15.5%	13.7%	12.25%

Current Asset Management

8

THEME

Principles for controlling investment in cash, marketable securities, accounts receivable, and inventories are developed, and the general application of these principles are discussed.

I. Controlling investment in cash and marketable securities.
    A. There are three primary reasons for holding cash.
        1. The transactions motive enables the firm to conduct its ordinary business-making purchases and sales.
        2. The precautionary motive depends on two factors:
            a. The predictability of cash inflows and outflows.
            b. The firm's ability to borrow on short notice.
        3. Speculative motive.
            a. Primarily to take advantage of profit-making opportunities that may arise.
            b. Large accumulations of cash for speculative purposes are rarely found.
            c. Both the precautionary and speculative motives are largely satisfied by holdings of marketable securities, which may be regarded as "near money" assets.
    B. Adequate cash provides certain benefits.
        1. Sufficient cash permits taking trade discounts.
        2. Adequate cash is required to strengthen the current and acid test ratios, which are key items in the appraisal of the firm's credit position.
        3. Ample cash also is desirable to take advantage of favorable business opportunities.

4. Adequate cash is necessary to provide the firm with sufficient liquidity to meet various emergencies.

C. Methods of improving the inflow-outflow pattern of cash and thereby conserving cash include:

1. Synchronization of cash flows.

   a. Frequent requisitioning of funds by division offices from the central office improves cash flow.

   b. Effective forecasting reduces the cash on hand to meet actual requirements.

2. Expediting collections and check clearing.

   a. Checks received must clear the bank before funds can be spent.

   b. Expediting the process involves reducing the time required for clearing the checks. This is a function of the distance between the payer's and the payee's banks.

   c. The lock-box plan expedites this process by providing for a post office collection box in a customer's city where pickups are made by a bank in the city. The checks are then cleared in the local area and the collecting bank remits by wire to the seller's bank of deposit.

   d. If the firm's own collection and clearing process is more efficient than that of the recipients of its checks, the firm can utilize "float," that is, maximize the use of its funds in transit. This allows the firm to show a negative balance on its own records and still retain a positive balance on the bank's records.

3. Slowing down disbursements.

   a. Firms could simply delay payments.

   b. Maintain deposits in distant banks.

   c. Use slow or awkward payment procedures.

D. Implementing the cash management procedures mentioned in C above involves an expense to the firm.

1. This expense is worth incurring wherever marginal returns exceed marginal expenses.

2. The minimum cash balance should be determined.

   a. This is required for transactions, however, an additional amount may be held as safety stock.

   b. Banks require firms to maintain "compensating balances" with them in lieu of additional service charges as well as to compensate for lenient terms made in loan agreements.

   c. The minimum balance should be the larger of transaction balances plus safety stocks or required compensating balances.

3. The overdraft system provides a convenient arrangement whereby a bank automatically extends a loan to cover any shortage when a check is written.

   a. Maximum loan limits must be agreed upon beforehand.

   b. This system is used by most countries outside the U.S.

        c. Its use by some U.S. financial institutions both for personal checking accounts and for firms seems to be increasing.

II.   Investment of funds.

    A. A firm may have cash to invest for the following reasons:

       1. Seasonal or cyclical fluctuations.

       2. Accumulation of resources as provision for and protection against a number of predicted and unpredictable contingencies.

    B. Criteria used in selecting security portfolios.

       1. Risk of default.

          a. Most corporate security portfolios are composed of securities with minimum risks of default.

          b. However, minimum risk securities provide the lowest return.

       2. Marketability. Precautionary and speculative motives require that a firm's portfolio be readily marketable.

       3. Maturity.

          a. Longer-term maturities have a higher degree of risk, but provide for higher returns.

          b. Interest rate fluctuations cause considerable price changes to longer-term maturities.

          c. As this portfolio is used to supply current requirements, it is generally advisable to confine security selection to the shorter maturities.

    C. Alternative marketable securities for investments:

       1. U.S. Treasury bills.

       2. U.S. Treasury certificates.

       3. U.S. Treasury notes.

       4. U.S. Treasury bonds.

       5. Negotiable certificates of deposit.

       6. Prime commercial paper.

       7. Eurodollar bank time deposits.

       8. Bonds and stocks of other corporations.

       9. Bonds and stocks of the firm in question.

III.   Management of investment in receivables.

    A. Typical ratios.

       1. For manufacturing firms a ratio of receivables to sales of 8-12 percent.

       2. An average collection period of one month.

       3. A ratio of receivables to total assets centering around 16-20 percent.

    B. Determinants of the level of receivables.

       1. Volume of credit sales.

       2. Average period between sales and collections, which is dependent upon:

          a. Economic conditions.

          b. Credit policy variables (controllable factors).

            1) Credit standards.

            2) Credit period.

            3) Discounts for early payment.

        4) Collection policy.

C. Credit standards.

   1. Credit quality costs must be considered.

     a. Defaults or bad debt losses.

     b. Investigation and collection costs.

     c. Costs of capital tied up in receivables.

   2. The evaluation of credit risk—the Cs of credit.

     a. Character—the probability that the customer will try to honor his obligation.

     b. Capacity—subjective judgment or evaluation of the ability of the customer to pay.

     c. Capital—measured by the general financial position of the firm as indicated by financial ratio analysis.

     d. Collateral—represented by assets the customer may offer as a pledge for security.

     e. Conditions—the impact of general economic trends on the firm or special developments in certain areas of the economy.

D. Sources of credit information.

   1. Previous experience with the customer.

   2. Work of the local credit associations, including:

     a. Credit interchange through the National Association of Credit Management.

     b. Periodic meetings of local industry groups.

   3. Some credit reporting agencies.

     a. Dun & Bradstreet.

       1) Widest coverage.

       2) A reference book, published six times a year, with credit ratings of firms.

     b. Agencies specializing in coverage of a limited number of industries.

       1) National Credit Office.

       2) Lyon Furniture Mercantile Agency.

E. Use of credit ratings in credit decisions.

   1. Two types of information are provided.

     a. Financial strength.

     b. Composite credit appraisal.

   2. Credit reports provide more detailed information.

     a. History of customer.

     b. Discussion of business operations and location.

     c. Financial information.

     d. Payment experience.

   3. Risk class groupings can be developed on basis of above information indicating probable loss ratio as a percentage of total sales to firms in that risk group.

   4. The probable loss ratio may be related to the firm's margin of profit

and overhead in relation to revenues.
  5. Credit limits set a maximum on the total amount of credit without a detailed review of the customer.
    a. It may be related to experience with the customer.
    b. If there has been no experience, it may be related to probable loss ratio.
    c. It may be a fraction of the firm's net worth.
F. Terms of credit.
  1. Specify the period for which credit is extended, and the discount, if any, for early payment.
  2. The credit term "2/10, net 30" means that a two percent discount is allowed if the purchase is paid for within 10 days; otherwise the entire amount is due in 30 days.
  3. The credit term "net 30" indicates that no discount is offered, and the full amount is due in 30 days.
  4. A credit term "2/10, net 30, May 1 dating," means that the effective invoice date is May 1. The discount may be taken until May 10, and the net is due May 30.
G. The credit period.
  1. Lengthening the credit period stimulates sales.
  2. Cost of receivables increases with lengthening credit periods.
H. Cash discounts.
  1. Increasing the size of the discount will attract customers desiring to take discounts.
  2. Average collection period will change.
  3. Cost of the discount will change.
  4. Optimal discount point should be established at the point where costs and benefits are exactly offsetting.
I. Collection Policy.
  1. The firm can attempt to collect past due accounts in several ways.
    a. Letter.
    b. Telephone call.
    c. Collection agency.
  2. The collection process may be expensive.
    a. Firmness is required to prevent increased collection periods.
    b. Losses must be minimized.
  3. Optimal policy again is where costs and benefits are offsetting.
IV. Inventories must be held by all firms in order to operate. Inventory-to-sales ratios are generally concentrated in the 12-20 percent range, while inventory-to-total assets ratios range from 16-30 percent. Management strives to minimize investment in inventories.
A. Types of inventories.
  1. Raw materials.
  2. Work in process.

    3. Finished goods.

  B. Determinants of the levels of raw materials inventories.

    1. Anticipated production.

    2. Seasonality of production.

    3. Reliability of supply sources.

    4. Efficiency of scheduling purchases.

    5. Production operations.

  C. Determinants of work in process inventories.

    1. Length of the production period.

    2. Make versus buy decisions.

  D. Determinants of the level of finished good inventories.

    1. Coordination of production and sales.

    2. Credit terms and credit policies.

  E. General determinants of investment in inventory.

    1. Level of sales.

    2. Length and technical nature of the production processes.

    3. Durability versus perishability or style factor in the end product.

  F. Inventory analysis is generalized.

    1. Managing all types of assets is basically an inventory-type problem.

      a. A basic stock to balance inflows and outflows is necessary.

      b. Safety stocks for the unexpected are needed.

      c. Anticipation stocks for future growth needs should be considered.

    2. Size of investment results in rising and falling costs.

      a. Costs that rise with larger inventories are designated as *carrying costs*.

        1) Warehousing.

        2) Interest on funds tied up in inventories.

        3) Insurance.

        4) Obsolescence.

      b. Costs that fall with size of inventories are designated as *ordering costs*.

        1) Fewer production interruptions.

        2) Fewer losses of sales because of inventory shortages.

        3) Possible purchase discounts.

    3. Decision rule: choose that inventory investment where the curves for the two types of cost intersect; this will minimize the combined inventory investment costs.

  G. The inventory decision model—Economic Order Quantity.

    1. It offers a method of controlling investment in inventory.

    2. Formula:

$$EOQ = \sqrt{\frac{2 \times F \times S}{P \times C}} = \sqrt{\frac{2 \times 10 \times 100}{1 \times 0.2}} = 100 \text{ units}$$

where

EOQ = economic order quantity

S = sales for the period in units = 100 units

C = carrying cost = 20 percent of inventory value

P = purchase price per unit of inventory = $1 per unit

F = fixed cost per order = $10

A = average inventory $= \dfrac{EOQ}{2}$ = 50 units + safety stock

a. The larger the sales per period or processing costs per order, the larger the EOQ.

b. The larger the inventory carrying charge, the smaller the EOQ.

3. There are two contributions of the EOQ control method.

a. It helps achieve sound inventory management.

b. It provides a basis for projecting requirements for investments in inventories.

V. Cash management may be considered as an inventory problem.

A. Optimum cash balances can be found by the use of inventory type models.

B. Cash inflows are represented by the "orders" of an inventory model. These come from the following:

1. Receipts.

2. Borrowing.

3. Sale of securities.

C. Primary "carrying costs" of cash are the opportunity costs of the lost interest payments.

D. The principal "ordering costs" are brokerage fees.

PROBLEMS

8-1. The Jensen Corporation reports $2,500,000 in purchases of materials for the year. Outstanding accounts payable total $325,000. How many days' purchases remain outstanding?

Solution:

a. $\dfrac{\$2,500,000 \text{ purchases}}{360 \text{ days}}$ = $6,944 purchases per day.

b. $\dfrac{\$325,000 \text{ A/P}}{\$6,944 \text{ purchases/day}}$ = 46.8 days payables outstanding

8-2. If a firm sells on terms of net 60 days and its accounts are, on the average, 30 days overdue, what will its investment in receivables be? (Annual credit sales are $800,000.)

Solution:

60 net
<u>+30 overdue</u>
90 days

90/360 = ¼ x $800,000 credit sales = $200,000 accounts receivable.

8-3. The Porterfield Production Company has sales of $60 million a year in a good year and $40 million in a poor year. Its fixed assets are $25 million; receivables and inventories are 35 percent of sales; total assets are constant at $50 million. The firm must have liquidity because of substantial risks involved in the production of a new product. In addition, the firm must be ready to meet foreign competitors. How much cash does the firm have available for investment in good years? In poor years?

Solution:

	Good Year†	Bad Year†
Sales	$ 60	$ 40
Fixed assets	25	25
Receivables and inventories††	21	14
Total operating assets	$ 46	$ 39
Total assets	$ 50	$ 50
Total operating assets	−46	−39
Cash available for investment	$ 4	$ 11

†Amounts in millions.
††.35 times sales.

The above results indicate that higher levels of sales utilize greater amounts of cash.

8-4. The Quadraphone Company expects its annual sales rate to double within the next few months. Current sales are 50,000 units at a cost of $5 a unit. Order processing costs will remain at $20.00 an order, but inventory carrying charges are expected to increase from $.75 to $1.00 because of additional storage and handling requirements.
   a. If the firm wishes to minimize inventory costs, what is the optimal number of orders it will utilize once the annual sales level is achieved?
   b. At what inventory level should a reorder be made, if the desired safety

stock is 300 units (on hand initially), and one week is required for delivery? Assume 50 weeks in a year.

Solution:

a. EOQ = economical order quantity
$\quad\quad S$ = sales for period in units = 100,000 units
$\quad\quad P$ = price paid per unit = \$5 per unit
$\quad\quad F$ = purchasing cost per order = \$20 per order
$\quad\quad C$ = percentage inventory carrying charge per unit = 20%.

$$\text{EOQ} = \sqrt{\frac{2 \times S \times F}{P \times C}}$$

$$\text{EOQ} = \sqrt{\frac{2 \times 100,000 \times 20.00}{\$5 \times .2}} = \sqrt{\frac{4,000,000}{\$1}}$$

EOQ = 2,000 units.

$$\frac{\text{sales}}{\text{EOQ}} = \frac{100,000}{2,000} = 50 \text{ orders.}$$

b. Weekly rate of use $= \dfrac{100,000 \text{ units}}{50 \text{ weeks in a year}} = 2,000 \text{ units.}$

Reorder point = safety stock + weekly rate of use
$\quad\quad\quad\quad\quad\quad = 300 + 1(2,000) = 2,300 \text{ units.}$

Major Sources of Short-Term Financing

9

THEME

Major sources of short-term financing are analyzed from the viewpoint of the financial manager.

I.   Trade credit is the largest category of short-term financing and is especially important for smaller firms which do not have access to other capital markets.
   A. Purchase of materials or supplies on credit from other firms is recorded as accounts payable.
   B. Trade credit is a "spontaneous" source of financing in that it arises from ordinary business transactions.
   C. Credit terms are determined by the following:
      1. Economic nature of the product.
         a. Turnover.
         b. Perishability.
      2. Seller circumstances.
         a. Financial strength of seller.
         b. Size of seller.
         c. Use of credit terms in sales promotion.
         d. Degree of excess capacity.
      3. Buyer circumstances.
         a. Degree of financial strength.
         b. Risks associated with the product.
   D. Cash discounts may be given.
      1. Savings from the discount frequently exceed the rate of interest on

borrowed funds; therefore, trade credit can be expensive.
  2. The length of credit is influenced by the size of the discounts offered.
E. Forms in which credit terms are expressed.
  1. Individual order terms: for example, 1/10, n/30; 2/10, n/60; and so on.
  2. Lumped-order terms and billing: End of Month (EOM); Middle of Month (MOM).
  3. Dating: 7/10-60; 2/10-60; Receipt of Goods (ROG).
F. Implicit cost of trade credit.
  1. Price of the merchandise may be higher or its quality lower.
  2. The implicit cost may be measured directly if a cash discount is involved.
    a. Formula:

$$\text{cost} = \frac{\text{discount percent}}{(100 - \text{discount percent})} \times \frac{360}{\substack{\text{max. days} - \text{discount} \\ \text{credit} \qquad \text{period}}}$$

    b. Illustration—terms of 2/10, net 30.

$$\text{cost} = \frac{2}{100 - 2} \times \frac{360}{30 - 10} = 0.0204 \times 18 = 36.73\%$$

G. Advantages of trade credit as a source of financing.
  1. It is convenient and informal.
  2. Its wise use promotes sound customer relations.
  3. A firm that does not qualify for credit from a financial institution may receive credit from the seller because of the latter's acquaintance with the firm.
  4. The cost may be higher or lower.
    a. Cost is commensurate with risks to the seller.
    b. The buyer may not have better alternatives.
    c. Sometimes the buyer has not calculated the cost of trade credit.
II. Commercial bank loans.
A. Importance.
  1. Banks occupy a pivotal position in the short-term money market.
  2. Banks often provide the marginal credit that allows firms to expand.
B. Characteristics.
  1. Forms of loans—single loan, credit line.
  2. Size of loans—mostly small in number, large in dollar amount.
  3. Maturity—concentration on the short-term lending market.
  4. Security—high-risk borrowers must provide collateral.
  5. Minimum average balance—usually 15-20 percent of loan is required as "compensating balance."
  6. Repayment of bank loans—"clean up" required for firms to demonstrate ability to repay.
C. Measuring the effective costs of bank loans.
  1. Interest rates are quoted in three ways.

        a. Regular compound interest.

        b. Discount interest.

        c. Installment interest.

    2. Compensating balances may increase effective cost.

    3. Fees may also be charged.

  D. In choosing a bank, the financial manager should consider:

    1. The bank's policy toward risk.

    2. The availability of management counseling services.

    3. The loyalty of the bank when the firm encounters difficulties.

    4. The stability of the bank's deposits as a measure of possible repayment pressure.

    5. Coinciding of the loan areas in which the bank specializes with the borrower's area of operations.

    6. The maximum size loan a bank can make.

    7. The financial and business services offered by the bank.

III. Commercial paper consists of promissory notes of large firms that are sold primarily to other business firms, insurance companies, investment funds, pension funds, and small banks.

  A. Maturities vary from two to six months with an average of about five months.

  B. Costs are generally about one-fourth to one-half of 1 percent below the prime rate.

  C. The open market for commercial paper is limited to firms which are good credit risks.

    1. Advantages.

        a. The commercial paper market is the broadest and most advantageous of the capital markets.

        b. It provides more funds at lower rates than do other methods, especially since compensating balances are not required.

        c. The borrower avoids the inconvenience and expense of financing arrangements.

        d. Publicity and prestige are enhanced.

        e. Some counseling from the commercial paper dealer is available.

    2. Disadvantages.

        a. The amount of funds available is limited to the excess liquidity of the main suppliers of funds at a particular time.

        b. A commercial paper borrower who is in temporary financial difficulty receives little consideration because of the impersonal nature of the commercial paper market.

    3. Its use has increased greatly during the tight money period since mid-1966.

        a. From the borrower's standpoint, the availability of bank credit has been reduced.

        b. From the viewpoint of lenders, its yields are often higher than on other low-risk, short-term investments.

IV. Use of security in short-term financing.
   A. Conditions for offering security.
      1. If the borrower's credit is not sufficient to justify a loan.
      2. If lenders will quote lower interest rates for a secured loan.
   B. Types of collateral offered:
      1. Marketable stocks or bonds are held by a few firms.
      2. Real property and equipment are usually used to secure long-term loans.
      3. Short-term assets are most frequently offered. They include:
         a. Accounts receivable.
         b. Inventories.

V. Accounts receivable financing.
   A. Two major forms.
      1. In *pledging* no notification is made to the buyer of the goods, and the lender has recourse to the holder of the account receivable in case of default. The receivable is *not* sold to the lender; it is merely used to secure a loan.
      2. In *factoring* the buyer of the goods makes payment directly to the factor, and the factor has no recourse to the seller of the goods in case of default. The receivable *is* sold outright to the lender.
   B. Procedure for pledging accounts receivable.
      1. A contract setting forth legal rights and procedures is agreed upon.
      2. The firm takes its invoices to the financial institution, where they are reviewed and either accepted or rejected.
      3. Upon acceptance, payment is made to the firm.
      4. When the buyer of the goods makes payment to the firm, the proceeds are turned over to the financial institution.
      5. Normally, the firms which use this service are small, and about half of the individual invoices are under $250.
   C. Procedure for factoring accounts receivable.
      1. A legal contract is drawn up.
      2. The firm receives an order for goods.
      3. The purchase order is drawn up and sent to the factor for a credit check.
      4. If the factor disapproves the purchase order, the selling firm can make the sale, but the seller bears the credit risk.
      5. If the factor approves the purchase order, it is processed and the invoice is stamped with instructions to remit payment to the factor.
      6. For a small firm, the credit checking service of the factor can be utilized as a cost-saving device.
   D. The cost of receivable financing.
      1. Accounts receivable pledging rates normally range from 8 to 12 percent a year.
      2. Factoring charges are composed of two elements:

      a. A fee for credit checking ranging from 1 to 3 percent.

      b. An interest charge of 8 to 12 percent that is prorated over the period for which the funds are outstanding; that is, it is an annual rate.

E. Advantages of receivable financing.

   1. It is a flexible method.

   2. The security provided may make financing possible.

   3. Factoring may provide the services of a credit department.

F. Disadvantages of accounts receivable financing.

   1. When invoices are numerous, administrative costs may be high.

   2. The firm is using a highly liquid asset as security.

G. In the future, accounts receivable financing will increase in relative importance as automation reduces the costs and increases the convenience of employing receivables financing. Credit card use is a prime example of a type of automated accounts receivable financing.

VI. Inventory financing.

A. Major forms.

   1. Blanket inventory lien.

   2. Trust receipts.

   3. Field warehousing.

B. The blanket inventory lien gives the lending institution a lien against all inventories of the borrowing firm.

   1. The firm is considered a relatively poor risk.

   2. The firm is free to sell the inventories. This reduces the value of the collateral.

C. A trust receipt is an instrument acknowledging that the borrower holds goods in trust for the lender.

   1. Disadvantages.

      a. Must be issued for specific goods.

      b. Other complex legal requirements.

   2. The borrower may keep the goods in his possession, but he must remit the proceeds of the sale of the specific goods to the lender.

D. Field warehousing.

   1. Establishment requires two elements:

      a. Public notification of the arrangement.

      b. Providing supervision over the warehouse.

   2. Financing procedure.

      a. Goods are delivered to the field warehouse.

      b. Custodian describes the goods and notifies the lender of the delivery.

      c. The lender deposits funds for the use of the borrower.

      d. The borrower receives purchase orders and transmits them to the lender.

      e. The lender notifies the custodian to release the goods.

PROBLEMS

9-1. How much additional trade credit will be spontaneously generated if a firm which previously averaged $1,500 of purchases a day (on terms of net 20) now doubles its purchases and simultaneously gets new credit terms of net 30?

Solution:

$3,000 purchases x 30 days = $90,000 payables
$1,500 purchases x 20 days = $\underline{30,000}$ payables
$60,000 additional trade credit

9-2. If a firm is unable to take advantage of available cash discounts at all times, which credit terms should it find least desirable, all other things constant?
  a. 1/10 net 20.
  b. 2/10 net 20.
  c. 1/10 net 30.
  d. 2/10 net 30.
  e. Indifferent between *a* and *c*.

Solution:

  a. 1/10 net 20 offers the smallest discount and the shortest terms.

9-3. Given credit terms of 1/10 net 20, what is the cost, on an annual basis, of not taking the cash discount?

Solution:

Use the following formula:

$$\text{Cost} = \frac{\text{discount percent}}{(100 - \text{discount \%})} \times \frac{360 \text{ days}}{(\text{max. days credit} - \text{discount period})}$$

$$= \frac{1}{99} \times \frac{360}{10} = 36.36\%.$$

9-4. The Jones Company needs $90,000 to pay off outstanding obligations. A local bank will make the loan but requires a 15 percent compensating balance. (The company would ordinarily keep a zero balance.) If the stated rate of interest is 6 percent, what is the effective cost?

Solution:

$$\frac{0.06 \text{ nominal cost}}{0.85\% \text{ of funds received}} = 7.06\% \text{ effective rate.}$$

Alternative Solution:

a. $0.85 \, X = \$ \, 90,000$ net loan
$X = \$105,882$ gross loan.

b. $105,882.00
$\underline{\times \qquad 0.06}$
$\$ \quad 6,352.92$ interest cost

c. $\dfrac{\$6,352.92 \text{ interest cost}}{\$90,000 \text{ funds received}} = 7.06\%$ effective rate.

9-5. The Rice Company borrows on a one-year bank note at 7 percent effective rate of interest. The total interest payment, $400, is deducted from the loan amount at the time the loan is issued. If the firm repays the loan in 12 equal monthly installments, what is the amount of the note? (Interest tables are not necessary for this problem.)

Solution:

$$\$400 = \text{ interest payment}$$
$$X = \text{ gross loan}$$
$$(X - \$400) = \text{ net loan}$$
$$(X - \$400/2) = \text{ average funds available over the year}$$

$$\frac{\$400 \text{ interest cost}}{(X - \$400)/2 \text{ average funds received}} = 0.07 \text{ effective rate of interest}$$

$$\$800 = 0.07 \, (X - \$400)$$
$$X = \$11,829.$$

9-6. A large manufacturing firm has been selling on a 1/10 net 30 basis. If the firm changes its credit terms to 2/10 net 20, what change might be anticipated on the balance sheet of its customers?

Solution:

Other things constant, the higher cash discount will give customers more incentive to make payment early, and payables will decrease. Also, the shorter credit terms will cause an increase in bank loans for the purpose of meeting payments.

9-7. The Friendly Finance Company has just sold an issue of six-month commercial paper. The paper carries an interest rate of 4 percent. Which of the choices below is most likely to be the current prime rate?

a. Above 5½%.   d. 4 percent.

b. 5 percent.   e. Below 4 percent.

c. 4½ percent.

Solution:

c. Commercial paper issues by large, reputable firms typically carries an interest rate slightly below the prime rate. Therefore, 4½ percent is the most likely value for the prime rate.

9-8. A firm has just negotiated a $25,000 loan with a bank. The stated rate of interest is 6 percent. If the bank discounts the loan, what is the effective rate of interest? (The loan is repaid at the end of the year).

Solution:

$$\frac{X \text{ interest}}{\$25,000 \text{ gross loan}} = 0.06 \text{ stated interest rate}$$

X = $1,500 interest

$25,000 gross loan

$\underline{-1,500}$ interest

$23,500 net loan

$$\frac{\$\ 1,500 \text{ interest}}{\$23,500 \text{ net loan}} = 6.38\% \text{ effective rate of interest.}$$

9-9. In problem 9-8, what is the approximate effective rate of interest if interest is computed on the initial balance, the loan is not discounted, and the loan is paid back in 12 equal monthly installments?

Solution:

$$\frac{\$\ 1,500}{\$25,000} = 0.06$$

$$\frac{\$25,000}{2} = \$12,500 \text{ average funds outstanding}$$

$$\frac{\$\ 1,500}{\$12,500} = 12\% \text{ effective rate of interest.}$$

9-10.

Kendall Corporation—Balance Sheet as of December 31, 1976

Cash	$ 40,000	Accounts payable	$ 90,000
Marketable securities	60,000	Bank loans (5%)	65,000
Accounts receivable	75,000	Notes payable	50,000
Inventories	100,000	Current maturity of long-	
Other current assets	25,000	term debt	20,000
Total current assets	$300,000	Total current	
		liabilities	$225,000
		Long-term debt	75,000
Fixed assets (net)	300,000	Net worth	300,000
Total assets	$600,000	Total liabilities	$600,000

Sales for the year: $1,200,000

a. If the sales/total assets ratio remains at 2 times, how much new financing will Kaplan need if sales rise by 12 percent?

Solution:

$1,200,000
　　x1.12
$1,344,000 new sales level

$$\frac{\$1,344,000}{X} = 2$$

$672,000 new total assets level
−600,000 total assets 1974
$ 72,000 new financing needed

b. Kendall suppliers sell on credit terms of 30 days. Kendall's payables presently represent 45 days of purchases. Other things remaining the same, what will Kaplan's debt ratio be after new short-term financing is used to bring the firm current on its trade obligations?

Solution:

No change. The new short-term financing will equal the overdue payables, thus leaving the debt ratio unchanged.

c. In b, what will Kendall's current ratio be if marketable securities are sold off to generate the funds necessary to become current on trade obligations?

Solution:

1. $\dfrac{45-30}{45} = \dfrac{15}{45} = \dfrac{1}{3}$

$\dfrac{1}{3}$ x $90,000 accounts payable (1974) = $30,000 marketable securities to be sold.

2. $300,000 total current assets
   $\underline{-30,000}$ marketable securities to be sold
   $270,000 new current assets

3. $225,000 present current liabilities
   $\underline{-30,000}$ excess payables
   $195,000 new current liabilities.

4. $\dfrac{\$270,000}{\$195,000}$ = 1.38 current ratio.

9-11. The Tarrington Products Company has been growing rapidly. It is suffering from insufficient working capital, however, and has therefore become slow in paying bills. Of its total accounts payable, $200,000 is overdue. This threatens its relationship with its main supplier of equipment used in the manufacture of various kinds of warships for the U.S. Navy. Over 90 percent of its sales are to four large defense contractors. Its balance sheet, sales and net profit for the year ended December 31, 1976, are shown here.

Tarrington Products—Balance Sheet, December 31, 1976

Cash	$ 40,000	Trade credit†	$ 400,000
Receivables	600,000	Bank loans	280,000
Inventories		Accruals†	90,000
Raw material	50,000		
Work in progress	300,000	Total current debt	770,000
Finished goods	80,000	Chattel mortgages	390,000
		Capital stock	140,000
Total current assets	1,070,000	Surplus	130,000
Equipment	360,000		
Total assets	$1,430,000	Total claims	$1,430,000
Sales	$2,500,000		
Profit after tax	130,000		

†Increases spontaneously with sales increases.

a. If the same ratio of sales to total assets continues and if sales increase to $3,000,000 how much nonspontaneous financing, including retained earnings, will be required?

Solution:

$$\left[\frac{\text{assets}}{\text{sales}} - \frac{\text{spontaneous sources}}{\text{sales}}\right] \times \text{increase in sales}$$

$$= [0.572 - 0.196] \times \$500,000 = \$188,000 = \text{financing required.}$$

Note: This figure is calculated on the assumption that accounts payable will continue to be overdue.

b. Assume the following:
   Receivables turn over five times a year (sales/receivables = 5).
   All sales are made on credit.
   The factor requires a 9 percent reserve for returns and disputed items.
   The factor also requires a 3 percent commission to cover the costs of credit checking.
   There is a 7 percent annual interest charge based on receivables less any reserve requirements and commissions. This payment is made at the beginning of the period and is deducted from the advance.
   1. What is the total amount of receivables outstanding at any time, when sales are $2.5 million?
   2. How much cash does the firm actually receive by factoring the average amount of receivables?
   3. What is the average duration of advances, on the basis of 360 days a year?
   4. What is the total annual dollar cost of the financing?
   5. What is the effective annual financing charge (percentage) paid on the the money received?

Solution:

1. Average receivables outstanding = ($2,500,000)/5 times = $500,000.
2. Cash actually received by firm:

$500,000 average receivables outstanding
 −45,000 reserve (9% of $500,000)
$455,000
 −15,000 commission (3% of $500,000)

$440,000 amount of advance after commission
  −6,160 interest charge at 7% (see below)
$433,840 cash actually received

Computation of interest charge:
Since the turnover rate of five times represents one-fifth of a year, or 72 days, the interest rate is one-fifth of 7 percent, or 1.4 percent. Applied to the base of $440,000 this rate is equal to $6,160.

3. Average duration of the advance is the collection period for the receivables, or 360 days/5, which equals 72 days.

4. Total annual cost of financing is the sum of the commission and interest costs: ($15,000 + $6,160) = $21,160.

5. Effective annual financing charge $= \left[\dfrac{\$\ 21{,}160}{\$433{,}840}\right] \times 5 = 24.4\%.$

Decisions Involving Long-Term Assets

Part Four

The Interest Factor in Financial Decisions

THEME

Most financing decisions involve commitments over extended periods. The interest factor will therefore have a crucial impact on the soundness of the decisions.

I.   A compound amount or compound value is defined as the sum (P_n) to which a beginning amount of principle (P_o) will grow over n years when interest is earned at the rate of i percent a year.

    A. $P_n = P_o (1 + i)^n$.

    B. Letting (CVIF) = (compound value interest factor) = $(1 + i)^n$, the above equation may be written as $P_n = P_o$ (CVIF). It is necessary only to go to an appropriate interest table to find the proper interest factor. See Appendix, compound value interest factor (CVIF) Table A-1.

    C. The compound value of $1,000.00 at 4 percent for 5 years may be found as $P_5 = \$1,000 (1.217) = \$1,217$.

II. *The present value of a future payment* (P_o) is the amount which, invested at a specified interest rate (i) today, would equal the future payment (P_n).

    A. Finding present values (or discounting) is simply the reverse of compounding.

    B. The present value of $1,217 at 4 percent is found by

$$P_o = P_n \left[\frac{1}{(1 + i)^n}\right] = \$1,217 \ (0.822) = \$1,000.$$

    The term in brackets is called the present value interest factor (PVIF);

$P_O = P_n$ (PVIF). See the present value interest factor (PVIF), Table A-2 in the Appendix.

III. An annuity is defined as a series of payments of a fixed amount (R) for a specified number of years. The first payment is assumed to occur at the *end* of the first year. The *compound value of an annuity* is the total amount one would have at the end of the annuity period if each payment was invested at a given interest rate and held to the end of the annuity period.

   A. S_n = compound value of an annuity, R = the periodic receipt,
   i = the interest rate, n = the number of years, and
   $S_n = R$ (CVIF$_a$) where CVIF is the interest factor shown in brackets directly below. See Appendix, compound value of an annuity interest factor (CVIF), Table A-3.†

$$S_n = R \left[\frac{(1 + i)^n - 1}{i} \right].$$

   B. A compounded value of a $1,000 annuity invested at 4 percent for 3 years is calculated. Compound value = CVIF$_a$ × annual receipt = 3.122 × $1,000 = $3,122.

IV. The *present value of an annuity* is the required lump sum on hand today to permit withdrawals of equal amounts (R) at the end of each year for n years.

   A. A_n = the present value of an annuity, R = the annual receipt, and

$$A_n = R \left[\frac{1 - (1 + i)^{-n}}{i} \right]$$

   $A_n = R$(PVIF)$_a$ where PVIF$_a$ is the interest factor shown in brackets above found in Appendix, the present value of annuity interest factor (PVIF$_a$), Table A-4.

   B. To withdraw $1,000 a year for 3 years when the interest rate is 4 percent, for example, requires:

$$A_n = R \text{(PVIF}_a)$$
$$= \$1,000 \times 2.775 = \$2,775.$$

V. There are other uses of the basic equations.

   A. To determine annual payments required to accumulate a future sum:

   1. $R = \dfrac{S_n}{\text{CVIF}_a}$

   2. What amount of money must be deposited at 5 percent for each of the next five years in order to have $10,000 at the end of the fifth year?

$$R = \frac{\$10,000}{5.526} = \$1,810.$$

   B. To find the annual receipts from a specified annuity:

   1. Beginning with a fixed amount of money, earning a fixed interest rate,

---

†The equation for an annuity is not derived here.

you plan to make a series of equal withdrawals. You wish to know the size of the withdrawals that will leave a balance of zero after the last one has been made.

2. $R = \dfrac{A_n}{\text{PVIF}_a}$

3. You have $7,000 earning 4 percent interest and you plan to make three equal yearly withdrawals starting in one year.

$$R = \frac{\$7{,}000}{2.775} = \$2{,}523.$$

C. *Interest rates* may be determined.

1. Frequently one knows the present value and cash flows associated with a payment stream but not the interest rate involved.

2. $\text{CVIF} = \dfrac{P_n}{P_o}$

3. A bank offers to lend $1,000 today upon agreement to repay $1,217 at the end of five years. What is the rate of interest involved?

$$\text{CVIF} = \frac{1{,}217}{1{,}000} = 1.217, \text{ the CVIF for 4\%}$$

See (CVIF) Table A-1 for 5 years.

D. To calculate the *present value of a series of uneven annual payments,* use the following formula (subscripts refer to time periods, X's refer to payments):

$$\text{PV} = X_1(\text{PVIF}_1) + X_2(\text{PVIF}_2) + \ldots + X_t(\text{PVIF}_t).$$

E. To calculate the *present value of a payments stream composed of one lump sum plus a stream of equal payments,* use the formula: PV = PV of lump sum + PV of series.

F. *Semiannual and other compounding periods* are often used.

1. Semiannual compounding means that interest is actually paid each six months.
   a. The interest rate is divided by two.
   b. The number of compounding periods is doubled since interest is paid twice a year.

2. The results of more frequent compounding may also be calculated.
   a. Divide the nominal interest rate by the number of times compounding occurs each year.
   b. Multiply the years by the number of compounding periods per year.

3. The general formula for this type of compounding is

$$P_n = P_o(1 + \frac{i}{m})^{mn}$$

where

m = number of compounding periods per year

n = number of years.

VI. Determination and evaluation of interest rates.

A. The general level of interest rates in the economy is determined by the interaction of the supply and demand for funds.

1. Funds are supplied by individuals, corporate savers, and banks, within the overall control of the Federal Reserve System.

2. Funds are demanded by business, individual borrowers, and government bodies.

B. The structure of interest rates is determined by the following influences:

1. The level of risk.

2. The term or maturity of the debt.

3. Other characteristics of the borrowers.

C. In evaluating the yields of a prospective investment, one must consider its opportunity costs.

1. A wide range of alternative potential investments is available in the economy.

2. An individual relates alternative prospective yields and risks to his needs and attitudes toward the possibility of losses.

3. A new investment is compared with the best of existing alternatives.

4. The opportunity cost of investing in a new alternative is the yield on the old alternative, which the new replaces.

PROBLEMS

10-1. At an annual growth rate of 10 percent, how long will it take to triple a sum of money?

Solution:

(Refer to the Compound Sum Table in the Appendix) 3,000 appears halfway between the 11th year (2.853) and the 12th year (3.138) in the 10 percent column; it therefore requires about 11.5 years to triple the sum of money.

10-2. If you bought a nondividend paying stock 13 years ago for $34 and the stock is now selling for $97, at what rate of interest has your capital grown?

Solution:

(Refer to the Compound Sum Table)

$97/34 = 2.853
2.853 appears in the 13th year at about 8.5 percent

10-3. Which amount is worth more at 8 percent: $2,000 today or $3,500 after five years?

Solution:

The PV of $3,500 at 8 percent over 5 years is calculated by:
P_o = $3,500 x 0.681 = $2,384, which is larger than $2,000.
Therefore $3,500 after five years at 8 percent is worth more than $2,000 today.

10-4. Because of illness, your 45-year-old aunt is expected to live only another ten years. You have placed her life savings of $22,000 in a bank earning 8 percent annually. She makes the first withdrawal one year from today. How much can she withdraw at the beginning of each of the remaining years to leave exactly zero in the account at the end of the tenth year?

Solution:

(Refer to the Present Value of an Annuity Table A-4 in Appendix).
Factor for nine years at 8 percent annually is 6,247
$22,000/6.247 = $3,522

10-5. How much must be invested today, at a 23 percent rate, in order to accumulate $5 in two years? (Work this problem without the use of the interest tables.)

Solution:

$X (1.23)^2$ = $5
$S (1.51)$ = 5
$X = 5/1.51$ = $3.31.

10-6. A savings and loan association advertises a 7 percent rate of interest compounded semiannually. What effective rate of interest is the savings and loan paying?

Solution:

$$(1 + 0.035)^2 - 1 = (1.0712) - 1 = 7.12\%.$$

10-7. What amount would an investor be willing to pay for a $1,000, five-year bond which pays $40 interest semiannually and is sold to yield 6 percent?

Solution:

a. $1,000 maturity value of the bond
x0.744 present value factor, 3% for 10 semiannual periods
$ 744

b. $ 40.00 semiannual interest
x   8.530 present value of an annuity factor of 3% for 10 semiannual
————————periods
$314.20

c. $ 744.00
    341.20
$1,085.20

10-8. The Atlas Coal Company is establishing a fund to fill in and replant forests over a strip mine. $700,000 will be required to do the job, and the funds will be needed ten years from now. The company plans to put a fixed amount into the fund each year for ten years, the first payment to be made in one year. Assume the fund will earn 5 percent a year. What annual contribution must be made to accumulate the $700,000 at the end of ten years?

Solution:

The answer is found as the sum of an annuity at the end of ten years. Use $CVIF_a$, Table A-3.

$$\text{Annual payment} \times 12.578 = \$700,000$$
$$\text{Annual payment} = \frac{\$700,000}{12.578} = \$55,653 \text{ a year.}$$

10-9. Your uncle will lend you $2,000 today if you agree to pay him $2,208 in five years. What rate of interest is your uncle charging you?

Solution:

$$CVIF = \frac{\$2,208}{\$2,000} = 1.104.$$

Looking across the five-year row in the CVIF Table A-1, we find the CVIF = 1.104 in the 2 percent column. Your uncle is charging you 2 percent interest, which is a good deal today!

Capital Budgeting Techniques

THEME

Capital budgeting is of the greatest significance because it involves commitments for large outlays whose benefits (or drawbacks) extend well into the future.

I. The capital budget is a plan of expenditures for fixed assets. It is significant for these reasons:
    A. It represents a decision whose results continue over an extended period.
    B. It represents an implicit sales forecast. Inaccurate forecasts will result in over-investment or under-investment in fixed assets.
    C. Good capital budgeting will improve the timing of asset acquisitions and the quality of assets purchased.
    D. Asset expansion involves substantial expenditures. The requisite financing must be arranged in advance.
    E. Failure occurs both because of too much capital investment and because of undue delay in replacing old equipment with modern equipment.

II. Overall view of capital budgeting.
    A. It is an application of the classic economic theory that marginal revenue should be equated to marginal cost.
    B. The demand for capital goods is represented by an investment return schedule.
    C. The supply of funds is represented by the firm's marginal cost of capital.

III. Investment proposals are assembled in categories.
    A. Replacements.
        1. Assets wear out or become obsolete.

    2. Estimates of cost savings in replacing an old asset can be made with a relatively high degree of confidence.

B. Expansion investments.

    1. Additional capacity is provided in existing product lines.

    2. Estimates are based on prior experience.

C. New product activities.

    1. This represents a form of expansion and possibly diversification.

    2. Estimates are subject to a wider margin of error.

D. Others, including intangible items.

    1. Pollution control equipment.

    2. Safety requirements.

    3. Social and environmental considerations.

IV. Administration of capital budgeting.

A. Approvals.

    1. Typically larger dollar amounts require higher levels of approval.

    2. Review and approval of major outlays is an important function of boards of directors.

B. Planning horizon.

    1. It varies with the nature of the industry.

    2. It is becoming longer as technology advances.

C. Payment schedule and post-audits.

    1. Finance department works with other departments to compile systematic records on the uses of funds.

    2. Data are also compiled on equipment purchased.

    3. Feedback data on actual savings should be compiled.

    4. Comparisons between earlier estimates and actual data provide a basis for review of past decisions and the formulation of new decisions.

V. Choosing among alternative proposals.

A. Frequently there are more proposals for projects than the firm is able or willing to finance.

    1. The proposals are ranked.

    2. A cutoff point is determined.

B. There are two basic types of proposals:

    1. *Mutually exclusive* proposals are alternative methods of performing the same job, such as a choice of conveyor belts versus fork-lift trucks for materials handling.

    2. *Independent items* are capital equipment considered for performing difficult tasks.

C. Good data is important.

    1. Reliable estimates of cost savings or revenue increases are critical.

    2. Effective record keeping for meaningful post-audits is essential.

    3. Good data require competent individuals to make the estimates.

VI. Three methods for ranking investment proposals are described.

A. The payback period is the number of years required to return the original investment from the net cash flow generated by a project. It is conceptually weak, because it ignores income beyond the payback period and does not take into account the fact that a dollar received today is more valuable than a dollar received in the future.

    B. The net present value method (NPV) is the present value of future returns discounted at the firm's cost of capital, minus the cost of the investment. If the net present value is positive, the project should be accepted; if negative, it should be rejected. If the two projects are mutually exclusive, the one with the higher NPV should be chosen.

       1. This method meets the objections to the payback method, in that it recognizes the time value of money.

       2. This method is generally preferable for ranking investment proposals.

    C. The internal rate of return (IRR) is the interest rate that equates the present value of the expected future cash flows, or receipts, to the initial cost outlay.

       1. The internal rate of return method also overcomes the conceptual flaws noted in the use of the payback method.

       2. The "break-even" characteristics of IRR make it an important decision-making tool.

VII. Calculation procedures.

    A. Determination of the payback period is demonstrated in Problem 11-5.

    B. The net present value is calculated using four basic steps.

       1. Estimate the actual cash outlay of the investment. This includes considering the sale of any old equipment and any tax savings or loss which is caused by the sale.

       2. Determine the incremental cash flows generated by the project, using the cash flow difference equation:

$$\Delta CF = (\Delta S - \Delta C - \Delta D)\,(1 - t) + \Delta D$$

where ΔS is the change in the sales level, ΔC is the change in costs, ΔD is the change in depreciation, and t is the firm's tax rate.

       3. Using the firm's cost of capital, calculate the present value of the incremental cash flows and the present value of the new machine's expected salvage value in the final time period and sum these figures.

       4. Compare the present value of the cash flows to the actual cash outlay to determine the investment decision to be made. See Problems 11-4, 11-5, and 11-6 as examples for the use of this method.

    C. The internal rate of return is calculated in basically the same way as the net present value.

       1. Estimate the actual cash outlay of the investment.

       2. Determine the incremental cash flows.

       3. Find the discount rate which forces the net present value to zero.

       4. Compare the calculated internal rate of return to the cost of capital to make the investment decision. See Problems 11-3 and 11-5.

VIII. The total capital budget is then formulated.
   A. It is necessary to select from a broad range of capital budgeting opportunities, and interrelationships among investment proposals must be noted:
      1. A capital budget is tentatively formulated.
      2. The allocation of corporate funds and decisions as to whether to raise additional funds are ordinarily made by the board of directors, the finance committee, or the executive committee—it is a high level decision.
      3. The capital budgeting program and financing decisions are simultaneously and interactively determined.
   B. A composition problem may arise.
      1. Individual projects may promise attractive yields, but difficulties might be involved in assuming all favorable projects simultaneously.
      2. If other firms in the same industry are expanding capacity or reducing costs, it may be impossible for all the firms to achieve their goals.
   C. The size of the total budget must be determined.
      1. Some firms follow the rule of thumb that growth will be financed only out of internally generated funds.
      2. Maintenance of a constant debt-to-equity ratio causes restricted growth if equity financing is not undertaken.
      3. If there is an absolute limit on the amount of debt financing, expenditures will be cut back in these instances:
         1. Internally generated funds are too small to make up the deficit.
         2. The firm will not undertake equity financing.

PROBLEMS

11-1.   As the cost of capital increases without limit, what happens to present value?
   a. Goes to plus infinity.
   b. Stays unchanged.
   c. Goes to zero.
   d. Must have dollar amount of investment to answer.
   e. Goes to minus infinity.

Solution:

   c. Goes to zero.

11-2.   What is one major advantage of the payback method?
   a. Explicit consideration of all receipts generated during the life of an investment.
   b. Adjustment for the time value of all inflows.

c. Focus on speed of return of invested funds.
d. Discounting of incremental outflows.
e. Focus on cash flows over time.

Solution:

c. Focus on speed of return of invested funds.

11-3. A $770 investment has the following cash returns:

Year	Return
1	$500
2	$125
3	$250

Find the internal rate of return.

Solution:

Cash Flow	9% PV Factors (from PVIF table)	Discounted Cash Flow	8% PV Factors (from PVIF table)
$500	0.917	458.5	0.926
125	0.842	105.3	0.857
250	0.772	193.0	0.794
		756.8	

Cash Flow	Discounted Cash Flow	7% PV Factors (from PVIF table)	Discounted Cash Flow
$500	463.0	0.935	467.5
125	107.1	0.873	109.1
250	198.5	0.816	204.0
	768.6		780.6

Internal rate of return = approximately 8 percent.

11-4. The Goodman Corporation has been presented with an investment opportunity which will yield ten years of increased annual profits as given below. If the cost of the investment is an immediate outlay of $125,000 and the firm requires a 10 percent return on its investment, what is the net present value of the investment? (Ignore taxes.)

Year(s)	Return
1	$80,000
2-9	$25,000
10	$30,000

Solution:

a.

Year(s)	Table	PV Factors	Returns	Discounted Return
1	A-2	0.909	$80,000	$ 72,720
2-9	A-4	4.850	$25,000	$121,250
10	A-2	0.386	$30,000	$ 11,580
				$205,550 present value of future returns

Note: The 2-to-9-year factor can be obtained from Table A-4 by subtracting the first-year value from the ninth-year value in the 10 percent column (5.759 − .909 = 4.850).

b. $205,550 present value of future returns
   −125,000 present cost of the investment
   $ 80,550 net present value of the investment

11-5. Each of two projects requires an investment of $800. The firm's cost of capital is 10 percent. The cash flow patterns (income return after taxes plus depreciation) are as follows:

Year	A	B
1	$400	$ 50
2	400	150
3	100	200
4	100	250
5	50	300
6	50	400

      a. Calculate the present value and net present value of each project at each of the following costs of capital: 0, 4, 6, 8, 10, 15, 20 percent.

      b. Rank the investments by the following methods:

        1. Payback.

        2. Internal rate of return.

        3. Net present value at cost of capital of 8 percent.

      c. Graph the results of part 1 with cost of capital on the horizontal axis and (1) present value on the vertical axis and (2) net present value on the vertical axis.

      d. What is the practical significance of your findings in a, b, and c?

Solution:

      a. Original investment = $800

      b. 1. Payback period: A. 2 years; B. 4½ years

                          A is better than B.

        2. Internal rate of return: A. 16½ percent; B. 13¼ percent

                          A is better than B.

        3. Net present value at 8% cost of capital: A. $132; B. $174

                          B is better than A.

Year	A	B	Year	Interest Factor	0% A	0% B	Interest Factor	4% A	4% B	Interest Factor	6% A	6% B	Interest Factor	8% A	8% B
1	400	50	1	1.0	400	50	0.962	385	48	0.943	377	47	0.926	370	46
2	400	150	2	1.0	400	150	0.925	370	139	0.890	356	134	0.857	343	129
3	100	200	3	1.0	100	200	0.889	89	178	0.840	84	168	0.794	79	159
4	100	250	4	1.0	100	250	0.855	86	214	0.792	79	198	0.735	74	184
5	50	300	5	1.0	50	300	0.822	41	247	0.747	37	224	0.681	34	204
6	50	400	6	1.0	50	400	0.790	40	316	0.705	35	282	0.630	32	252
			Present value		1100	1350		1011	1142		968	1053		932	974
			Net present value		300	550		211	342		168	253		132	174

Year	Interest Factor	10% A	10% B	Interest Factor	11% A	11% B	Interest Factor	15% A	15% B	Interest Factor	20% A	20% B
1	0.909	364	45	0.901	360	45	0.870	348	44	0.833	333	42
2	0.826	330	124	0.812	325	122	0.765	302	113	0.694	278	104
3	0.751	75	150	0.731	73	146	0.658	66	132	0.579	58	116
4	0.683	68	171	0.659	66	165	0.572	57	143	0.482	48	121
5	0.621	31	186	0.593	30	178	0.497	25	149	0.402	29	121
6	0.564	28	226	0.535	27	214	0.432	22	173	0.335	17	134
Present value		896	902		881	870		820	754		754	638
Net present value		96	102		81	70		20	(46)		(46)	(162)

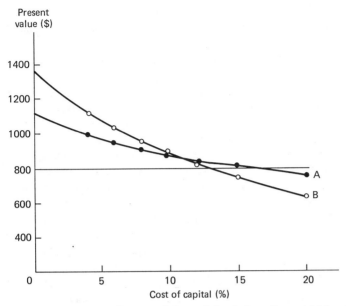

c.   **Figure 11-1.   Influence of Cost of Capital on Present Value Comparisons**

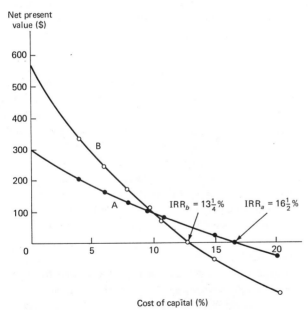

Figure 11-2.   Cost of Capital—The Net Present Value Crossover and the Internal Rate of Return

d. Significance of findings: (1) The different methods result in different rankings. (2) The payback has the defects indicated in the text.

(3) At a cost of capital of 8 percent, B is better than A. At a rate of

10½ percent a potential investor should be indifferent between the two investment alternatives. Note that the present value of A is less than the present value of B at 10 percent, but the relation is reversed at 11 percent. Beyond the internal rates of return (A: 16½ percent; B: 12 3/4 percent) both investments have negative net present values; thus, at costs of capital higher than these levels, the projects would not be accepted. This indicates that projects cannot be ranked without taking the cost of capital into account; otherwise, errors may result.

Also note that projects that have higher returns in early years and lower returns in later years (for example, mining enterprises in which yields may drop off) are penalized less by higher costs of capital. Conversely, projects with lower returns in early years and higher returns in later years (such as fruit orchards where the trees require time to mature) have higher present values at lower rates of interest. Project A is the mining type, while Project B is the orchard type. Note that at low costs of capital, the present value of Project B is higher than A. At higher costs of capital, the present value of Project A is higher than B.

In general, a firm with a high cost of capital will tend to make short-term investments in the sense that most of the returns are realized in the early years of the life of the project. If the firm has a low cost of capital, it will tend to make longer-term investments in the sense that higher returns in later years will not be penalized by high discount factors—low present value multipliers.

11-6. The Eastern Company is using a computer whose original cost was $25,000. The machine is now five years old and has current market value of $5,000. The computer is being depreciated over a 10-year life toward zero estimated salvage value. Depreciation is on a straight-line basis. Management is contemplating the purchase of a new computer whose cost is $50,000 and whose estimated salvage value is $1,000. Expected savings from the new computer are $5,000 a year, and it will raise sales by one percent. Depreciation is on a straight-line basis over a five-year life and the cost of capital is 10 percent. Assume a 50 percent tax rate. Eastern's total sales are $500,000, operating costs are $350,000 and depreciation is currently $500,000 per year.

a. Should the firm replace the asset?

b. How would your decision be affected if the expected savings from the investment in the new computer increase to $10,000 a year and its salvage value increases to $5,000?

c. With regard to the changes in b, how would your decision be affected if a second new computer is available that costs $60,000, has a $10,000 estimated salvage value, increases sales by 2 percent, and is expected to provide $15,000 in annual savings over its five-year life? Depreciation is still on a straight-line basis. Use only the NPV method.

Note: Compare the NPV of replacing the old computer by the second new computer, to the NPV of part b.

Solution:

a. Net cash outflow:

Book value, old machine	$12,500
Salvage value, old machine	(5,000)
Operating loss due to sale	7,500
x tax rate (t)	x .50
Tax savings	$ 3,750
Price of new machine	$50,000
Less: Tax savings	(3,750)
Salvage value, old machine	(5,000)
Net cash outflow	$41,250

Change in cash flows:

$$\Delta CF = (\Delta S - \Delta C - \Delta D)(1 - t) + \Delta D$$
$$= (\$5,000 + \$5,000 - \$7,300)(1 - .50) + \$7,300$$
$$= (\$2,700)(.50) + \$7,300$$
$$= \$8,650$$

Present value of annual cash flows:

$$PV = \$8,650 \times 3.791$$
$$= \$32,792$$

Present value of salvage value of new machine:

$$PV = \$1,000 \times 0.621$$
$$= \$621$$

PV of annual cash flows	$32,792
PV of salvage value, new machine	621
Net cash outflow	(41,250)
NPV	($ 7,837)

On the basis of the above analysis, the firm should not replace the asset.

The annual cash flow can also be determined using the income statement format in the text.

	(1) Without New Investment	(2) With New Investment	(3) = (2) − (1) Difference (Δ)
Sales (S)	$500,000	$505,000	$5,000
Operating costs (C)	$350,000	$345,000	−$5,000
Depreciation (D)	50,000	57,300	7,300
Deductible costs (DC)	400,000	402,300	2,300
Taxable income (I)	$100,000	$102,700	$2,700
(t = 50%)			
Less: Income taxes	50,000	51,350	1,350
Profit after taxes (P)	$ 50,000	$ 51,350	$1,350
Cash flow (P + D)	$100,000	$108,650	$8,650

b. Net cash outflow unchanged:

$$\Delta CF = (\Delta S - \Delta C - \Delta D)(1 - t) + \Delta D$$
$$= (\$5,000 + \$10,000 - \$6,500)(1 - .50) + \$6,500$$
$$= (\$8,500)(.50) + \$6,500$$
$$= \$10,750$$

PV of annual cash flows:
$$PV = \$10,750 \times 3.791$$
$$= \$40,753$$

PV of salvage value of new machine:
$$PV = \$5,000 \times 0.621$$
$$= \$3,105$$

PV of annual cash flows	$40,753
PV of salvage, new machine	3,105
Net cash outflow	(41,250)
NPV	$ 2,608

Since the NPV is positive, the firm should replace the asset.

c. Net cash outflow:

Price of new machine	$60,000
Less: Tax savings	(3,750)
Salvage value, old machine	(5,000)
Net cash outflow	$51,250

Change in cash flows:
$$\Delta CF = (\Delta S - \Delta C - \Delta D)(1 - t) + \Delta D$$
$$= (\$10,000 + \$15,000 - \$7,500)(1 - .50) + \$7,500$$
$$= (\$17,500)(.50) + \$7,500$$
$$= \$16,250$$

PV of annual cash flows:
$$PV = \$16,250 \times 3.791$$
$$= \$61,603$$

PV of salvage value of new machine:
$$PV = \$10,000 \times .621$$
$$= \$6,210$$

PV of annual cash flows	$61,603
PV of salvage value, new machine	6,210
Net cash outflow	(51,250)
NPV	$16,563

The firm will select to invest in the second new computer.

Investment Decisions Under Uncertainty

12

THEMES

The essential elements of risk analysis and the place of risk analysis in capital budgeting are presented in this chapter.

I.   Some basic definitions.
   A. The *riskiness* of a project is defined in terms of the variability of future returns on the project.
   B. *Variation of future returns* is used as a measure of risk.
      1. The degree of uncertainty or risk can be defined and measured in terms of a probability distribution.
         a. The tighter the probability distribution (the more peaked the distribution) the lower the risk on a project.
      2. In a distribution of rates of return on a set of projects, the *mean return* is defined as the expected return ($\overline{R}$), and the *standard deviation* (σ) is used as a measurement of risk.
         a. All other things the same, the higher the expected return, the more attractive the project.
         b. The higher the standard deviation, the greater the variability of returns and, by definition, the greater the riskiness of the project.
      3. The coefficient of variation (v) should be used to compare investments where the use of the standard deviation would be misleading.

$$v = \frac{\text{standard deviation}}{\text{expected return}} = \frac{\sigma}{\overline{R}}$$

        a. Generally, the coefficient of variation should be used to compare returns on individual assets.

        b. The standard deviation is used to appraise returns on portfolios of assets.

        c. The covariance (σ_{ij}) measures the risk of an individual asset by its contribution to the risk of the portfolio of assets into which it is placed.

    4. Figure 12-1 illustrates the distribution of probable returns from investments A and B and allows one to compare the riskiness of the two projects.

        a. Expected returns for A and B both equal $3,000.

        b. Project A has a standard deviation of $200, and B has a standard deviation of $1,000.

        c. Investment A is defined to be less risky than investment B.

II.   Riskiness over time.

    A. Visualize investments A and B in Figure 12-1 as expected cash flows from the same project but in different years.

       1. The expected return is the same for both years.

       2. The subjectively estimated standard deviation is larger for the more distant return. Riskiness is *increasing over time.*

    B. If risk were thought of as being constant over time, then the standard deviation would be constant. This is not generally the case; usually distant returns are more risky, as illustrated in Figure 12-2. (Figure 12-2b should be viewed as a three-dimensional plot extending from the page.)

III.   Utility theory and risk aversion.

    A. Assumption of risk aversion is basic to many decision models used in finance.

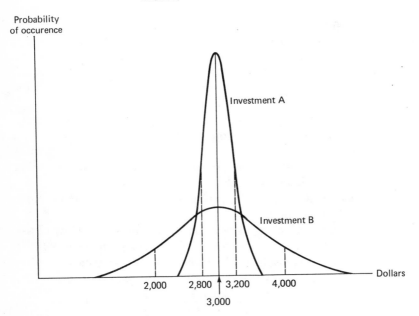

Figure 12-1. Probability Distributions of Two Investments with the Same Expected Dollar Return

III. Utility theory and risk aversion.
  A. Assumption of risk aversion is basic to many decision models used in finance.
    1. Risk takers are classified as risk seekers, risk indifferent, or risk averters.
    2. Risk aversion generally holds in financial decision-making due to the notion of diminishing marginal utility of money.

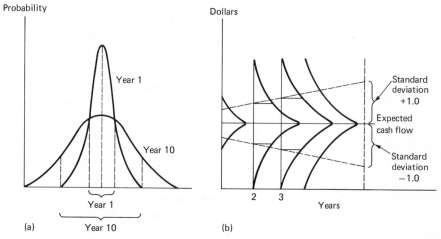

Figure 12-2. Risk as a Function of Time

  B. Figure 12-3 graphs the relationship between money and its utility. Curve A represents the investor with a diminishing marginal utility of money, who is less willing to assume greater risk for each additional dollar of money. His utility of money increases at a decreasing rate.

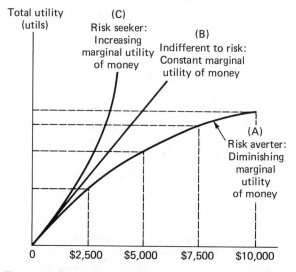

Figure 12-3. Relationship between Money and Its Utility

IV. Portfolio effects.
   A. If the returns from a number of projects in which the firm invests are not all determined by the same factors, changing economic conditions affect the returns from the projects differently. Thus, the size of variations from expected returns may be reduced by investing in a number of different types of projects, or *portfolios* or projects.
   B. Effects of investment in diversified projects on portfolio risk.
      1. When considering the riskiness of a particular investment, it is frequently useful to consider the relationship between the investment in question and other existing assets or potential investment opportunities.
      2. If negatively correlated projects are available in sufficient number, then diversification can completely eliminate risk. Perfect negative correlation (a correlation coefficient of −1.0) is, however, almost never found in the real world.
      3. If there is a high positive correlation between the new project and the firm's other assets, the overall risk is not reduced significantly by diversification. A correlation of + 1.0 results in no risk reduction.
      4. Uncorrelated projects benefit the firm to some extent. If an asset's returns are not closely related to the firm's other major assets, this asset is more valuable to a risk-averting firm than is a similar asset whose returns are positively correlated with the bulk of the assets.
      5. The covariance of a project measures its net influence on portfolio risk.
         a. The measure of covariance includes the correlation between project returns and portfolio returns.
         b. The covariance of a project is its correlation with portfolio returns times the product of its standard deviation and the standard deviation of the portfolio.
   V. There are advantages for both management and stockholders in corporate diversification.
   A. Since stockholders can diversify investments among different firms, it would be unnecessary for managers to consider diversification of the firm's capital projects under the following conditions:
      1. Perfect capital markets.
      2. No income taxes.
      3. No frictions in expanding and contracting business organizations.
      4. No bankruptcy costs, including money costs and the stigma attached to business failure.
   B. Managements are concerned with corporate diversification for these reasons:
      1. Bankruptcy resulting from the failure of a firm is costly to investors and injures the reputations of managers.
      2. Potential managers would avoid firms where risks of failure were high because of lack of diversification.
      3. Tax laws favor losses by a *division* of a firm over those of a separate firm.

    C. Portfolio theory, therefore, remains an important aspect of capital budgeting decisions from the standpoint of the managers of a firm.
      1. Diversification reduces the risks of failure of the firm.
      2. Reducing the risks of failure lowers or eliminates the costs of reorganization and bankruptcy to investors, as well as saving taxes in the aggregate.
  VI. Alternate methods of treating risk.
    A. *Informal treatment.*
      1. For example, the net present values based on single-valued estimates of annual returns (using the firm's cost of capital) might be calculated.
      2. If the net present values of two mutually exclusive projects are "reasonably" close to one another, the "less risky" one is chosen. The decision rules are strictly internal to the decision-maker.
      3. To formalize the approach, the mean expectation and the standard deviation of the NPV's may be presented to the decision-maker. However, the decision is still made in an unspecified manner.
    B. *The risk-adjusted discount rate.* (See Problem 12-3).
      1. The process of choosing among risky assets can be formalized by using higher discount rates for more risky projects.
      2. By developing a risk/return tradeoff function, estimates for the risk premiums can be added to the riskless rate of return. A project with higher risk requires a larger risk premium.
      3. When the risk-adjusted discount rate approach is employed, different discount rates are prescribed for the various divisions of the company. The divisions then differentiate among the types of investments by the investments' individual riskiness.
      4. Risk adjustments should reflect both the estimated standard deviation (or coefficient of variation) of expected returns and investors' attitudes toward risk, as well as portfolio effects.
    C. *The certainty equivalent method.*
      1. Following directly from the concept of utility theory, it requires the decision-maker to specify how much money he requires with certainty to make him indifferent between this certain sum and the expected value of a risky sum.
      2. Certainty equivalent factor (α) = certain return/risky return, or:

$$(\alpha) \times (\text{risky return}) = \text{certain return}.$$

  VII. Techniques for decision-making under uncertainty.
    A. Since decisions are generally made in stages, *decision trees* can be employed.
    B. *Computerized simulation* aids in finding solutions to varying real world conditions.

PROBLEMS

12-1. In relation to two-product diversification, the *least* beneficial effect of diversification is achieved if the correlation between the two projects is:
a. +1.0
b. +0.5
c. 0
d. −0.5
e. −1.0

Solution:

a. +1.0. If any two projects are perfectly correlated, then diversification does nothing to eliminate risk.

12-2. The probability distribution of cash flows from a project with relatively high risk is:
a. A vertical line extending up from the expected value.
b. A horizontal line.
c. Relatively peaked.
d. Relatively flat.
e. Skewed to the left.

Solution:

d. Relatively flat. The flatter the probability distribution of expected future returns, or alternatively stated, the less peaked the distribution, the higher the risk on a project.

12-3. The Martin Company is faced with two mutually exclusive investment projects. Each project costs $4,000 and has an expected life of four years. Annual net cash flows from each project begin one year after the initial investment is made and have the following characteristics:

	Probability	Cash Flow
Project A	.1	$2,000
	.4	3,000
	.2	3,600
	.3	3,400
	1.0	
Project B	.1	$ 100
	.4	3,500
	.2	7,500
	.3	6,500
	1.0	

Martin has decided to evaluate the riskier project at a 12 percent cost of capital versus 9 percent for the less risky project. (If using *Essentials*, skip part c.)

a. What is the expected value of the annual net cash flows from each project?

b. What is the risk-adjusted NPV of each project?

c. Assume that the Martin Company desires to evaluate the projects using certainty equivalent factors developed in their newly formed research division of the treasurer's staff. It has been decided to assign $\alpha = .732$ to the more risky project and $\alpha = .951$ to the less risky one. The riskless rate of return is 7 percent for Martin. Using this data, calculate the NPV for each project.

Solution:

a. Expected annual cash flow (A) = $2,000 x 0.1 + $3,000 x 0.4
   + $3,600 x 0.2 + $3,400 x 0.3
   = $3,140.

   Expected annual cash flow (B) = $100 x 0.1 + $3,500 x 0.4
   + $7,500 x 0.2 + $6,500 x 0.3
   = $4,860.

b. Project B is the riskier project because it has the greater variability in its expected cash flows. Hence, project B is evaluated at the 12 percent cost of capital, while project A requires only 9 percent cost of capital.

   NPV (A) = $3,140 ($PVIF_a$, 9%, 4-year annuity) − $4,000
   = $3,140 (3.240) − $4,000
   = $10,174 − $4,000 = $6,174.

   NPV (B) = $4,860 ($PVIF_a$, 12%, 4-year annuity) − $4,000
   = $4,860 (3.037) − $4,000
   = $14,760 − $4,000 = $10,760.

   The above calculations indicate that the Martin Company should accept project B in spite of its higher risk.

c. Certainty equivalent adjustment of the expected annual cash flows.

   Expected annual cash flows (A) = (.951) ($3,140)
   = $2,986.

   Expected annual cash flows (B) = (.732) ($4,860)
   = $3,557.

   NPV (A) = $2,986 ($PVIF_a$, 7%, 4-year annuity) − $4,000
   = $2,986 (3.387) − $4,000
   = $10,113 − $4,000 = $6,113.

   NPV (B) = $3,557 ($PVIF_a$, 7%, 4-year annuity) − $4,000
   = $3,557 (3.387) − $4,000 =
   = $12,048 − $4,000 = $8,048.

   Although the certainty equivalent method reduces both projects, NPV, project B should still be accepted.

12-4. The Anderson Products Co., Inc., is considering replacing a 15-year-old machine that has a salvage value of $5,000 and is completely depreciated. It is looking at two mutually exclusive alternatives:

1. Replacement with a similar new machine with a $70,000 cost and before-tax cash flows of $17,600 a year. The tax rate is 50 percent.

2. Replacement with a new type of machine, previously untried by either the company or its competitors, for sale by its inventor for $125,000. The expected net cash flows with the new machine are $32,000 a year. The first machine has an expected salvage value of $4,000 at the end of its 15-year life, and the new machine has an expected salvage value of $5,000 at the end of its 15-year life. The firm's cost of capital is 12 percent.

a. Should the firm replace the existing machine, and if so, should replacement be with a similar new machine or with the new type of machine? (Refer to Chapter 11 on Capital Budgeting Decisions.)

b. How would your results be affected if a risk-adjusted discount rate of 14 percent were used for the new type of machine?

Solution:

a. Similar new machine:

1. *Investment in new equipment* $70,000
      Receipt from sale of old machine   (5,000)
      Taxes resulting from gain on old machine   2,500
          Total outflows, or initial costs $67,500

2. *Annual Benefits*

$$\Delta CF = (\Delta S - \Delta C - \Delta D)\,(1 - t) + \Delta D$$

ΔS	$ 0				
less: ΔC	(17,000)				
less: ΔD	4,400				
Δ Taxable income	$13,200				
less: tax	6,600		*Year*		
Δ After-tax profit	$ 6,600		*event*	*PV factor*	
Add: depreciation	4,400		*occurs*	*at 12%*	
3. Δ *Cash flow*	$11,000		1-15	6.811	$74,921

4. *Expected salvage value of new machine* $ 4,000   15   0.183   732
      Total PV of inflows $75,653

5. *Net present value* (PV inflows–PV outflows) $ 8,153

b. New type of machine:

    1. *Investment in new equipment* $125,000

        Receipt from sale of old machine   (5,000)

        Taxes resulting from gain on sale of old machine   2,500

            Total outflows, or initial costs $122,500

    2. *Annual benefits*

$$\Delta CF = (\Delta S - \Delta C - \Delta D)(1 - t) + \Delta D$$

			Year		
	ΔS	$ 0			
less: ΔC		(32,000)			
less: ΔD		8,000			
ΔTaxable income		$ 24,000			
less: tax		12,000	*Year*		
ΔAfter-tax profit		$ 12,000	*event*	*PV factor*	
Add: Δ depreciation		8,000	*occurs*	*at 12%*	
3. Δ *Cash flow*		$ 20,000	1-15	6.811	$136,220

		Year		
4. *Expected*		*Year*		
salvage value		*event*	*PV factor*	
of new ma-		*occurs*	*at 14%*	
chine	$ 5,000	15	0.183	915
Total PV of				
inflows				$137,135

    5. *Net present value* (PV inflows–PV outflows) $ 14,635

On the basis of the above analysis, the firm should replace with the new type of machine. Outflows remain at $122,500 at new discount rate.

		Year event occurs	PV factor at 14%	
Δ Cash flow	$ 20,000	1-15	6.142	$122,840
Expected salvage value	5,000	15	0.140	700
				$123,540
Net present value (PV inflows– PV outflows)				$ 1,040

At the higher discount rate, the new process appears less profitable ($1,040 < $8,153), so the replacement is made with a machine similar to the old one.

Sources and Forms
of Long-Term Financing

Part Five

The Market for Long-Term Securities

13

THEME

The operation of the capital markets and the laws which regulate them influence the timing and use of long-term financing. The effective use of long-term financing has a major impact on the value of the firm because long-term financing decisions, like long-term investment decisions, can be altered only at substantial costs.

I.   Capital markets.
     A. Investment bankers are the main intermediaries in the new issue market.
     B. Securities already issued are traded on securities exchanges and over-the-counter.
II. Organized security exchanges are physical entities operating as auction markets.
     A. Direct participation in these "auctions" is limited to individuals or representatives of organizations who buy "seats" on the exchange.
     B. Two practices said to contribute to effectively functioning securities markets are *margin trading* and *short selling.*
        1. Margin trading is the purchase of securities on credit. Limitations on credit purchases are set by the Federal Reserve Board.
        2. Short selling is the sale of securities not owned at time of sale in the expectation of a price decline.
        3. Effects of margin trading and short selling.
           a. They provide a more continuous market by increasing activity.
           b. They provide a more rapid price adjustment mechanism by increasing the flexibility of traders.

  C. Benefits of security exchanges to the economy.
   1. Exchanges lower the cost of capital to businesses.
   2. Exchanges provide a continuous test of the values of securities.
   3. Exchanges increase the frequency of security price fluctuations and reduce the amplitude of their changes.
   4. Exchanges aid in the absorption of new issue flotations.

III. Over-the-counter security markets provide for security transactions not conducted on the organized exchanges.
  A. In these markets brokers and dealers buy and sell securities into and out of their own inventories.
  B. A comparison of trading in this market with trading in the organized exchanges shows:
   1. The stocks of most companies are traded over-the-counter, but the stocks of larger firms are listed, and two-thirds of the dollar volume of stock trading takes place through exchanges.
   2. Over 95 percent of bond transactions take place over-the-counter.

IV. In deciding whether to list his securities on an exchange, the financial manager weighs the following arguments:
  A. Arguments for listing.
   1. Public reporting of transactions advertises the firm.
   2. Prestige and goodwill is obtained by providing the information required for listing.
   3. Listed securities are more acceptable as loan collateral.
   4. Supervision of transactions prevents manipulation.
  B. Arguments against listing.
   1. Over-the-counter dealers maintain a market and stimulate trading.
   2. Over-the-counter dealers develop a market until a security is ready for listing.
   3. It is more difficult to remove securities from listing than to list them; thus, to some degree, the decision is irreversible.
   4. Over-the-counter stocks are subject to lower margin requirements than are listed securities.
   5. More information on operations must be provided if stocks are listed.

V. Investment banking includes the following aspects:
  A. *Public flotation* of a security issue is carried out through investment bankers who perform the following functions:
   1. *Underwriting*—The investment banker purchases the new security issue, pays the issuer, and markets the securities. The banker bears the risk of price fluctuation from the time of purchase to the time that the issue is distributed.
   2. *Distribution*—The investment banker maintains a sales staff which performs the marketing function.
   3. *Advice and counsel*—The experience of the investment banker enables him to advise the issuer regarding the characteristics of the issue to insure successful flotation. Often the banker serves on the board of

directors in order to give advice and to protect his own reputation by securing sound management for the firm.

4. *Source of funds*—The investment banker provides a source of funds to the issuing firm during the distribution period.

B. The process of floating a public issue follows these steps:

1. *Preunderwriting conferences* are held between the issuing firm and the investment banker to discuss alternative forms of financing and to reach the decision to float an issue.

2. An *underwriting investigation* is made by the underwriters into the firm's prospects. Specialists are called in to examine legal, accounting, engineering, and other aspects of the firm.

3. The *underwriting agreement* is formulated and specifies all underwriting terms except the actual price of the securities.

4. A *registration statement* is filed with the Securities and Exchange Commission. A minimum waiting period of 20 days is required before clearance by the Securities and Exchange Commission is received. The underwriter can make no sales during this time but can distribute preliminary prospectuses.

5. The price paid for securities by the underwriter is determined in the following manner, typically at the close of the registration period:

   a. When a company "goes public" for the first time, the investment banker and the firm negotiate the price in accordance with valuation principles, and a final price is established at the close of the S.E.C. waiting period.

   b. When additional offerings are involved, the firm and the underwriter agree to price the securities in relation to the closing price on the last day of registration.

   c. Generally, the investment banker prefers a low price and a high yield, while the issuer of the securities naturally wants the opposite.

   d. Competition usually forces investment bankers to price close to market determined levels.

6. An underwriting syndicate may be formed by the investment banker for these reasons:

   a. To reduce the extent of his risk.

   b. To use the selling organizations of other investment bankers.

   c. He may be unable to finance a large issue by himself.

7. A *selling group* is a group of dealers who act as retailers of the issue. The operations of the group are governed by an agreement which covers these points:

   a. Description of the issue.

   b. Price concession, which is the selling group's commission.

   c. Handling of repurchased securities. (Note: The syndicate manager takes subscriptions until the issue is sold. He also stabilizes the market while the books are open in order to facilitate the placement of the issue.)

        d. Duration of the selling group.

    8. After the selling group has been formed, the actual offering takes place. The formal public offering is called "opening the books."

    9. During the offering period, the price of the security is pegged by placing orders to buy at a specified price in the market. This is done to prevent a cumulative downward movement in the price.

C. Analysis of the costs of public flotations shows these relationships:

    1. Ranking of costs from highest to lowest.

        a. Common stock.

        b. Preferred stock.

        c. Debt.

            1) This ranking is explained by the larger marketing task for stock flotations, since this market is narrower than the debt market.

    2. Costs as a percentage of the proceeds of the issue are greater for small than for large issues. Fixed expenses are high, and the selling job and risks are greater for the securities of small firms.

D. The role of the investment banker is not limited to his traditional functions of handling issues. He has extended his activities in these fields:

    1. The procurement of risk capital for new enterprises.

    2. Acting as a broker for private placements.

    3. The organization of investment trusts.

    4. Acting as a middleman in merger negotiations.

    5. Contracting to maintain the market for rights during the trading period.

VI. Regulation of security trading.

A. The financial manager should be aware of the federal laws regulating issuance and trading of securities because they influence his liability and affect financing costs.

B. The Securities Act of 1933 relates to the marketing of new issues. It seeks to provide full disclosure of information, a record of representations, and penalties for violations. The major provisions are:

    1. The Act applies to public interstate offerings over $300,000 (subject to certain exceptions).

    2. It requires registration 20 days in advance of the offering to the public.

    3. It allows purchasers who suffer loss due to misrepresentation or omission of material facts to sue for damages.

C. The Securities Exchange Act of 1934 extends the disclosure principle to the trading of existing issues. Its major provisions are:

    1. The Act establishes the S.E.C. (Securities and Exchange Commission).

    2. It requires registration and regulation of the national securities exchanges.

    3. It requires corporate insiders to file monthly reports of changes in ownership of stock of the corporation and provides legal redress for stockholders.

    4. It gives the S.E.C. power to prohibit manipulations through wash sales, pools, and pegging operations except during stock flotations.

      5. It gives the S.E.C. control over proxy machinery and practices.

      6. It gives the board of governors of the Federal Reserve System power to determine margin requirements.

  D. Appraisal of regulation of security trading.

      1. Social well-being requires that orderly markets be promoted.

      2. Objectives of the regulation.

         a. To protect the amateur investor from fraud.

         b. To control the volume of bank credit.

         c. To provide orderly markets in securities.

PROBLEMS

13-1.   Margin trading is the process of _____.

Solution:

Buying securities on credit.

13-2.   When an investor is buying on margin, the securities are:

    a. Delivered to the buyer within the next four business days.

    b. Held by the brokerage house.

    c. Delivered to the exchange for certification.

    d. Retained by the seller.

    e. None of the above.

Solution:

b.

13-3.   A member of an exchange who is responsible for maintaining an "orderly market" is known as _____.

Solution:

A specialist.

13-4.   True or false? The Securities and Exchange Commission determines margin requirements.

Solution:

False. The Board of Governors of the Federal Reserve determines margin requirements.

13-5. True or false? Most bond issues are traded in the over-the-counter market.

Solution:

True.

13-6. Securities flotation costs increase as one moves from bonds to preferred stock, and then to common stock. What best explains this phenomenon?

Solution:

Large block purchases of bonds by institutions.

Common Stock

14

THEME

To utilize the various forms of financing effectively, the financial manager must be aware of the ramifications of using each form. This chapter describes in some detail the typical provisions of common stock financing.

I.   Income and control differ among the various forms of ownership.
    A. Individual proprietorships:
        1. When the firm is funded entirely by the owner, all rights to income, control, and responsibility for debt lie with the owner.
        2. When it is funded at least in part through debt, limitations are placed on control and the apportionment of income.
    B. Partnership rights are apportioned by agreement or by state law.
    C. Business corporation rights are apportioned by the state of incorporation and are set forth in the corporate charter.

II.   Owners of common stock in business corporations have these general rights:
    A. Collective rights.
        1. Make charter amendments if the changes are approved by state officials.
        2. Adopt and amend the bylaws.
        3. Elect the corporate directors.
        4. Authorize the sale of fixed assets.
        5. Ratify mergers.
        6. Change the amount of authorized common stock.
        7. Authorize issuance of preferred stock, debentures, bonds, and other securities.

B. Each stockholder also has specific rights as an individual owner enabling him to:
1. Vote as prescribed by the corporate charter.
2. Transfer stock to another party.
3. Inspect the books of the corporation.
4. Share in the residual assets in case of dissolution.

C. Apportionment of income and control.
1. Common stock is the recipient of the residual income of the corporation.
2. Through the right to vote, holders of common stock have legal control of the corporation.
3. An element of risk is also involved in equity ownership due to its low priority of claims at liquidation.

D. Nature of voting rights.
1. Each stockholder has the right to cast votes in proportion to the number of shares owned.
   a. A *proxy* is a transfer of the right to vote.
   b. The use of proxies is supervised by the Securities and Exchange Commision to prevent:
      1) Self-perpetuation of management.
      2) Small stockholder groups from gaining special advantages.
2. In *cumulative voting* the stockholder is allowed to cast multiple votes for one director. For example, 100 shares can be cast as 500 votes for one director if five directors are being elected, rather than 100 votes for each of five directors.
   a. Formula:

   $$r = \frac{d \times S}{D + 1} + 1$$

   where

   r = number of shares required to elect a desired number of directors
   d = number of directors desired to elect
   S = total number of shares of common stock outstanding and entitled to vote
   D = total number of directors to be elected.

   b. Illustration:
   d = 2
   S = 100,000
   D = 6

   $$r = \frac{2 \times 100,000}{6 + 1} + 1 = 28,572$$

3. The *preemptive right* gives the existing equity owners the option to purchase any additional new issues of common stock.
   a. State laws vary with regard to the preemptive right.
      1) In some states it is a part of every corporate charter.

    2) In other states it must be included as a specific provision.

   b. The preemptive right is designed to protect:

    1) The power of control of present stockholders.

    2) The pro rata share of earned surplus and earning power for the present stockholders.

  4. With regard to risk:

   a. Common stockholders have limited liability in the case of loss.

   b. Common equity provides a cushion for creditors if losses occur on dissolutions. The equity-to-total assets ratio is an indicator of the degree by which the amounts realized on the liquidation of assets may decline from stated book values before creditors suffer losses.

III. Evaluation of common stock financing.

 A. In reaching a decision to issue common stock, the financial manager should consider these factors:

  1. Advantages of common stock over other forms of financing.

   a. No fixed charges are incurred.

   b. There is no maturity date.

   c. The credit worthiness of the firm is increased.

   d. At times may be sold more easily than debt.

  2. Disadvantages of common stock.

   a. The control of the firm is shared with the new shareholders.

   b. The new shares participate fully in earnings and dividends.

   c. Flotation costs are relatively high.

   d. Stock normally sells on a higher yield basis than debt.

   e. Dividends are not deductible from income for tax purposes.

  3. Circumstances favoring the use of common stock.

   a. The firm's sales and profits fluctuate widely.

   b. Profit margins do not cover the cost of debt.

   c. The firm already has a high debt ratio in relation to the prudent maximum for its line of business.

   d. The firm is new, lacking access to debt financing.

   e. Dilution of control is not a problem.

   f. Cash flow considerations are important.

   g. The relative costs of common stock financing appear favorable.

   h. Available debt financing would carry onerous loan agreement restrictions.

   i. Investors, perhaps worried by the threat of inflation, favor equity to debt securities at the present time. (This point is discussed in detail in Chapter 22.)

IV. The use of rights in financing.

 A. Definitions.

  1. A *right* is an option to buy a part of newly issued stock at a specified price during a designated period of time.

  2. A *rights offering* involves the sale of additional stock to existing stock-

holders, and is mandatory if the preemptive right exists for the firm in question.

B. Several questions face the financial manager in a rights offering:
1. How many rights will be required to purchase a share of the new stock?
2. What should be the value of each right?
3. What effect will the rights offering have on the price of the existing stock?
4. What will be the subscription price of the stock?

C. To determine the number of rights required to purchase a new share of stock:
1. Calculate the number of new shares to be issued:

Number of new shares = (funds to be raised) ÷ (subscription price)

2. Calculate the number of rights needed to buy a new share:

Number of rights required = number of old shares/number of new shares

D. To determine the value of each right, the following formulas may be used.

$$R = \frac{M_o - S}{N + 1} \text{ (Rights-on calculation)}$$

$$R = \frac{M_e - S}{N} \text{ (Ex-rights calculation)}$$

where
R = value of one right
M_o = rights-on price of the stock
M_e = ex-rights price of the stock
S = subscription price
N = number of rights required to purchase one share.

1. Stock is sold rights-on until a predetermined ex-rights day.
2. The ex-rights value of the stock differs from the rights-on value of the stock by the value of a right as determined in the above equation.

V. Effects on the position of the stockholders.

A. If a stockholder exercises his rights, a rights offering does not affect the value of his stock.
1. A stockholder may suffer a loss if:
   a. He forgets to exercise or sell his rights.
   b. Brokerage costs of selling the rights are excessive.
2. The oversubscription privilege contained in most rights offerings allows stockholders to buy on a pro rata basis all shares not taken in the initial rights offering. This privilege also helps to assure a full sale of the new stock issue.

B. Considerations affecting the financial manager's decision to make a rights offering.

   1. There are three major alternative-methods of selling stock:

      a. Alternative I—sell the issue through investment bankers with or without rights.

         1) Advantages.

            a) Wide distribution of shares.

            b) Certainty of receiving funds.

         2) Disadvantages.

            a) The relatively high cost of underwriters services.

      b. Alternative II—issue rights but provide only a small discount from the market price, using investment bankers to sell the unsubscribed shares.

         1) Advantages.

            a) Smaller underwriters expense.

            b) Small decrease in unit price of shares.

            c) Certainty of receiving funds.

            d) Increased stockholder loyalty.

         2) Disadvantages.

            a) Somewhat narrower distribution of shares.

            b) Losses to forgetful shareholders.

      c. Alternative III—issue rights, allow a large discount and do not use investment banking facilities.

         1) Advantages.

            a) No underwriting expense.

            b) Substantial decrease in the unit price of shares.

            c) Increase stockholder loyalty.

         2) Disadvantages.

            a) Pressure on owners to exercise rights, large losses realized by those who do not.

            b) Narrower distribution of shares.

C. The choice of method depends on the individual company's needs.

   1. A company may feel that a rights offering has a higher probability of raising funds without lowering the market price of stock because:

      a. If existing shareholders wish to maintain their pro rata share in the earnings and control of the firm, they will exercise their rights.

      b. Existing shareholders are most likely to have a favorable opinon of the firm.

      c. Margin requirements on rights purchases are only 25 percent, as compared to 65 percent for regular stock purchases.

   2. Some observed differences between market price and subscription price.

      a. Subscription prices have been about 15 percent lower than market prices in recent years.

      b. Generally, subscription prices are from 10 percent to 20 percent lower than market prices.

3. No generalization can be made regarding the effects of a rights offering on the market price of the stock; the effect of the offering depends upon the market's evaluation of the future prospects of the issuing company.

PROBLEMS

14-1. Bordon Corporation needs $30 million in new outside equity funds. The current market price of its stock is $50 per share, and it is selling at ten times earnings. If current earnings are $40 million and the subscription price is set at $30, what is the value of one right?

Solution:

$$\frac{\$50 \text{ price}}{10 \ P/E} = \$5 \text{ EPS}$$

$$\frac{\$40,000,000 \text{ earnings}}{\$5 \text{ EPS}} = 8,000,000 \text{ old shares}$$

$$\frac{\$30,000,000 \text{ new equity needed}}{\$30 \text{ subscription price}} = 1,000,000 \text{ new shares needed}$$

$$\frac{8,000,000}{1,000,000} = 8 \text{ rights per new share}$$

$$R = \frac{M_O - S}{N + 1} = \frac{\$50 - \$30}{8 + 1} = \frac{20}{9} = \$2.22 \text{ value of one right.}$$

14-2. Atlantic Corporation's 3 million shares of common stock are currently selling at a market price of $50 per share. The firm plans to raise an additional $20 million through rights by selling 500,000 new shares of stock at $40 per share.
a. What will be the theoretical price of the common stock after the financing is completed?
b. What is the theoretical value of one right?

Solution:

a.   3,000,000 current shares
          X$50 market price
    $150,000,000 market value of firm
    +20,000,000 additional funds to be raised
    $170,000,000 total value of firm after rights issue

3,000,000 current shares outstanding
+500,000 new shares
3,500,000 total shares outstanding after rights issue

$$\frac{\$170,000,000}{3,500,000} = \$48.57 \text{ theoretical price}$$

b. $\dfrac{3,000,000}{500,000} = 6$ rights per share

$$R = \frac{M_o - S}{N + 1} = \frac{\$50 - \$40}{7} = \frac{10}{7} = \$1.43 \text{ value of one right}$$

14-3.   Assume you owned 30 shares of stock before the rights offering. How much better off is your financial position if you do exercise your rights? (rather than sell)?

Solution:

No change. Whether or not rights are exercised or sold leaves the net present wealth of the stockholder unchanged. This is insured by the arbitrage operations of the market. It is true even when commission costs are taken into account.

14-4.   The Gulf Corporation needs additional funds and has three alternatives open to it.
a. Sell stock at the current market price using investment bankers (ABC will net 95 percent of the market price).
b. Sell stock using rights through investment bankers (using a subscription price set at 85 percent of the market price).
c. Sell stock using rights without utilizing investment bankers (using a subscription price set at 15 percent of the market price).
Which alternative (or alternatives) should Gulf adopt if it wishes to minimize the reduction in market price per share?

Solution:

a. There is a "stock dividend effect" in any successful rights offering which tends to lower the market price per share.

14-5.   The Barrington Company is financed solely with common stock. Its balance sheet is given below.
Earnings available to common stock after taxes are $30,000. The price-earnings ratio is 16, so the current market price is $48 per share ($3 x 16).

Barrington Company—Balance Sheet, End of Year, 1976

		Common stock (10,000 shares)	$ 30,000
		Surplus	120,000
Total assets	$150,000	Total claims	$150,000

The company sells an additional 10,000 shares at $25 per share with a rights offering whereby one new share can be purchased for each old share held.

New Balance Sheet

		Common stock, $3 par	$ 60,000
		Capital surplus	220,000
		Surplus	120,000
Total assets	$400,000	Total claims	$400,000

After the rights offering has been completed and the assets obtained have become productive, earnings available to common stock after taxes go up to $80,000.

a. What is the value of each right?

b. What will be the new market price of the stock when it goes ex-rights if the market price of the stock falls by the value of one right?

c. What will be the new market price of the stock if the same price-earnings ratio prevails before and after the rights offering?

Solution:

a. $R = \dfrac{M_O - S}{N + 1} = \dfrac{48 - 25}{1 + 1} = \dfrac{23}{2} = \$11.50$

b. $\$48 - \$11.50 = \$36.50$

c. Earnings per share times P/E ratio
$\$4.00 \times 16 = \$64.00$

14-6. Henry Clay has 200 shares of Southern Industries. The market price per share is $70. The company now offers stockholders one new share to be purchased at $52 for every five shares held.

a. Determine the value of each right.

b. Assume that Mr. Clay (1) uses 75 rights and sells the other 125, or (2) sells the 200 rights at the market price you have calculated.

Prepare a statement showing the changes in his position under the above assumptions.

Solution:

a. $\dfrac{M_O - S}{N + 1} = \dfrac{\$70 - \$52}{5 + 1} = \dfrac{\$18}{6} = \$3$ per right.

b. 1.

Original holdings		Market value of	
(200 shares at $70)	$14,000	215† shares at $67	$14,405
Use of 75 rights		Gain on sale of	
(15 shares at $52)	780	125 rights at $3	375
Total investment	$14,780	Stockholder position	$14,780

2.

Original holdings		Market value of	
(200 shares at $70)	$14,000	200 shares at $67	$13,400
Total investment	$14,000	Gain on sale of	
		200 rights at $3	600
		Stockholder position	$14,000

14-7. You are a dissident stockholder of Billingham Corporation and have collected 20 percent of the 100,000 voting shares outstanding. If a total of seven directors is to be elected to the board, how many directors can you elect, assuming cumulative voting is used?

Solution:

$$r = \dfrac{d \times S}{D + 1} + 1 \quad or \quad d = \dfrac{(r - 1)(D + 1)}{S}$$

$$d = \dfrac{19{,}999 \times 8}{100{,}000} = \dfrac{159{,}992}{100{,}000} = 1.60.$$

You could elect one director.

14-8. A firm with 300,000 shares of stock outstanding—market price $15 per share—decided to raise additional funds through a new equity issue. After the issue was sold, total shares outstanding doubled, and the market value of the firm rose to $8 million. At what price was the new stock sold? (Ignore flotations costs.)

†The 75 rights are exercised into 15 new shares. Total shares = new 15 + old 200 = 215 shares.

Solution:

a.   300,000 shares
      x$15 price per share
      $4,500,000 market value

b. $8,000,000 market value after new funds
   −4,500,000 market value before new funds
   $3,500,000 market value of new funds

c. $\dfrac{\$3,500,000 \text{ market value of new funds}}{300,000 \text{ new shares}}$ = $11.67 price of new share.

14-9.   If ABC Corporation has 8,000 shares of common stock outstanding, and the balance sheet given below, what is the book value of the common stock?

Balance Sheet

		Payables	$ 2,500
		Loans	47,500
		Mortgages	100,000
		Preferred stock	100,000
		Common stock	400,000
		Capital surplus	50,000
		Earned surplus	50,000
		Total liabilities and	
	Total assets $750,000	capital	$750,000

Solution:

a. $400,000 common stock
     50,000 capital surplus
     50,000 earned surplus
   $500,000

b. $\dfrac{\$500,000}{8,000 \text{ shares}}$ = $62.50 book value of common stock.

14-10.   Universal Airlines, Inc., provides transcontinental service throughout the United States. In 1974 Universal's domestic services were fifth in size among airlines of the United States. The company was seeking to raise $10 million for general corporate purposes. Relevant financial information is given in the balance sheet. The data have been altered slightly.

Universal Airlines, Inc.—Balance Sheet, June 30, 1976 (in millions of dollars)

Cash	$ 13.0	Accounts payable	$ 14.0
U.S.Government securities	4.0	Notes payable	6.0
Receivables	15.0	Accruals	10.0
Supplies	2.0		
Other current assets	1.0	Total current liabilities	$ 30.0
		Long-term debt	90.0
Total current assets	$ 35.0	Total debt	$120.0
Net property	113.0	Common stock, par $3:	
Other assets	2.0	Outstanding: 1.5	
		million shares	4.5
		Capital surplus	15.0
		Retained earnings	10.5
		Net worth	$ 30.0
Total assets	$150.0	Total claims on assets	$150.0

Income Data (in millions of dollars)

	1976	1975	1974	1973
Sales	$150	$120	$104	$88
Earnings after tax avail-able to common	4.50	3.00	4.00	1.00
Earnings per share	3.00	1.80	2.70	0.60
Dividends per share	0.90	0.90	0.45	0.70

Commercial Airlines' Financial Ratios

Current ratio (X)	1.4
Sales to total assets (X)	0.9
Sales to inventory (X)	23.0
Average collection period (days)	38
Current debt/total assets (%)	15-20
Long-term debt/total assets (%)	50-55
Preferred/total assets (%)	0-5
Net worth/total assets (%)	25-30
Profits to sales (%)	2.6
Profits to total assets (%)	2.4
Profits to net worth (%)	7.5
Expected growth rate for earnings and dividends (%)	7.0

Common stock could be sold for $45 per share. Sinking fund debentures (ten-year life) could be sold to yield 6 percent. Flotation costs would not be sufficient to affect the decision. Which form of financing should Universal Airlines use to raise the $10 million?

This question should not be answered in terms of precise cost of capital calculations. Rather, a more qualitative and subjective analysis is appropriate. The only calculations necessary are a few simple ratios. Careful interpretation of these ratios is necessary, however, to understand and discuss the often complex, subjective judgment issues involved.

Solution:

The following factors will be considered in the analysis.

a. Relative costs of the financing alternatives:

Price-earnings ratio $\qquad \dfrac{\$45}{\$3} = 15$ times.

Earnings yield $\qquad \dfrac{\$3}{\$45} = 6.7\%.$

Dividend yield $\qquad \dfrac{\$0.90}{\$45} = 2.0\%.$

Estimated cost of retained earnings: $k = \dfrac{D}{P} + g = 2.0\% + 7.0\%.$

$$= 9.0\%.$$

Cost of debt before tax 6%; after tax 3%.

There is some cost advantage to debt, but the earnings yield is also quite low.

b. Level and stability of profits:

Profits to total assets $\qquad \dfrac{\$4.5}{\$150} = 3.0\%.$

Profits to net worth $\qquad \dfrac{\$4.5}{\$30.0} = 15\%.$

Profits to sales $\qquad \dfrac{\$4.5}{\$150} = 3.0\%.$

Profits and earnings per share have been fluctuating a great deal, and the greater risk involved in a debt financing situation could present problems in meeting fixed costs and even lead to insolvency. Note that the earnings rate on net worth is 6.7 percent, compared with the profit rate on book net worth of 15 percent. The earnings rate on total assets is nearly that of the after-tax rate on debt financing, illustrating again the slim margin involved with debt financing.

c. Universal Airlines' current debt-total asset ratio is almost equal to the norm for the industry, but its long-term debt ratio is considerably higher. The pro forma statement (below) shows the further consequences of debt versus equity alternatives. With a debt issue the total debt percentage rises to 12 percent above the industry average. The equity alternative, on the contrary, brings Universal's ratios more in line with those of the industry. Even so, the total debt ratio is 5 percent above the norm. This reinforces the argument for equity financing.

Percentage of Total Assets

	Industry	Pacific	Pro Forma	
			Debt	Equity
Current debt	20%	20%	19%	19%
Long-term debt	50	60	62.5	56
Total debt	70	80	81.5	75
Preferred stock	0-5	0	0	0
Net worth	30	20	18.5	25

d. Sinking fund requirement (cash flows): The fact that the company must provide for a sinking fund on the debt alternative is another disadvantage from the corporate standpoint. To retire the bonds over a ten-year-life means a 10 percent rate, plus the 3 percent interest cost, which amounts to 13 percent a year, or $1.3 million. There is little doubt that the common stock alternative is superior from a cash flow standpoint. This is true even with the added dividend payments created by the issuance of over 220,000 new shares. Assuming a $1 dividend, this added cash outlay amounts to only 17 percent of the outlay required under the debt alternative.

e. Dilution of control to present stockholders: Universal Airlines is a fairly well-established firm incorporated in 1930, and its 1.5 million shares are widely held. Thus, the additional 222,222 shares required to finance the equity issue will not present a dilution of control problem.

In conclusion, the common stock issue is favored. Actually, common stock was sold according to the company's prospectus of April 2, 1974.

Fixed Income Securities: Debt and Preferred Stock

15

THEME

This chapter provides the financial manager with the technical materials to analyze debt decisions and to formulate financial policies regarding the use of alternative methods of obtaining financial leverage.

I. Some key definitions.
   A. A *bond* is a long-term promissory note.
   B. A *mortgage* is a pledge of real assets as security for a loan.
   C. A *debenture* is unsecured long-term debt.
   D. *Funded debt* is any long-term debt.
   E. An *indenture* is a document which contains the details of the long-term contractual relationship between the issuing corporation and the bondholders. It includes:
      1. The form of the bond.
      2. A description of any pledged property.
      3. The authorized amount of the issue.
      4. Protective clauses or covenants such as limitations on indebtedness, restrictions on dividends, or the minimum current ratio requirement during the period of bonded indebtedness.
      5. Provisions for redemption or call privileges.
   F. The trustee is an agent of the bondholders, but he is appointed by the issuer before the bonds are sold.
      1. The *trustee* has three main responsibilities.
         a. He certifies the issue of the bonds.

    b. He polices the behavior of the corporation in its performance of the responsibilities set forth by the indenture.

    c. He represents the interests of the bondholder in the event of default.

G. A *call provision* gives the issuing corporation the right to call the bond for redemption.

    1. If it is used, the company must pay a call premium over and above the par value of the bond.

    2. Since this provision is valuable to the firm but potentially detrimental to an investor, interest rates on new issues of callable bonds exceed those on new issues of noncallable bonds.

H. A *sinking fund* facilitates the orderly retirement of a bond issue or preferred stock issue.

    1. Nature of sinking fund requirements.

        a. Typically, the firm is required to buy and retire a portion of the bond issue each year.

        b. The amount is sometimes related to the level of sales or earnings of the current year.

        c. Usually the requirement is a mandatory fixed amount.

        d. If it is mandatory, failure to meet a sinking fund payment usually constitutes a default on the bond issue.

    2. Alternative procedures for handling sinking funds.

        a. The sinking fund may be used to call a certain percentage of the bonds at a stipulated price, with bonds selected by lottery from serial numbers.

        b. The sinking fund payment may be used to buy bonds on the open market.

        c. The firm will choose the method that results in the greatest reduction of indebtedness for a given expenditure.

    3. The call provision of the sinking fund can work to the detriment of bondholders since the call is generally at par while the bond may have been purchased well above par.

    4. Since a sinking fund provides additional protection to investors, bonds that have them are likely to carry lower yields than comparable bonds with no sinking fund provisions.

II. Secured long-term debt can be classified on three bases:

A. Priority of claims.

    1. A *senior mortgage* has first claim on assets and earnings.

    2. A *junior mortgage* has a subordinate lien.

    3. *Subordinated debt* is unsecured debt, which is junior to others.

B. Right to issue additional securities.

    1. A *closed-end mortgage* specifies that no additional bonds may be sold which have a lien on the property specified in the original mortgage.

    2. An *open-end mortgage* exists if the bond indenture fails to mention additional bond issues. Therefore, the property can be repledged.

        3. A *limited open-end mortgage* allows the sale of a specified amount of additional bonds.

    C. Scope of the lien.

        1. A specific lien specifies certain designated property.

        2. A blanket mortgage pledges all real property owned by the company.

    D. The factors given above have important influences on the following:

        1. The degree of protection for the creditor.

        2. The rate of interest paid by the firm.

        3. The rating of the bond by rating agencies.

III.   Unsecured long-term debt.

    A. *Debentures* are unsecured bonds which are issued:

        1. When the firm's property is unsuitable for a lien.

        2. When the firm's finances are very strong.

        3. When the firm is too weak to have alternatives.

    B. A *subordinated debenture* is an unsecured bond that has a claim on assets after unsubordinated debt in the event of liquidation. This places the debenture below present and future senior debt with regard to priorities.

        1. Advantages.

           a. Subordination strengthens the position of the senior creditors.

           b. Debentures have a tax advantage over preferred stock.

           c. Debentures do not restrict the ability of the borrower to obtain senior debt.

        2. Finance companies are high-leverage operations with debt-to-equity ratios, including subordinated debt, of around three-to-one.

        3. For industrials, a rule of thumb requires firms to maintain an equity-to-subordinated-debt ratio of 150 to 200 percent.

    C. *Income* bonds are bonds which pay interest only if income is earned by the company.

        1. In the past, they arose from reorganizations.

        2. In recent years, they have been used in normal financing to replace a preferred stock issue because of the tax advantage of interest over dividends.

        3. They typically contain:

           a. A cumulative provision.

           b. A sinking fund provision.

           c. A convertible provision.

           d. Voting rights upon default of a specified number of interest payments.

        4. Although interest is not a fixed charge, the principal must be paid when due.

    D. A general principle of finance is that new forms of financing will be developed in order to meet changes in the needs of firms related to changes in the economic environment.

IV.   Appraisal of long-term debt.

A. From the viewpoint of the holder.
　　1. Debt is favorable because it gives priority in both earnings and liquidation. It has a definite maturity and protective covenants.
　　2. The bondholder generally receives a fixed return.
　　3. The bondholder may exercise no control except in the case of default.
B. From the viewpoint of the issuer.
　　1. Advantages.
　　　　a. Debt has a limited cost, and expected yield is lower than the cost of common or preferred stock.
　　　　b. Stockholders retain voting control.
　　　　c. Interest expense is tax deductible.
　　　　d. Call provisions add flexibility to the financial structure.
　　2. Disadvantages.
　　　　a. A fixed interest commitment is made.
　　　　b. Higher risk may result in lowering the value of common stock outstanding.
　　　　c. A definite maturity date exists requiring repayment or refunding.
　　　　d. Stringent indenture provisions may be imposed.
　　　　e. Financial standards limit the amount of debt in the liability structure.
　　3. Decisions to use debt are favored by the following:
　　　　a. Sales and earnings are relatively stable.
　　　　b. Profit margins are adequate.
　　　　c. A rise in profits or the general price level is expected.
　　　　d. The existing debt ratio is relatively low.
　　　　e. Common stock price-earnings ratios are low.
　　　　f. Control considerations are important.
　　　　g. Cash flow requirements under the bond agreement are not burdensome.
　　　　h. Restrictions on the bond indenture are not onerous.
V. Preferred stock.
　　A. Under some circumstances, the financial manager will decide that preferred stock is a suitable source of funds because it limits cash payout and provides financial leverage.
　　B. Preferred stock is by nature a hybrid security. It is classified as debt or equity depending upon the analysis being made.
　　　　1. Preferred stock is *not* like equity (but *is* like debt) in that it does not carry voting rights.
　　　　2. Preferred stock is *not* like debt (but *is* like equity) in that failure to pay dividends does not cause default on the obligation.
　　C. The risks of preferred shareholders in relation to the risks of equity owners are reduced by these features:
　　　　1. Preferreds have prior claims to earnings and to assets in liquidation.
　　　　2. Occasionally, a sinking fund provides for the retirement of the issue.
　　　　3. Ordinarily, consent of the preferred shareholders must be obtained

before securities with equal or prior claim on earnings can be issued.

4. Common stock dividends are restricted if the current ratio, debt ratio, or surplus account falls below prescribed limits.

VI. Major provisions of preferred stock issues.

A. Preferred dividend provisions.

1. The dividend may be stated as a percentage of the par value of the stock or as an annual dollar amount.

2. Preferreds are normally nonparticipating.

3. They are usually cumulative, so a preferred dividend which is passed is still owed.

   a. To protect preferred holders, all preferred dividend arrearages must be paid before any common dividends are paid.

   b. No interest is paid upon arrearages.

   c. Common stock may be substituted for large arrearages.

B. Other provisions.

1. About 40 percent of the preferred stock issued in recent years has been convertible into common stock.

2. For nonvoting issues, the right to vote is usually given upon the failure of the firm to pay dividends for six, eight, or ten quarters.

3. About 25 percent of preferred issues carry the preemptive right.

4. Some preferred issues have sinking fund and call provisions. When they are used, a call premium must be paid.

5. Most preferreds have no maturity date.

C. Summary of usual preferred stock provisions:

1. It is nonparticipating.

2. It is nonvoting.

3. It has a prior claim on earnings and assets.

4. It is cumulative.

5. It has no maturity.

6. It is callable.

VII. Appraisal.

A. From the viewpoint of the issuer.

1. Advantages.

   a. The obligation to make fixed payments is avoided.

   b. It obtains higher earnings for original owners if leverage is successful.

   c. It avoids provision of equal participation in earnings.

   d. It usually does not dilute existing control of the firm.

   e. Since it usually has no maturity value and no sinking fund, it is more flexible than bonds.

   f. It enables the firm to conserve mortgageable assets.

2. Disadvantages.

   a. Sells at a higher yield than bonds.

   b. Dividends are not an expense for tax purposes.

B. From the viewpoint of the investor.

1. Advantages.
   a. Provides reasonably steady income.
   b. Preferred stockholders have priority over common stockholders in the event of liquidation.
   c. Corporations often like to hold preferred stock as an investment; 85 percent of dividends received are not taxable.
2. Disadvantages.
   a. Returns are limited.
   b. Price fluctuations are far greater.
   c. The stock has no legally enforceable right to dividends.
   d. Accrued cash dividends are seldom settled in an amount comparable to the amount of the obligation.

C. Recent trends.
   1. To avoid the tax disadvantage of nondeductibility of preferred stock dividends, companies have made offers to exchange preferred stock for debentures or subordinated debentures.
      a. When preferred stock is not callable, total securities offered usually exceed the market value of the preferred.
      b. A common formula is to offer bonds equal in market value to the preferred, plus cash or common stock as extra inducement to exchange.
   2. Use of convertible preferred stock in connection with mergers.
      a. Use of cash or bonds in payment to the shareholders of the acquired company would constitute realized gains from a tax standpoint.
      b. If convertible preferred stock is paid to the selling stockholders, this constitutes a tax-free exchange of securities.
      c. Selling stockholders thus obtain a fixed income security while postponing the capital gains taxes.

VIII. Decision-making in the use of preferred stock.
   A. Since it is a hybrid security type, the use of preferred stock is favored by conditions that fall between those favoring the use of common stock and those favoring the use of debt.
      1. If profit margins are adequate, the firm will gain from the additional leverage provided by preferred stock.
      2. Relative costs of alternative sources of financing are important.
      3. When the use of debt involves excessive risk and the issuance of common stock poses control problems, preferred stock may be a good compromise.
   B. Refunding a bond or preferred stock issue involves these points:
      1. A refunding operation involves the sale of a new issue of lower-yield securities. Proceeds from this sale are used to retire bonds or preferred stocks sold earlier at higher interest rates.
      2. Costs of refunding include:
         a. The call premium paid for the privilege of calling the old issue.

b. The flotation costs involved in selling the new issue.

3. Annual benefits of the refunding operation are equal to the difference in the interest payments associated with the old issue and those of the issue replacing it.

4. To determine whether refunding will be beneficial to the firm:

a. Find the present value of the interest savings by discounting at the *after-tax* cost of the debt.

b. Then compare this discounted value with the cash outlays associated with the refunding.

IX. Why are there so many different kinds of securities?

A. Different investors have different risk-return tradeoff functions.

B. In order to appeal to the widest possible market, various securities are offered.

C. Used wisely a policy of differentiated securities can lower a firm's average cost of capital below what it would be if it only issued one class of debt and common stock.

D. The listing below ranks securities from the safest down to securities with the highest risk but also the highest return.

1. U.S. Treasury bonds.

2. 1st mortgage bonds.

3. 2nd mortgage bonds.

4. Subordinated debentures.

5. Income bonds.

6. Preferred stock.

7. Convertible preferred.

8. Common stock.

PROBLEMS

15-1. The preferred stock of the Canadian Corporation has a cumulative annual dividend of $1.00. In the six-year period of 1971 through 1976, the firm retained 100 percent of its earnings (paid no preferred dividends). If projected earnings after tax but before preferred dividends for 1976 are $125,000, what is the largest common dividend that could be paid out of current earnings? (Shares outstanding, 1971-1976: 10,000 preferred, 15,000 common.)

Solution:

$1.00 cumulative annual dividend

x6 years (1971-1976)

$6.00 total cumulative dividend due

10,000 shares preferred
x$6 cumulative dividend due
$60,000 preferred dividends due

$125,000 earnings
60,000 preferred dividends due
$ 65,000 available for common dividends

$$\frac{\$65,000}{15,000} = \$4.33 \text{ largest possible common dividend.}$$

15-2. The Nebraska Corporation has one million shares of $50 par value preferred stock outstanding. Which of the following is a reasonable call price for such an issue (*not* a call for sinking fund purposes)?

a. $47.50   d. $65.00
b. $50.00   e. all the above
c. $55.00

Solution:

c. Call prices are always set at some premium above par value.

15-3. Which combination of current ratio and debt ratio below would preferred stockholders prefer?

	Current ratio	*Debt ratio*
a.	Low	Low
b.	Low	High
c.	High	Low
d.	High	High

Solution:

c. High current ratio—more liquid
   Low debt ratio—less risky

15-4. What is the major reason that many firms have retired their preferred stock?

Solution:

The nondeductibility of dividends for tax purposes.

15-5. Given the balance sheet below, what percentage of the bank's claims will be satisfied if $500 is available for claims on liquidation?

Balance Sheet

	Bank debt	$ 600
	Accounts payable	300
	Subordinated debt (subordinated *only* to bank loan)	300
	Common stock	2,000
	Retained earnings	400
Total assets = $3,600	Total claims	$3,600

Solution:

Total debt = $1,200

	Initial Position	Initial Percentage	Initial Distribution	Final Distribution
Bank debt	$600/1200	0.50	$250	$375
Accounts payable	300/1200	0.25	125	125
Subordinated debt	300/1200	0.25	125	—
		1.00	$500	$500

$$\frac{\$375}{\$600} = 62.5\%.$$

15-6. The Obrien Corporation has a $30 million bond issue outstanding. It carries a 6 percent coupon and will be outstanding for ten years. The bonds can be called at a 5 percent premium. The firm has an opportunity to float a new ten-year bond issue of $30 million with a 4 percent coupon. It is predicted that market interest rates will not fall below 4 percent. If flotation costs on the new issue are $1,500,000, and tax effects are ignored, should the firm refund the old bonds and issue the new ones? What is the net present value of savings?

Solution:

Call premium: $30,000,000 × 0.05	= $1,500,000
Flotation costs:	= 1,500,000
Total costs	= $3,000,000

Old interest payments: $30,000,000 x 0.06   = $1,800,000
New interest payments: $30,000,000 x 0.04   =   1,200,000
   Annual saving $ 600,000
P.V. of annuity 10 years at 4 percent, Table A-4
      8.111 x $600,000 = $4,866,600.

$4,866,600
−3,000,000
Net present value $1,866,600

Since the net present value is positive, the refunding should be undertaken.

15-7. Leverage is always disadvantageous to a firm if the rate of return on assets is less than _____ .

Solution:

The cost of debt.

15-8. The orderly retirement of a bond issue can be facilitated by _____ .

Solution:

A sinking fund.

15-9. If market rates of interest have risen above the coupon rate on a publicly traded bond issue, the firm is likely to fulfill its sinking fund obligations through _____ .

Solution:

Market purchases of its own bonds.

15-10. What is the major advantage to the firm of subordinated debt over preferred stock?

Solution:

The interest on subordinated debt is deductible as an expense for income tax purposes.

15-11. Why should the interest rate on the new debt, rather than the average cost of capital, be used as the discount factor when calculating the net present value of a refunding operation?

Solution:

There is no risk to the savings—their value is known with relatively complete certainty. With a lower risk, a lower capitalization rate should be employed.

15-12. In what way is an income bond like a share of preferred stock?

Solution:

Management is not required to pay interest if it is not earned.

15-13. Which of the following is a reason for using long-term debt?
a. The firm's management expects a substantial price level rise in future (investors don't share this view).
b. Existing debt ratio is low relative to the industry.
c. Common stock price is temporarily depressed relative to bond prices.
d. b and c.
e. a, b, and c.

Solution:

e. All are reasons for using long-term debt.

15-14. The Doan Chemical Company is a leading manufacturer of industrial chemicals, plastics, and metals. During 1976 the company sought to raise $150 million to retire short-term obligations of $50 million and to add working capital for further growth.

The alternatives available to the company were 20-year, 9 percent sinking fund debentures or the sale of common stock at $60 per share. Under the debenture financing, the firm was obligated to provide for the retirement of $4 million of principal annually, starting in 1979. Relevant balance sheet and income statement data are listed below. Assume a 40 percent tax rate.

Which financing alternative should Doan Chemical have chosen?

Chemical Industry Financial Ratios

Current ratio (x)	2.6
Sales to total assets (x)	1.3
Sales to inventory (x)	6.1
Average collection period (days)	46
Current debt/total assets (%)	25
Long-term debt/total assets (%)	25
Preferred/total assets (%)	0-5
Net worth/total assets (%)	50
Profits to sales (%)	4.3
Profits to total assets (%)	5.7
Profits to net worth (%)	9.7
Expected growth in earnings and dividends (%)	6.34

Doan Chemical Company, Balance Sheet, June 30, 1976 (in millions of dollars)

Cash	$ 60	Accounts payable	$ 90
Net receivables	150	Notes payable, 7%	150
Inventories	190	Accruals	60
Total current		Total current	
assets	$ 400	liabilities	$ 300
Investments	50	Long-term debt, 8%	100
Net property	550	Common stock, par $5	100
		Capital surplus	150
		Retained earnings	350
Total assets	$1,000	Total claims on assets	$1,000

Doan Chemical Company, Consolidated Statement of Income
Years Ended June 30, 1974, 1975, and 1976
(in millions of dollars)

	1975	1976	1977
Sales (net)	$820	$900	$970
Rental and service income	15	20	20
Total income	835	920	990
Cost of products sold	610	685	720
Depreciation	90	95	100
Selling, administrative, and other expenses	15	20	20
Total expenses	715	800	840
Net operating income (average 18% of sales)	120	120	150
Interest	20	22	18.5
Profit before taxes	100	98	131.5
Income taxes, 40%	40	39	53
Net profit for period	60	59	79
Earnings per share of common	3.00	2.95	3.95
Cash dividends per common share	1.20	1.20	1.60
Price range for common stock: high	54	35	63
low	27	15	32

Solution:

a. Relative costs:

Price-earnings ratio $\dfrac{\$60}{\$3.95}$ = 15 times

Earnings yield $\dfrac{\$3.95}{\$60}$ = 6.6%

Dividend yield $\dfrac{\$1.60}{\$60}$ = 2.66%

Estimated cost of newly issued common stock $\quad k = \dfrac{D}{P} + g$

$$= 2.66\% + 6.34\%$$
$$= 9\%$$

Debt cost: before tax $\quad$ = 9%

after tax $\quad$ = 5.4%

The company's earnings and dividend yield are quite low, and common stock could be sold on a favorable basis. The cost of this newly issued common stock is estimated at 9 percent. Although the cost of debt before tax is approximately the same, the effective debt cost is still much lower (at 5.4 percent) because of the advantage of tax deductions on interest payments.

b. Financial structure

| | Industry Average | Doan Chemical Percentage of Total Assets | | |
		Now	Debt	Equity
Current debt	25	30	23	23
Long-term debt	25	10	23	9
Total debt	50	40	46	32
Net worth	50	60	54	68

Compared with the indicated industry composite financial structure, Doan is relatively heavy in net worth and low in the use of debt. (Admittedly, the dispersion of leverage ratios found in the chemical industry makes its composite a less meaningful guide than those of industries in which leverage ratios are similar among most of the firms in the industry.) In the *pro forma* analysis above, it is clear that to raise the funds by common stock would increase the net worth ratio far above the industry average.

On the other hand, the debt issue would bring the ratios closer to the industry average. The total debt figure (46 percent) would still be below the average, and the further leveraging opportunity would continue to exist. This analysis strongly favors the debt alternative.

c. Control

Currently outstanding shares 20.00 million

New shares $\dfrac{\$150,000,000}{\$60}$ = $\underline{2.5\text{ million}}$

Total shares   22.5 million

% increase = $\dfrac{2.5}{20}$ = 13%

There would be an increase of 13 percent in shares outstanding, of which the added 2.5 million shares would be widely distributed, so there is no danger of loss of control in the event of a common stock issue. Generally, control is not an issue in the case of large, listed corporations.

d. Sinking fund: The $4 million sinking fund requirement, plus the additional interest cost of $13.5 million, less an implicit short-term debt cost reduction of $3.5 million ($50 million x 7 percent), would require an added fixed cash outlay of $10 million until 1979, for the use of debt, and $14 million after 1979.

If the net operating income (earnings before interest and taxes) in 1976 were compared with the anticipated total fixed cash outlays after debt financing, the result would be a 5.3 times coverage (150/28.5) until 1979 and a 4.6 times coverage (150/32.5) on operations after 1979. This is down from an 8.1 times coverage (150/18.5) before financing. However, earnings are expected to grow at a rate of 6.34 percent per year. Thus, the added fixed cash outlays would actually be a much smaller burden than indicated above.

e. Break-even chart and graph for Doan Chemical's financing alternatives appears on the following pages.

The difference between the two alternatives, in terms of the resulting net income, is the interest cost on debt and the number of shares outstanding. Prior to the financing, the total interest cost was $18.5 million. Under the new debt issue, total new debt increases by $100 million as the other $50 million of the new issue is used to retire notes payable. This increases interest cost to $28.5 million. These figures are explained as follows:

Before Financing	Amount	Cost	After-Debt Financing	Amount	Cost
	($ millions)			($ millions)	
Notes payable (7%)	$150	$10.5	Notes payable (7%)	$100	$ 7.0
Long-term debt (8%)	100	8.0	Long-term debt	250	21.5
			(8% on $100)		
			(9% on $150)		
Total	$250	$18.5	Total	$350	$28.5

The required fixed cash outlay is an added burden to the firm although earnings increases are expected to alleviate the problem.

For the common stock issue, the interest cost is reduced to $15 million ($18.5 million-3.5 million) and the number of shares outstanding increases by 2.5 million shares. The latter poses no control problem for the company, however.

The approximate break-even point is at $750 million in sales, after which the debt alternative becomes more advantageous in terms of earnings per share because of the increased leverage. Since the Doan Company's sales exceed the break-even sales and there is reason to believe that this will continue to increase, the debt alternative seems favored from this standpoint.

The conclusion is that the Doan Chemical Company should finance by debt. Both relative costs and the financial structure pattern clearly favor debt. The break-even analysis also shows debt to be advantageous at the company's sales volume. See Figure 15-1. Furthermore, the added fixed cost burden is not expected to present any problem.

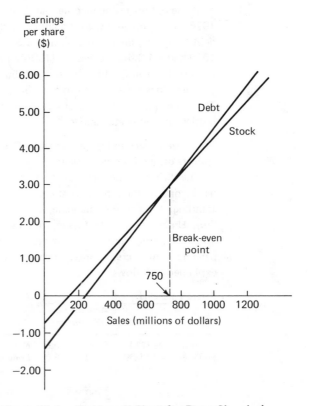

Figure 15-1. Break-even Chart for Doan Chemical
Company's Financing Alternatives

Break-even Worksheet for Doan Chemical's Financing Alternatives

Use of Debt

Sales (millions)	$ 0	$200	$500	$600	$700	$800	$900	$1,000	$1,100	$1,200
Net income before taxes (18%)	0	$ 36.0	$ 90.0	$108.0	$126.0	$144.0	$162.0	$180.0	$198.0	$216.0
Interest on debt	28.5	28.5	28.5	28.5	28.5	28.5	28.5	28.5	28.5	28.5
Income subject to tax	—	7.5	61.5	79.5	97.5	115.5	133.5	151.5	169.5	187.5
Tax (40%)	—	3.0	24.6	31.8	39.0	46.2	53.4	60.6	67.8	75.0
Net income after tax	$(28.5)	4.5	36.9	47.7	58.5	69.3	80.1	90.9	101.70	112.5
Earnings per share (20 million shares)	$ (1.43)	$ 0.23	$ 1.85	$ 2.39	$ 2.93	$ 3.47	$ 4.01	$ 4.55	$ 5.09	$ 5.63

Use of Stock

Sales (millions)	$ 0	$200	$500	$600	$700	$800	$900	$1,000	$1,100	$1,200
Net income before taxes (18%)	0	$ 36.0	$ 90.0	$108.0	$126.0	$144.0	$162.0	$180.0	$198.0	$215.0
Interest on debt	15.0	15.0	15.0	15.0	15.0	15.0	15.0	15.0	15.0	15.0
Income subject to tax	0	21.0	75.0	93.0	111.0	129.0	147.0	165.0	183.0	201.0
Tax (40%)	0	8.4	30.0	37.2	44.4	51.6	58.8	66.0	73.2	80.4
Net income after tax	$(15.0)	$ 12.6	$ 45.0	$ 55.8	$ 66.6	$ 77.4	$ 88.2	$ 99.0	$109.8	$120.6
Earnings per share (22.5 million shares)	$(0.67)	$ 0.56	$ 2.0	$ 2.48	$ 2.96	$ 3.44	$ 3.92	$ 4.40	$ 4.88	$ 5.36

Term loans and leases

16

THEME

Intermediate-term financing is defined as liabilities originally scheduled for repayment in more than one but less than ten years. It has been playing an increasingly important role because of its flexibility. The two major forms of intermediate-term financing include term loans and lease financing.

I. Term loans.
   A. A term loan is a business loan with a maturity of more than one year.
   B. Because term loans represent long-term fixed commitments, restrictive provisions are generally attached to them for the protection of the lender.
      1. The borrower must maintain a specified current ratio, and a specified minimum net working capital.
      2. Purchase of fixed assets is limited.
      3. Additional borrowing and future assumption of contingent liabilities are limited.
      4. An effort is made to insure the continuity of management.
      5. Financial statements and budgets are forwarded to the lender.
   C. The costs of term loans vary with the size of the loan and the strength of the borrowing firm.
      1. On loans of less than $500 the interest rate may be as high as 15 percent.
      2. On loans of $1 million and above, interest charges approximate the prime rate.
      3. Frequently, the interest charge is fixed as a function of the rediscount rate or the published prime rate of New York City banks; in this case,

the cost of the loan could fluctuate.

D. Other characteristics of term loans vary with the type of lender.

    1. Commercial bank term loans.

        a. Mature in from one to five years.

        b. Generally they are for amounts ranging from $100,000 to $250,000.

        c. Frequently they are made to companies with assets of less than $5 million.

        d. Often they are secured by stocks, bonds, machinery, or other equipment.

    2. Life insurance company and pension fund term loans.

        a. Mature in from five to fifteen years.

        b. Generally they are for amounts ranging from $1 million to $5 million.

        c. They usually are made to large companies.

        d. Collateral is required about one-third of the time, frequently in the form of real estate.

    3. Commercial banks and life insurance companies sometimes combine to make loans.

        a. Loans of over $10 million may be broken down into smaller amounts and financed in combination.

        b. A bank may make the loan for five years, with an insurance company taking it over for the segment with longer maturity.

E. Repayment provisions of term loans generally provide for amortization, or systematic repayment over the life of the loan.

    1. Repayment frequently is made possible from increased earnings due to the loan.

    2. The amortization schedule seeks to protect both the borrower and the lender.

    3. The amortization schedule is determined through the use of the formula:

$$R = \frac{A_n}{IF}$$

where

    R = amortization payment

    A_n = amount of the loan

    IF = appropriate interest factor (Table A-4).

    4. If loans are repaid ahead of schedule, a prepayment penalty of from 3 to 8 percent of the outstanding balance is usually required.

    5. A few term loans are not fully amortized and have a balloon segment at the end.

    6. In addition to fixed interest charges, institutional investors have increasingly taken compensation in the form of options to buy common shares. These options usually are in the form of detachable warrants permitting the purchase of the shares at stated prices over a designated period of time.

F. The major suppliers and users of term loans have changed over time.
   1. Industries with large investments in fixed assets tend to use term loans most frequently.
   2. A 1957 study showed that the greatest relative increase in the use of term loans was by industries characterized by small, rapidly growing firms.
   3. In earlier periods, over half of all term loans were made to refund bonds sold at higher interest rates.
   4. More recently, term loans have been used for working capital, and to finance plant and equipment additions.
G. Evaluation of term loans.
   1. Advantages.
      a. Avoid possible nonrenewal of short-term loans.
      b. Avoid public flotation costs.
      c. Minimal negotiation time.
      d. Ease of indenture modification (relative to changing the terms of a public offering).
   2. Disadvantages.
      a. Relatively high interest costs.
      b. Large cash drain due to amortization payments.
      c. Restrictions on operations and higher credit standards which are insisted upon by lenders.
H. The use of term lending has broad implications for the entire economy. since term loans provide several advantages.
   1. Reduced vulnerability of the economy to forced liquidation.
   2. Movement of insurance firms (with their stable inflow of funds) into direct lending.
   3. A partial solution of the long-term debt problem of small business.
II. Lease financing.
A. Lease financing is quite similar to borrowing and is another method of providing financial leverage.
B. Major forms.
   1. *Sale and leaseback*—a firm owning land, buildings, or equipment sells the property and simultaneously executes an agreement to lease the property for a specified period under specific terms.
      a. The seller immediately receives the sale price of the property but retains the right to use it.
      b. Payments provided for by the lease are sufficient to return the full purchase price plus a stated return to the buyer.
   2. *Service leases* or *operating leases* include both financing and maintenance services.
      a. The lease contract is written for less than the expected life of the leased equipment.
      b. Such leases typically contain a cancellation clause permitting the

lessee to cancel the lease and return the equipment before the expiration of the basic lease agreement.

    3. *Financial leases*—do not provide for maintenance services and are not cancellable.

        a. These leases provide for full amortization of cost, plus a return on the unamortized balance.

        b. Sale-leaseback is a special type of financial lease.

  C. Annual lease payments are deductible for income tax purposes provided the following requirements stated by the Internal Revenue Service are included in the agreement:

    1. The term of the lease must be less than 30 years.

    2. The rental payments must provide a reasonable rate of return to the lessor.

    3. A renewal option is bona fide. A minimum requirement is that the lessee meet the best outside offer.

    4. There shall be no purchase option.

III. Cost comparisons of lease financing with alternatives.

  A. Lease cost is compared with a bank loan. Cash flow differentials are discounted at appropriate rates—cost of debt for most differentials, average cost of capital for salvage value.

  B. Effects of accelerated depreciation.

    1. Initially, it would appear that the use of accelerated depreciation provides greater tax benefits to owning.

    2. However, the lessor will be forced by competition to share these benefits with the lessee, so the final result depends upon competitive conditions.

  C. Interest rates are frequently assumed to be higher in leasing than in borrowing.

    1. But this may reflect higher risks to lessors than to other lenders.

    2. It may be difficult to separate money costs and the cost of other specialist services provided by the lessor.

  D. Residual property values:

    1. Rising real estate values favor the ownership of land and buildings.

    2. Obsolescence of equipment and low salvage values favor leasing such equipment.

    3. But it is argued that competition will force leasing rates down to the point where potentials of high residual values are recognized in the leasing rates.

  E. Costs of obsolescence.

    1. Lessor bears costs of obsolescence, which would tend to favor leasing if obsolescence rate is high.

    2. But the lessor's reconditioning and marketing may enable it to find users for whom older equipment is still economical. This may reduce costs of obsolescence to both lessor and lessee.

  F. Possible advantages of leasing.

1. Lease payments are tax deductible.
2. Credit availability is increased.
   a. Firm may be able to obtain more money for longer terms than they could under a loan.
   b. Future borrowing capacity is not hindered since debt ratio is unchanged.

PROBLEMS

16-1. Initially, the balance sheet of Holt Corporation shows a debt-assets ratio of 70 percent. It then leases a machine tool that has a cost equal to the amount of its original assets. What debt-assets ratio will the "postlease" balance sheet show if Holt does not capitalize the rental expense?

Solution:

No change. Holt is purchasing a service, not an asset, so the balance sheet will not be altered.

16-2. A firm has contracted to repay a term loan in ten annual installments of $300 each. If the interest is 8 percent, what is the amount of the loan?

Solution:

PV of annuity for 10 years at 8% = 6.710 (Table A-4)

$$R = \frac{An}{IF} \qquad \$300 = \frac{An}{6.710} \qquad An = \$2013$$

16-3. In the preceding problem what is the outstanding loan balance at the end of the *second* year?

Solution:

Year	Total Payment	Interest Payment	Loan Payment	Remaining Balance
1	$300	$161	$139	$1874†
2	$300	$150	$150	$1724

†$1,874 = ($2,013 − $139).

16-4. A firm has recently expanded production and now requires a new machine tool. The firm's management is considering two alternative means of financing the machine—an outright purchase or a financial lease (not cancellable). You have been asked to develop an analysis of the relative costs of owning versus leasing. Which of the interest rates below will you use to determine the proper discount factor?
a. Cost of debt.
b. Cost of preferred dividends.
c. Cost of retained earnings.
d. Cost of equity.
e. Weighted average cost of capital.

Solution:

a. The cost of debt is the appropriate choice since there is essentially no risk to the firm of obtaining the savings of the preferable alternative.

16-5. Assuming the terms of a particular lease option are not subject to change, which of the following would decrease the cost of owning?
a. The elimination of accelerated depreciation for tax purposes.
b. The introduction of the investment tax credit.
c. An increased salvage value.
d. An increased obsolescence rate.

Solution:

Both b and c would decrease the cost of owning.

16-6. Often, direct term loans issued by commercial banks can be distinguished from those issued by insurance companies. Which of the below are likely to be useful distinguishing characteristics?
a. Maturity of the loan.
b. Borrower's use of the funds.
c. Size of the loan.
d. Collateral on the loan.
e. Size of the borrower.

Solution:

All except b. The remaining choices typically indicate whether the loan was issued by a bank or an insurance firm. As maturity, size of loan, collateral, and size of borrower increase, it is more likely the loan was offered by an insurance company.

16-7. Which of the following is an advantage of owning as opposed to leasing?
   a. Protection against obsolescence.
   b. Tax deductibility of the lease expense.
   c. Protection against decline in salvage value.
   d. Tax deductibility of depreciation expense.
   e. Understatement of financial leverage on the balance sheet.

Solution:

d. However, the tax deductibility of the depreciation expense is offset by the tax deductibility of the lease expense.

16-8. The Jackson Company is faced with the decision whether to purchase or to lease a new fork-lift truck. The truck can be leased on a five-year contract for $2,200 a year, or it can be purchased for $8,000. The lease includes maintenance and service. The salvage value of the truck five years hence is $2,000. The company uses the sum-of-the-years digits method of depreciation. If the truck is owned, service and maintenance charges (a tax deductible cost) would be $400 a year. The company can borrow at 10 percent for amortized term loans. It has a 40 percent marginal tax rate, and the average after-tax cost of capital is 14 percent.

   Which method of acquiring the use of equipment should the company choose?

Solution:

Amortization of loan.

Present worth of 5 annual payments $= p \times$ [PVIF$_a$ at 10% for 5 years, Table A-4]

$$\$8,000 = p \times [3,791]$$

$$p = \$2,110 \text{ constant annual payment.}$$

The solution is continued in Table 16-1 on the next page.

We used the weighted cost of capital for discounting cash flows reflecting the view that the cash flows associated with a given project define the risk of that project. However, some authors hold the view that the appropriate discount rate to apply should reflect the riskiness of the individual cash flows involved in the lease-versus-own comparison. Cash flows known with relative certainty would be discounted at comparatively low rates, and conversely for risky cash flows. Applying this logic to lease analysis leads to the conclusion that each cash flow stream involved in a lease-versus-purchase decision (for example, the loan payment, maintenance cost, and so on) should be analyzed to determine its degree of risk, then discounted at an appropriate rate. This disagreement has not yet been settled.

Table 16-1. Comparison of Cost of Leasing versus Owning

	Applicable to Loan				Applicable to Net Cost of Owning					Applicable to Lease	Comparative Costs		
Year (1)	Total Payment (2)	Interest (3)	Amortization Payment (4)	Remaining Balance (5)	Maintenance Cost (6)	Depreciation (7)	(3)+(6)+(7)= Tax Deductible Expense (8)	(.4)(8)= Tax Savings (9)	(2)+(6)−(9)= Cash Outflow of Owning (10)	(1−.4)(Lease cost)= After Tax (11)	14% Present Value Factors (12)	(10)×(12)= Present Value of Costs of Owning (13)	(11)×(12)= Present Value of Costs of Leasing (14)
1	$ 2,110	$ 800	$1,310	$6,690	$ 400	$2,000	$ 3,200	$1,280	$ 1,230	$1,320	.877	$1,079	$1,158
2	2,110	669	1,441	5,249	400	1,600	2,669	1,068	1,442	1,320	.769	1,109	1,015
3	2,110	525	1,585	3,664	400	1,200	2,125	850	1,660	1,320	.675	1,120	891
4	2,110	366	1,744	1,920	400	800	1,566	626	1,884	1,320	.592	1,115	781
5	2,110	190	1,920	—	400	400	990	396	2,114	1,320	.519	1,097	685
									(2,000)		.519	(1,038)	
	$10,550	$2,550	$8,000		$2,000	$6,000	$10,550					$4,482	$4,530

Conclusion: The analysis favors owning the truck, since its net cost is lower than that of the leasing alternative.

16-9. The Town Department Store has been growing rapidly. Management estimates that it will need an additional $4 million during the next two years. Because of its weak current position, the store is considering the sale and leaseback of its land and building for $9 million. The annual net rental would be $600,000. The immediate use of the sales proceeds will be to retire bank loans and mortgages. The current balance sheet and recent earnings are shown below.

Town Department Store—Balance Sheet, December 31, 1974
(in millions of dollars)

Cash	$1	Accounts payable	$5
Receivables	7	Bank loans, 5%	5
Inventories	6	Other current debt	1
Total current assets	$14	Total current debt	$11
		Mortgage on property,	
Land	$1	5%	3
Buildings	4	Common stock	2
Equipment and fixtures	1	Retained earnings	4
Net fixed assets	6		
Total assets	$20	Total claims on assets	$20

Annual depreciation charges are $100,000 on the building and $400,000 on the equipment and fixtures. Profit before taxes in 1974 is $1,600,000; after taxes, $960,000.

a. How much capital gains tax will Town pay if the land and building are sold, and what are the net proceeds? (Assume all capital gains are taxed at the capital gains tax rate.)

b. If the lease had been in effect during 1974, what would Town's profit after the taxes have been? (Assume a 40 percent tax rate.)

c. If the firm uses the net proceeds of the sale to reduce the bank loan and accounts payable instead of the mortgage, what will be its new current ratio?

d. List some advantages and disadvantages of the sale-and-leaseback operation, and recommend whether or not the firm should adopt the proposal.

Solution:

a.

Sale price	$9,000,000
Basis (land + building)	5,000,000
Capital gains	$4,000,000
Tax at 30%	1,200,000

Net proceeds = sales price − tax = $9,000,000 − $1,200,000
= $7,800,000.

b. Profit before taxes $1,600,000
   Add: interest on bank loans   250,000
        interest on mortgage   150,000
        depreciation on building   100,000
        profit before taxes, interest and depreciation $2,100,000

   Less: rental   600,000
   Taxable income $1,500,000
   Tax at 40%   600,000
        Profit after taxes $ 900,000

c. Net proceeds $7.8 million
   Reduction in current liabilities   7.8 million
   Total current debt ($11 million − $7.8 million)   3.2 million
   New current ratio ($14 million/$3.2 million)   4.38 times

d. *Advantages.* Improves current position; opens the possibility for more borrowing from the bank in the future; increases the firm's ability to obtain funds; avoids restrictions in loan agreements.

Disadvantages. Leasing may have less flexibility than the alternatives; firm may lose benefits of increases in property values.

The lease is recommended. The firm can carry the fixed charges of the lease because of its high profitability. However, the firm is under-financed with equity money. It should plow back the high profits to build up net worth and consider outside equity money.

Warrants and Convertibles

17

THEME

The sale of debt or preferred stock with convertibility provisions or with warrants can be made at lower interest costs and can provide for a future broadening of the equity base.

I. *Warrants* are long-term options to buy a stated number of shares of common stock during a specified duration at a stated price.
    A. Customary provisions include the following:
        1. The exercise price at which stock may be bought.
        2. A statement of the period during which options can be exercised.
        3. An antidilution clause to protect the warrant in the event of a stock dividend or stock split.
    B. The market value of warrants increases as these factors increase:
        1. The duration of the option period.
        2. The market value of common stock relative to the stated purchase price (the exercise price).
        3. The number of common shares to be purchased by each warrant.
        4. The speculative possibilities—that is, the growth potential—of the common stock.

II. Determinants of the value of warrants.
    A. Formula value of warrants:

$$\begin{array}{c} \text{Formula} \\ \text{value of} \\ \text{warrant} \end{array} = \left(\begin{array}{c} \text{Market price} \\ \text{of} \\ \text{common stock} \end{array} - \begin{array}{c} \text{Option} \\ \text{purchase} \\ \text{price} \end{array} \right) \times \begin{array}{c} \text{Number of shares each} \\ \text{warrant entitles owner} \\ \text{to purchase} \end{array}$$

    B. Actual price of a warrant.

       1. Warrant usually sells above theoretical value.

          Market price of warrant = Formula value of warrant + Premium.

       2. Premium over value is largest when price of common is at a low unit level.

       3. The amount of the premium decreases as the price of the common rises.

       4. Above some absolute level of common stock price, the premium becomes constant.

    C. Reasons why the size of the premium diminishes as the price of the common stock rises.

       1. Declining leverage impact.

       2. Increasing magnitude of potential losses.

III. Reasons for using warrants.

    A. Warrants are usually used by growing firms to reduce the interest cost on debt and to avoid restrictive indenture provisions.

    B. Warrants tend to widen the market for the firm's debt.

    C. Warrants can provide for additional equity funds in the future.

IV. Appraisal of the use of warrants.

    A. Advantages.

       1. Warrants allow a balanced financing of debt and equity.

       2. They aid the sale of debt and reduce interest rates on debt.

       3. They can result in the future sale of equities at prices higher than the current market value.

    B. Disadvantages.

       1. The long-term call on the common stock is a form of dilution.

       2. Exercise of the warrants increases the equity base and, therefore, reduces the effects of trading on the equity.

       3. Warrants can be exercised and bring in funds at a time when the firm has no need for additional capital.

V. Convertible securities are bonds or preferred stock which are exchangeable for common stock at the holder's option. Typical terms of the conversion privilege include the following:

    A. The *conversion ratio*—the number of shares of common for which the convertible may be exchanged.

    B. The *conversion price*—the effective price paid per share of common upon conversion.

       1.   Conversion price $= \dfrac{\text{par value of convertible security}}{\text{number of shares received on conversion}}$

       2. Usually the conversion premium is 15 to 20 percent above market price at the time the convertible is issued; that is, the conversion price exceeds the market price of the stock by 15 to 20 percent.

    C. Some convertibles have decreasing ratios (increasing conversion prices) over time.

    D. Convertibles also include a clause protecting the holder against dilution due to stock splits or stock dividends.

VI.   Use of convertibles.

    A. Convertibles provide a hedge against uncertainty.

      1. In depression, they afford the protection of senior debt.

      2. In boom or inflation, both the price of the convertible and the value of the conversion privilege increase.

    B. Interest rates on convertible bonds are always lower than those on nonconvertible bonds of equivalent risk; investors who buy convertibles give up income for the hope of capital gain.

    C. There has been a pronounced increase in the use of convertibles in recent years; financial managers seem to be using convertibles more to facilitate the raising of future equity capital rather than as a sweetener to reduce the interest cost of debt issues.

VII. Advantages to the use of convertibles.

    A. Convertibles permit the sale of debt at low interest rates.

    B. Convertibles provide a method of selling equity at prices higher than the current market prices.

    C. The call provision gives the company a means of forcing conversion whenever the market price of the stock exceeds the conversion price.

    D. Convertibles provide low-cost capital during a period when earnings on assets are being developed.

VIII. Disadvantages of convertibles.

    A. A delay in financing could possibly enable the sale of an equity issue at prices higher than those obtained through a convertible issue.

    B. The market price of the common might not rise above the conversion price. Thus, a high debt-equity ratio would remain.

IX.   Warrants and convertibles perform the same basic functions, but differences should be noted.

    A. The exercise of convertibles does not ordinarily bring additional funds to the company. The exercise of warrants does bring in additional funds.

    B. Conversion results in reduced debt ratios. The exercise of warrants strengthens the equity position, but debt (or preferred) remains outstanding.

    C. Because of the call feature, convertibles give the firm greater control over the timing of capital structure changes than do warrants.

PROBLEMS

17-1. Grant Corporation's warrants are currently selling at an $8 premium over the formula value. Each warrant entitles its owner to purchase two shares of common stock for $50 (or $25 per share). If the common stock is presently selling for $45, what is the market price of the warrant?

Solution:

Step 1. Use the formula:

$$\text{Formula value} = \left(\begin{array}{c} \text{Market price of} \\ \text{common stock} \end{array} - \begin{array}{c} \text{Option} \\ \text{price} \end{array} \right) \times \begin{array}{c} \text{Number of shares each} \\ \text{warrant entitles owner} \\ \text{to purchase} \end{array}$$

$$= (\$45 - \$25) \times 2$$
$$= \$40 \text{ formula value of warrant}$$

Step 2. Use the formula:

$$\text{Market price of warrant} = \text{formula value of warrant} + \text{premium}$$
$$= \$40 + \$8$$
$$= \$48 \text{ market price of warrant.}$$

17-2. The call price on Lee's $1,000 par value convertible bond is $1,100. Given a conversion price of $25 per share (that is, each bond can be converted into 40 shares of stock), which of the choices below is the lowest price at which the stock can sell and still have bondholders convert rather than submit their bonds for redemption in the event of a call?
a. $30.01   d. $25.01
b. $28.51   e. $20.51
c. $27.50

Solution:

c. $\dfrac{\$1100 \text{ call price}}{40 \text{ conversion ratio}} = \$27.50$ minimum price for conversion.

17-3. In the preceding problem, what would you expect the conversion ratio (shares received on conversion per $1,000 bond) to be after Lee declared a 20 percent stock dividend?

Solution:

0.20 stock dividend x 40 shares = 8 additional shares
40 + 8 = 48 shares, the new conversion ratio.

17-4. At time of issue, what price relationship generally exists between the subscription price on warrants and the market price on common stock, and between the subscription price of rights and the market price of common stock?

Solution:

The subscription price of warrants is generally above the market price of the stock; that of rights is set below the stock price.

17-5. True or false: Warrants generally sell above their formula value.

Solution:

True. This is always true unless arbitrageurs fail to fulfill their function.

17-6. Where is the conversion price on a convertible bond generally set?

Solution:

Above the price of the stock.

17-7. True or false. The coupon rate on a convertible bond is usually higher than on an equivalent straight bond.

Solution:

False. It is typically lower because of the advantage to the investor of the conversion privilege.

17-8. In which of the following cases would current financing by means of debt with warrants be inappropriate?
   a. External funds needed now but no additional requirement expected for many years.
   b. External funds needed now with a continuing requirement for additional funds.
   c. A large amount of external funds needed now with diminishing requirements expected for next several years.
   d. Some external funds needed now with an expected increase in funds required for next several years.

Solution:

a.

17-9. The Johnson Company's capital consists of 9,000 shares of common stock and 3,000 warrants. Each warrant is capable of buying four shares of common at $75 per share. The warrants are protected against dilution (that is, the subscription price is adjusted downward in the event of a stock dividend or a stock split). The company also issues rights to buy one new share of common stock at $55 for every three shares held. With the stock selling with rights at $95, compute:

a. The theoretical value of the rights before stock sells ex-rights.

b. The new subscription price of the warrant after the rights issue.

Solution:

a. Value of one right $= \dfrac{M_O - S}{N + 1} = \dfrac{\$95 - \$55}{3 + 1} = \dfrac{\$40}{4} = \$10.$

b. Value of the warrant (before rights offering) = (market price of common stock less option price) x number of shares each warrant entitles owner to purchase = ($95 − $75) x 4 = $80.

In order to protect warrant holders against the dilution effect of the rights issue, the theoretical value of the warrants must remain the same after the stock goes ex-rights; therefore, with the market price of stock ex-rights = $95 − $10 = $85 and the value of the warrant held at $80,

$$\$80 = (85 - x)4$$
$$x = \$65 \text{ new subscription price.}$$

17-10. Hickman Paint, Inc., has the following balance sheet:

Balance Sheet 1

Current assets	$120,000	Current debt	$ 50,000
Net fixed assets	130,000	Common stock, par value $2	60,000
		Retained earnings	140,000
Total assets	$250,000	Total claims	$250,000

The firm earns 20 percent on total assets before taxes (assume a 50 percent tax rate).

In the following few years, sales are expected to double, and the financing needs of the firm will double. The firm decides to sell debentures to meet these needs. It is undecided, however, whether to sell convertible debentures or debentures with warrants. The new balance sheet would appear as follows:

Balance Sheet 2

Current assets	$240,000	Current debt	$ 90,000
Net fixed assets	260,000	Debentures	170,000
		Common stock, par value $2	60.000
		Retained earnings	180,000
Total assets	$500,000	Total claims	$500,000

The convertible debentures would pay 7 percent interest and would be convertible into 20 shares of common stock for each $1,000 debenture. The debentures with warrants would carry an 8 percent coupon and entitle each holder of a $1,000 debenture to buy ten shares of common stock at $70. John Hickman owns 80 percent of the company before the financing.

a. Assume that convertible debentures are sold and all are later converted. Show the new balance sheet, disregarding any changes in retained earnings.

b. Complete the firm's income statement after all the debentures have bene converted.

c. Now, instead of convertibles, assume that debentures with warrants were issued. Assume further that the warrants were all exercised. Show the new balance sheet figures.

d. Complete the firm's income statement after the debentures warrants have all been exercised.

Solution:

a. 20(shares) x 170(debentures) = 3,400(new shares) x $2(par value) = $6,800(addition to common stock account at par value).

$$\$170,000 - \$6,800 = \$163,200 \text{ paid-in surplus.}$$

Balance Sheet 3

		Current debt	$ 90,000
		Debentures	—
		Common stock, par $2	66,800
		Paid-in surplus	163,200
		Retained earnings	180,000
Total assets	$500,000	Total claims on assets	$500,000

b. Net income after all charges except debenture interest and before taxes,

(20 percent of total assets)	$100,000
Debenture interest	0
Taxable income	$100,000
Federal income tax, 50%	50,000
Net income after taxes	$ 50,000
Earnings per share after taxes	$1.50 ($50,000/33,400 = $1.50).

c. 10(shares) x 170(debentures) = 1,700(new shares) x $2(par value) = $3,400 (addition to common stock account at par value).
$70 (option price) x 1,700 (shares) = $119,000.
$119,000 − $3,400 = $115,600 (paid-in surplus).

Balance Sheet 4

		Current debt	$ 90,000
		Debentures	170,000
		Common stock, par $2	63,400
		Paid-in surplus	115,600
		Retained earnings	180,000
Total assets	$619,000	Total claims on assets	$619,000

d. Net income after all charges except debenture interest and before taxes.

$619,000 x 0.20 =	$123,800
Debenture interest	13,600
Taxable income	$110,200
Federal income tax	55,100
Net income after taxes	$ 55,100
Earnings per share after taxes	$1.74 ($55,100/31,700 = $1.74).

Financial Structure and the Cost of Capital

Part Six

Valuation and Rates of Return

18

THEME

The basic principles underlying valuation theory and investors' return on capital are discussed in Chapter 18.

I. There are several definitions of valuation.
    A. *Liquidating value* is the amount realizable if assets are sold separately from the organization that has been using them.
    B. *Going concern* value is the amount realizable if an enterprise is sold as an operating business.
    C. *Book value* is the accounting value at which an asset is carried.
    D. *Market value* is the price at which an asset (or firm) can be sold.
    E. *Fair or reasonable value* as viewed by different investors may differ from market value.
II. The capitalization of income method of valuation.
    A. This procedure, which is equivalent to the present value of a stream of earnings, is used to determine an asset's value.
    B. The first step in using this valuation method is to determine the proper capitalization rate, or the required rate of return.
III. The required rate of return.
    A. Efficient portfolios.
        1. Under the conditions set forth in Figure 18-1 all investors would hold portfolios lying on the line $R_F MZ$; this implies that they would hold only efficient portfolios which are linear combinations of the risk-free security and the risky portfolio M.

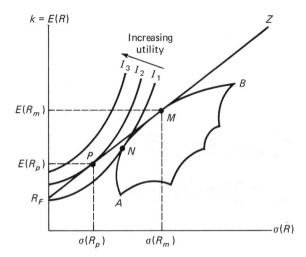

**Figure 18-1. Investor Equilibrium Combining the
Risk-Free Asset with the Market Portfolio**

2. In equilibrium, all investors will hold efficient portfolios with standard
   deviation-return combinations along the line $R_F MZ$. The particular
   location of a given individual on the line will be determined by the
   point at which his indifference curve is tangent to the line, and this in
   turn reflects his attitude toward risk, or his degree of risk aversion.

   The line $R_F MZ$ in Figure 18-1 (using the "rise over run" concept) is
   given by Equation 18-1.

   $$k = E(R) = R_F + \frac{(ER_m) - R_F}{\sigma(R_m)} \sigma(R_p).$$

3. The expected return on any portfolio is equal to the riskless rate plus a
   risk premium equal to $[E(R_m) - R_F] / \sigma(R_m)$ times the portfolio's
   standard deviation.

4. The capital market line for efficient portfolios bears a linear relationship
   between expected return and risk, and it may be rewritten as in Equation 18-2.

   $$k = E(R_p) = R_F + \lambda^\circ \sigma_p. \qquad (18\text{-}2)$$

   Here

   $\quad k = E(R_p) \;=\;$ expected return on an efficient portfolio
   $\qquad\quad R_F \;=\;$ risk-free interest rate

   $\qquad\quad \lambda^\circ \;=\;$ market price of risk; $\lambda^\circ = \dfrac{E(R_m) - R_F}{\sigma_m}$

   $\qquad\quad \sigma_p \;=\;$ standard deviation of returns on an efficient portfolio
   $\qquad E(R_m) \;=\;$ expected return on the market portfolio
   $\qquad\quad \sigma_m \;=\;$ standard deviation of returns on the market portfolio.

   All efficient portfolios, including the market portfolio, lies on the
   CML. Hence: $E(R_m) = R_F + \lambda^\circ \sigma_m.$ $\qquad\qquad (18\text{-}3)$

5. The relationship is graphed in Figure 18-2.

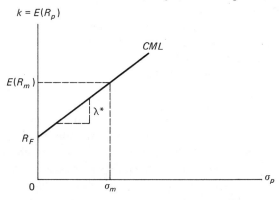

Figure 18-2. The Capital Market Line

6. The CML is drawn as a straight line with an intercept at R_F, the risk-free return, and a slope equal to the market price of risk ($\lambda°$), which is the market risk premium $[E(R_m) - R_F]$ divided by σ_m. Thus, the market price of risk, $\lambda°$, is a normalized risk premium.

B. Returns on individual assets or securities.

1. The expected returns for an individual security or investment can be represented as points on the following security market line:

$$E(Ri) \;=\; R_F + \lambda \; Cov(R_i, R_m). \qquad (18\text{-}4)$$

Here:

$$\lambda \;=\; \text{price of risk for securities} = [E(R_m) - R_F]/\sigma^2_m$$

$Cov(R_i, R_m) \;=\;$ covariance of the returns of security i
with returns on the market

$E(R_i) \;=\;$ expected return on an individual security i.

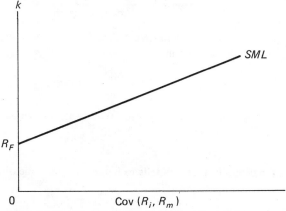

Figure 18-3. The SML for Individual Securities

2. Equation 18-4 for the security market line (*SML*) is graphed in Figure 18-3, which relates the covariance of the returns on the individual security to the expected return on the individual security.
3. The SML differs from the CML in two respects.
   a. First, for the individual securities or individual firm, the risk measure is the covariance instead of the standard deviation. This is an important conceptual difference because it conveys the recognition that the risk of an individual security or firm is measured in terms of its contribution to the risk of the portfolio into which it is placed.
   b. Second, the price of risk is shown as the excess market return normalized by the *variance* of market returns in the denominator instead of the standard deviation. The effect is to change the dimensionality or scale of the security market line as compared with the capital market line.
   c. The different values of k may represent different firms—or they may be the rates of return on the various securities of a single firm.
   d. Shifts in the CML may be caused by:
      1) Changes in the interest rate over time.
      2) Changes in the attitudes of the investor toward risk.
   e. The relationship between risk and return is positive. As the level of risk increases, the required rate of return, k, increases. The inverse is also true.

IV. Bond valuation.
   A. Expected cash flows are the annual interest payments plus the principal amount to be paid when the bond matures.
   B. Capitalization rates applied to bonds vary with differences in risk of default.
   C. The valuation method is applied to perpetual bonds that have no maturity (a perpetuity):

$$\text{Value} = V = \frac{\text{constant annual interest}}{\text{capitalization rate}} = \frac{I}{i}.$$

Assume that the annual interest (I) is $80 and the going capitalization rate (i) for this type of bond is 8 percent:

$$V = \frac{\$80}{.08} = \$1,000.$$

If the capitalization rate rises to 10 percent, the value of the bond will fall:

$$V = \frac{\$80}{.10} = \$800.$$

If the capitalization rate falls to 5 percent, the value of the bond will rise:

$$V = \frac{\$80}{.05} = \$1,600.$$

D. The valuation method is applied to short-term bonds with a fixed maturity value.

1. For a bond maturing in time period n,

$$V = \frac{I_1}{(1 + i)^1} + \frac{I_2}{(1 + i)^2} + \ldots + \frac{I_n + M}{(1 + i)^n}$$

where M is the maturity value of the bond and i is the appropriate interest rate.

2. Calculation of the value of a five-year bond at different interest rates:

Year	Receipts	Discount Factor 8%	10%	5%	Present Value of Receipts at Indicated Discount Rates 8%	10%	5%
1	$80	.926	.909	.952	$ 74	$ 73	$ 76
2	80	.857	.826	.907	69	66	73
3	80	.794	.751	.864	64	60	69
4	80	.735	.683	.823	59	55	66
5	80 + $1,000	.681	.621	.784	735	671	847
Value of Bond					$1,000	$925	$1,131

3. Calculation of the value of a one-year bond at different interest rates:

Year	Receipts	Discount Factor 8%	10%	5%	Present Value of Receipts at Indicated Discount Rates 8%	10%	5%
1	$80 + $1,000	.926	.909	.952	$1,000	$982	$1,028
Value of Bond					$1,000	$982	$1,028

4. Change in the value of a $1,000 bond with an 8 percent coupon when interest rates change:

	Decline in Value as Interest Rate Rises from 8% to 10%	Increase in Value as Interest Rate Falls from 8% to 5%
One-year bond	$ 18	$ 28
5-year bond	$ 75	$131
Consol (perpetuity)	$200	$600

E. A differential in responsiveness to changes in interest rates always holds true—the longer the maturity of a security, the greater its price change in response to a given change in capitalization rates.

F. Yield to maturity on a bond is the rate of return that is expected if the bond is held to its maturity.

1. Yield to maturity for a perpetual bond = $i = I/V$, where I is the interest paid and V is the current market value.
2. For a bond with a specific maturity, the procedure for finding yield to maturity is exactly like that of finding the internal rate of return in capital budgeting.
3. For a bond paying $50 interest per year, if the price of the bond is $947.20, the yield to maturity is 7 percent.

$$V = \frac{I_1}{(1+i)^1} \quad \frac{I_2}{(1+i)^2} \quad \frac{I_3 + M}{(1+i)^3}$$

$$
\begin{aligned}
\$947.20 &= \$50(\text{PVIF}) + \$50(\text{PVIF}) + \$1,050(\text{PVIF}) \\
&= \$50(.935) + \$50(.873) + \$1,050(.816) \\
&= \$46.75 + 43.65 + \$856.80.
\end{aligned}
$$

V. Preferred stock valuation.

A. Most preferred stocks assure their owners fixed dividend payments.

B. Most are perpetuities whose value is found:

$$V = \frac{\text{dividend on preferred}}{\text{capitalization rate}} = \frac{D}{k_p}.$$

C. The yield on a preferred stock is similar to that on a perpetual bond and is found by solving the above equation for k_p.

VI. *Common stock valuation.*

A. Major differences in debt and preferred stock valuation versus common stock valuation.

1. Income, or receipts, from common stock are subject to greater fluctuations and more uncertainty.
2. Common stock earnings and dividends are expected to exhibit growth over time, not to stay constant, so annuity formulas cannot be used.

B. Estimating the value of a stock: The single period case:

1. The price today of a share of common stock, P_o, depends upon the expected cash flow from the stock and the riskiness of these cash flows.
2. The expected cash flows consist of (1) the dividend received each year, D_t, and (2) the price received if the stock were sold at the end of year n, P_n.
3. If the stock is held for one year and the stock price grows at a rate g, the valuation equation is:

$$P_o = \frac{D_1}{k_s - g}.$$

where k_s is the required rate of return on the stock.

C. Estimating the rate of return.

1. The expected rate of return, $\hat{k}_s$, is analogous to the internal rate of return on a capital project. It is the discount rate that equates the present value of expected dividends, D_1, and the final stock price, P_1, to the present stock price, P_o.

2. The total return = dividend yield + capital gains yield

$$= \frac{\text{expected dividend}}{\text{present price}} + \frac{\text{expected increase in price}}{\text{present price}}.$$

3. An illustration.

a. Assume that the ACO stock has a current market price of $40. It is earning $3.60 per share and paying $2.00 a year in dividends. In recent years dividends, earnings, and the price of the company's stock have been growing 4 percent per year, and they are expected to continue to grow at this rate in the future.

b. The expected return ($\hat{k}$) on ACO's stock may be calculated:

$$\text{Present price} = \frac{\text{dividend}}{(1 + \hat{k}_s)} + \frac{\text{price at end of year 1}}{(1 + \hat{k}_s)}$$

$$= \frac{\text{dividend}}{(1 + \hat{k}_s)} + \frac{\text{present price} \times (1 + \text{growth rate})}{(1 + \hat{k}_s)}$$

$$\$40 = \frac{\$2.00}{(1 + \hat{k}_s)} + \frac{\$40(1.04)}{(1 + \hat{k}_s)}$$

$$= \frac{\$2.00}{(1 + \hat{k}_s)} + \frac{\$41.60}{(1 + \hat{k}_s)} = \frac{\$43.60}{(1 + \hat{k}_s)}$$

$$1 + \hat{k}_s = \frac{\$43.60}{\$40.00} = 1.090$$

$$\hat{k}_s = 1.090 - 1.00 = 0.090, \text{ or } 9\%.$$

c. The expected rate of return, $\hat{k}$, represents two components:

1) dividend yield = $\dfrac{\text{dividends}}{\text{present price}} = \dfrac{\$2}{\$40} = 0.05$, or 5%.

2) capital gains yield = $\dfrac{\text{price increase}}{\text{present price}} = \dfrac{\$1.60}{\$40.00} = 0.04$, or 4%.

d. An alternative expression of the above is:

$$\hat{k}_s = \text{expected rate of return} = \frac{D_1}{P_0} + g = 5\% + 4\% = 9\%.$$

where

D = dividend expected at the end of the year

P = current price of the stock

g = expected constant growth rate.

e. The decision of whether or not to purchase a stock depends upon the relationship between the expected and required rates of return.

If $\hat{k}_s$ exceeds k_s, buy; if $\hat{k}_s$ is less than k_s, sell; and if $\hat{k}_s$ equals k_s, the stock is in equilibrium.

  f. The following are critical assumptions in the calculations.

    1) The profitability rate on new investments will result in a continued earnings growth rate of 4 percent per year.

    2) The dividends will remain a constant proportion of earnings, so dividends will also grow at a 4 percent rate.

    3) The common stock will also grow at a 4 percent rate, rising as earnings and dividends rise.

D. Market equilibrium: required versus expected returns.

  1. When markets are in equilibrium the required rate of return and the expected rate of return will be the same.

  2. If the expected rate is increased (say by an increase in the expected value of g), investors will buy the stock, which will drive up its price and drive its dividend yield down. This will continue until again $\hat{k}_s$ = k_s and the stock is again in equilibrium. If the expected rate of return decreases, the opposite occurs.

  3. Evidence suggests that stocks adjust quite rapidly to disequilibrium and in general, $\hat{k}_s = k_s$.

E. Estimating the value of a stock: multi-period.

  1. Expected dividends as the basis for stock value.

    a. Value of stock = P_o = PV of expected future dividends

$$P_o = \sum_{t=1}^{\infty} \frac{D_t}{(1+k_s)^t}.$$

  2. Stock values with zero growth.

    a. If future growth is expected to be zero, the value of the stock reduces to the same formula as for the perpetual bond:

$$\text{Price} = \frac{\text{dividends}}{\text{capitalization rate}}$$

$$P_o = \frac{D_1}{k_s} \quad \text{or} \quad k_s = \frac{D_1}{P_o}.$$

  3. Normal or constant growth.

    a. If growth is expected to continue in the foreseeable future at about the same rate as GNP, the value of the stock can be calculated:

$$P_o = \frac{D_1}{k_s - g} \quad \text{or} \quad k_s = \frac{D_1}{P_o} + g.$$

  4. Supernormal growth.

A firm may be in the early stages of a "life cycle" in that it is growing much faster than the economy. At some future point in time, it is estimated to slow the growth rate to the normal rate. The value of this stock is composed of two parts, the present value of the dividends during the period of supernormal growth plus the present value of the stock at the end of the supernormal growth period. The value of a firm with such a growth pattern is determined by the following equation:

$$P_o = \sum_{t=1}^{N} \frac{D_o (1 + g_s)^t}{(1 + k)^t} + \sum_{t=N+1}^{\infty} \frac{D_N (1 + g_n)^{t-N}}{(1 + k)^t}$$

where g_s = supernormal growth rate and g_n the normal growth rate. The first summation is the present value of the dividends received during the early, rapid growth period, while the second is the present value of the expected dividends.

VII. The following factors lead to variations in return among securities.
   A. *Risk.*
      1. This is the most important factor leading to differential expected rates of return.
      2. *Risk* is defined as uncertainty about the return that will actually be realized.
      3. Investors as a group dislike risk and, therefore, are "risk averters."
      4. If investors are risk averters on the average, greater risk is associated with higher average returns.
   B. *Marketability.*
      1. The higher the liquidity, or marketability, the lower an investment's required rate of return.
      2. Listed stocks tend to sell on a lower yield basis than over-the-counter stocks.
      3. Publicly owned stocks sell at lower yields than stocks with no established market.
      4. Investments in small firms generally require higher yields.
   C. *Changes in stock price levels.*
      1. Its basic influence is determined by conditions of supply and demand.
      2. Stock prices are changed by the following:
         a. Changes in required rates of return.
         b. Changes in growth expectations.
VIII. *Historical rates of return.*
   A. *Ranges of equity yields* for different kinds of firms under varying market conditions are as follows:

Ranges for Rates of Return on Common Stocks

	Interest Rate and Stock Market Conditions†		
	Interest Rates Low, Investors Optimistic	Normal	Interest Rates High, Investors Pessimistic
Company characteristics			
Low risk, high marketability	7%	10%	14%
Average risk and marketability	9	12	16
High risk, low marketability	10	14	22

†We do not wish to imply that interest rates will be low when investors are optimistic, or vice versa. Rather, low rates and investor optimism both tend to lower the cost of equity capital, and if they both occur simultaneously, costs will be lower than if only one occurs. Also, it is quite possible that these two effects could be offsetting—for example, high interest rates and investor optimism might occur at the same time, resulting in "normal" equity capital costs. High interest rates may reflect an outlook for high inflation rates.

B. Debt yields.

1. Debt yields vary directly with the degree of tightness in money market conditions.

2. Interest rates decline as the size of the loan increases because of the fixed costs of making and servicing loans.

3. Small loans are made mostly to small firms, and small firms are inherently more risky than large ones.

PROBLEMS

18-1. a. In 1976 the Arcadia Corporation earned $20 million after taxes and paid a $2 quarterly dividend plus an extra dividend of $1.50 at the end of the year. Its current price is $80 a share. What is its dividend yield?

b. Assuming that 4 million shares are authorized and that 2 million shares are outstanding, what is the RST price-earnings ratio?

Solution:

a. $8.00 four quarterly $2 dividends
$\underline{1.50}$ extra $1.50 dividend
$9.50 total annual dividend

$$\frac{\$\ 9.50}{\$80.00} = 11.9\% \text{ dividend yield.}$$

b. $\dfrac{\$20,000,000}{2,000,000} = \$10$ EPS

$\dfrac{\$80 \text{ price}}{\$10 \text{ EPS}} = 8$ times = price-earnings ratio.

18-2.   A stockholder pays $34.50 for a share of stock which he plans to hold in-
         definitely. If he expects the firm to pay an annual $2.50 dividend and to
         experience an annual 6 percent stock price appreciation from reinvestment
         of retained earnings, what will be the rate of return on his original invest-
         ment? (Use formula given in the text.)

Solution:

$$k = D_1/P_o + g$$
$$= 2.50/34.50 + 0.06$$
$$= 0.0725 + 0.06$$
$$= 0.1325 \approx 13.25 \text{ percent.}$$

18-3.   A firm's stock is currently selling for $40 a share. The firm is earning $4 a
         share and pays a $3 dividend.
   a. At what rate must earnings, dividends, and stock price all grow if inves-
      tors require a 10 percent rate of return?
   b. Split expected rate of return, 10 percent, into two components—the
      dividend yield and the capital gains yield.
   c. If the firm reinvests its retained earnings to yield the expected rate of
      return, what will happen to earnings per share?

Solution:

a. $k\quad = D_1/P_o + g$
   $0.10 = \$3/\$40 + g$
   $0.10 = 0.075 + g$
   $g\quad = 0.025 = 2.5 \text{ percent.}$

or:

$P_o\ = D_1/(1+k) + P_1/(1+k)$
$\$40 = \$3/(1.10) + \$40(1+g)/(1.10)$
$\$44 = \$43 + 40g$
$\$1\ = 40g$
$g\ = 1/40 = 0.025 = 2.5 \text{ percent.}$

b. $\dfrac{\$3 \text{ dividend}}{\$40 \text{ price}} = 0.075 = 7.5$ percent dividend yield.

   $\$41$ price next year
   $\underline{-40}$ price this year
   $\$\ 1$ capital gain

   $\$1/40 = 0.025 = 2.5$ percent capital gains yield.

c. $ 4 EPS
   −3 DPS
   $ 1 retained earnings per share
   x0.10 rate of return
   $0.10 increase in EPS,

which is 0.10/4.00 = 0.025 = 2.5 percent.

18-4. a. The bonds of the Inferrity Corporation are perpetuities bearing an 8 percent coupon and rated AAA. Bonds of this type yield 7 percent. What is the price of Inferrity's bonds? Their par value is $1,000.

b. Interest rate levels rise to the point where such bonds now yield 10 percent. What will be the price of Inferrity's bonds now?

c. Interest rate levels drop to 8 percent. At what price will Inferrity's bonds sell?

d. How would your answer to parts a, b, and c change if the bonds had a definite maturity date of 30 years?

Solution:

$1,000 bond with 8 percent coupon rate:
   $1,000 x 0.08 = $80 interest per year.

a. $\dfrac{\$80}{0.07} = \$1,143.$

b. $\dfrac{\$80}{0.10} = \$800.$

c. $\dfrac{\$80}{0.08} = \$1,000$ or par.

d. 1) $80 x 12.409†   = $ 993
       $1,000 x 0.131††   =   131
                          $1,124 smaller than $1,143 (a)

   2) $80 x 9.427†   = $ 754
       $1,000 x 0.057††   =   57
                          $ 811 larger than $800 (b)

   3) $80 x 11.258†   = $ 901
       $1,000 x 0.099††   =   99
                          $1,000 the same as $1,000 (c)

†Present value of an annuity for $1 for 30 years discounted at 7, 10, and 8 percent (Table A-4).
††Present value of $1, 30 years from today, discounted at 7, 10, and 8 percent (Table A-2).

18-5. The Wood Company, a small electric car manufacturer, is planning to sell an issue of common stock to the public for the first time. It faces the problem of setting an appropriate price on the stock. The company feels that the proper procedure is to select a firm similar to it with publicly traded shares and to make relevant comparisons. The company learns that Pulp Inc., is similar to it with respect to (1) product mix, (2) size, (3) asset composition, and (4) debt-equity proportions.

Relation for 1976	Pulp	Wood (Totals)
Earnings per share	$ 2.50	$ 500,000
Price per share	37.50	—
Dividends per share	1.50	250,000
Book value per share	30,000	6,000,000

a. How would these relations be used in guiding Wood in arriving at a market price for the stock?

b. What price would you recommend if Wood sells 300,000 shares?

Solution:

a. As a first step to obtain the boundaries for a final decision on the indicated market price for Wood, compute the per share data:

Earnings per share, 1976	$ 1.67
Dividends per share, 1976	0.83
Book value per share, 1976	20.00

Next, obtain the relevant multiples from the Wood example. The market prices of Pulp are the following multiples:

Multiple of earnings per share, 1976	15
Multiple of dividends per share, 1976	25
Multiple of book value per share, 1976	1.25

Now apply the multiples to the Wood data to obtain indicated market prices:

	Indicated Market Price for Wood Stock Based on Data of Pulp
Based on earnings, 1976	$25.05
Based on dividends, 1976	20.75
Based on book value, 1976	25.00

b. The range is between $20.75 and $25.05 a share. Factors tending toward a high range: (a) Wood has had a good recent trend in sales earnings and relative stability of earnings, (b) stock market conditions are favorable, and (c) Wood is a company whose product activities are attractive to investors. Factors tending toward a low range are the opposite of factors tending toward a high range.

The actual price would be negotiated between Wood and the underwriter. It should be noted that in making an actual valuation of this kind, it is important to include data both for several years and for several similar firms to avoid basing the price on atypical data.

18-6.   Filter Industries is a manufacturer of specialized filtration techniques. During the past year expansion requirements have caused the firm to go public. The firm is expected to grow at a rate of 20 percent for the next four years before settling down to a growth rate of 8 percent for the indefinite future. Dividends are currently at $.50 per share and are expected to grow at the same rate as the firm.

a. If you required a 12 percent return on your investment, what price would you pay for the common stock?

b. Suppose you were only interested in holding the stock for a one-year period. How would you then value the stock?

Solution:

a.

Year	Dividend	Discount Factor	Present Value
1	$ .60	.893	.536
2	.72	.797	.574
3	.864	.712	.615
4	1.037	.636	.659
			$2.384

Value at end of year 4:

$$P = \frac{\$1.037\ (1.08)}{.12 - .08} = \frac{\$1.12}{.04} = \$28.00.$$

Present value of end of year 4 price:

$28.00 \times (.636) = $17.81.

Total value of stock today:

$2.385 + $17.80 = $\underline{20.185}$.

b. The present value of the stock to you would not change. All that would change is the proportions of the present value represented by prospective dividend yield and capital gains.

Financial Structure and the Use of Leverage

19

THEME

The purpose of this chapter is to formulate a sound basis for determining the effect of its financial structure on the firm's cost of capital.

I.   These are some basic definitions.
   A. *Asset structure* is the left-hand side of the balance sheet (the firm's assets which must be financed).
   B. *Financial structure* is the right-hand side of the balance sheet (the sources of financing).
   C. *Capital structure* is the permanent financing of the firm, represented by long-term debt plus preferred stock and common equity, but excluding all short-term credit.
   D. *Capital structure* includes common stock, capital surplus, and accumulated retained earnings.
   E. *Financial leverage* is the ratio of total debt to total assets. (Leverage is also measured by the ratio of total debt to net worth; this ratio is referred to as the debt-equity ratio).
   F. *Business risk* is the inherent variability of expected returns on the firm's "portfolio" of assets.
   G. *Financial risk* is additional risk to common stock resulting from the use of financial leverage.
II.   The theory of financial leverage is presented.
   A. If the return on assets exceeds the cost of debt, leverage is successful. Leverage may increase the returns to equity, but risk is also increased.

186

    B. Leverage increases returns to owners if successful, and decreases the returns to owners if unsuccessful.

    C. At some degree of leverage the cost of debt rises because of increased risk with the higher fixed charges.

    D. Risks of increased debt also affect the holders of common stock, causing expected returns on common stock to rise.

III. The procedure for calculating the comparative costs of alternative forms of financing is shown in Table 19-1.

    A. *Basic assumptions of the example.*

       1. Sales are currently $2,000,000. It is estimated that by an additional investment of $1,000,000 sales could be increased to $4,000,000. However, the industry is subject to fluctuations in demand, so the level of sales could also be as low as $500,000. The estimated probabilities for each level of sales are given in Table 19-1.

       2. The firm has no interest-bearing debt at present.

       3. If the $1,000,000 is obtained through debt, the cost of debt will be 10 percent.

       4. Alternatively, the additional funds could be raised by the sale of common stock, netting the company $50 per share.

       5. Fixed costs are $500,000, variable costs are 40 percent of sales, and the tax rate is 50 percent.

       6. The current P/E ratio is 15. If debt financing is used, the P/E ratio will fall to 14; with equity financing it will rise to 16.

    B. *Analysis of Table 19-1.*

       1. The firm suffers operating losses until sales are $1,000,000, but beyond that point it enjoys a rapid rise in gross profit.

       2. Stock financing has a tighter distribution and smaller coefficient of variation, so it is less risky than debt financing.

       3. But since expected EPS is lower for stock than for bonds, the firm must make a risk-return tradeoff.

    C. *Break-even analysis.*

       1. Figure 19-1 is a break-even chart for Universal's two financing methods.

       2. The debt line intersects the EPS axis at a lower point if sales are depressed to zero, but has a steeper slope so EPS will rise faster as sales increase.

       3. Below the break-even level of sales, the firm would be better off issuing common stock; above that level, debt financing would produce higher earnings per share.

IV. Financial leverage is related to operating leverage.

    A. Note that in the illustration in Table 19-1 the results were influenced by both operating and financial leverage.

    B. Both operating and financial leverage have similar effects on profits, and a greater use of either has these results:

       1. The break-even point is raised.

Table 19-1. Universal Machine Company Profit Calculations at Various Sales Levels

Probability of Indicated Sales	.10	.20	.40	.20	.10
Sales in units	50,000	100,000	200,000	300,000	400,000
Sales in dollars	$ 500,000	$1,000,000	$2,000,000	$3,000,000	$4,000,000
Fixed costs	$ 500,000	$ 500,000	$ 500,000	$ 500,000	$ 500,000
Variable costs (40% of sales)	200,000	400,000	800,000	1,200,000	1,600,000
Total costs (except interest)	$ 700,000	$ 900,000	$1,300,000	$1,700,000	$2,100,000
Earnings before interest and taxes (EBIT)	$(200,000)	$ 100,000	$ 700,000	$1,300,000	$1,900,000
Financing with debt					
Less: Interest (10% x 1,000,000)†	$ 100,000	$ 100,000	$ 100,000	$ 100,000	$ 100,000
Earnings before taxes	$(300,000)	–0–	$ 600,000	$1,200,000	$1,800,000
Less: Income taxes (50%)†	(150,000)	–0–	300,000	600,000	900,000
Net profit after taxes	$(150,000)	–0–	$ 300,000	$ 600,000	$ 900,000
Earnings per share on 100,000 shares of common (EPS)	$ (1.50)	–0–	$ 3.00	$ 6.00	$ 9.00
Market price of common (14 times earnings)††	—	—	$ 42.00	$ 84.00	$ 126.00
Expected EPS‡	$ 3.15				
Coefficient of variation‡‡	.962				
Financing with stock					
Earnings before taxes	$(200,000)	$ 100,000	$ 700,000	$1,300,000	$1,900,000
Less: Income taxes (50%)†	(100,000)	50,000	350,000	650,000	950,000
Net profit after taxes	$(100,000)	$ 50,000	$ 350,000	$ 650,000	$ 950,000
Earnings per share on 120,000 shares of common (EPS)††	$ (.83)	$ 0.42	$ 2.92	$ 5.42	$ 7.92
Market price of common (16 times earnings)††	—	$ 6.72	$ 46.72	$ 86.72	$ 126.72
Expected EPS‡	$ 3.05				
Coefficient of variation‡‡	.830				

† Assumes tax credit on losses.
†† Negative values are not realistic.
‡ Calculated by multiplying the EPS at each sales level by the probability of that sales level, then summing these products.
‡‡ Calculated as follows: Coefficient of variation = (Standard deviation of EPS) (Expected EPS).

$$\text{Standard deviation} = \sigma = \sqrt{\sum_{i=1}^{n} (R_i - \bar{R})^2 P_i}$$

2. The impact of a change in the level of sales on profits is magnified.
C. Operating and financial leverage have reinforcing effects:
1. Operating, or *first stage*, leverage affects earnings before interest and taxes.
2. Financial, or *second stage*, leverage affects earnings after interest and taxes.

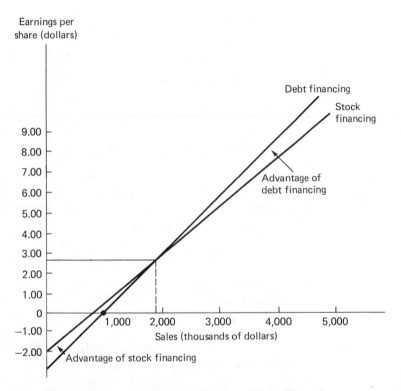

Figure 19-1. Earnings per Share for Stock and Debt Financing

D. *The degree of operating leverage* was defined in Chapter 4 as the percentage change in operating profits associated with a given percentage change in sales volume:

$$\text{Degree of operating leverage at point } Q = \frac{Q(P - V)}{Q(P - V) - F}$$

For the data from Table 19-1 at the $2,000,000 sales volume, leverage

$$= \frac{1,200,000}{1,200,000 - 500,000} = 1.71.$$

Here Q is units of output, P is the average sales price per unit of output, V is the variable cost per unit, and F is total fixed costs.

E. *The degree of financial leverage.*

The degree of financial leverage is defined as the percentage change in earnings available to common stockholders that is associated with a given percentage change in earnings before interest and taxes (EBIT). An equation has been developed to aid in calculating the degree of financial leverage for any given level of EBIT and interest charges (I).

$$\text{Degree of Financial Leverage} = \frac{Q(P-V)-F}{Q(P-V)-F-I} = \frac{\text{EBIT}}{\text{EBIT}-I} \qquad (19\text{-}1)$$

Using the data from Table 19-1 at the $2,000,000 sales volume,

1. Leverage with no additional financing $= \dfrac{700{,}000}{700{,}000} = 1.00.$

2. Leverage with debt $= \dfrac{700{,}000}{600{,}000} = 1.17$

3. Leverage with equity $= \dfrac{700{,}000}{700{,}000} = 1.00.$

F. *Combining operating and financial leverage.*

The equation for the degree of operating leverage can be combined with equation (19-1) for financial leverage to show the total leverageing effect of a given change in sales on earnings per share:

$$\text{Combined leverage effect} = \frac{Q(P-V)}{Q(P-V)-F-I}. \qquad (19\text{-}2)$$

For the data from Table 19-1 at the $2,000,000 sales volume,

1. No additional financing $= \dfrac{1{,}200{,}000}{1{,}200{,}000 - 500{,}000} = 1.71.$

2. Financing with debt $= \dfrac{1{,}200{,}000}{1{,}200{,}000 - 500{,}000 - 100{,}000} = 2.00.$

3. Financing with equity $= \dfrac{1{,}200{,}000}{1{,}200{,}000 - 500{,}000} = 1.71.$

G. The usefulness of the degree of leverage concept lies in the fact that (1) it enables us to specify the effect of a change in sales volume on earnings and (2) it permits us to show the interrelationships between operating and financial leverage.

V. Detailed study of financial ratios among different industries and among firms in the same industry reveals a considerable range of variation. However, in firms in the same industry there is a tendency toward a clustering of financial structures.

VI. Among the factors influencing financial structure are these:

A. Growth rate of future sales.

B. Stability of future sales.

C. Competitive structure of the industry.

D. Asset structure of the industry.

E. Control position and attitudes toward risk of owners and management.

F. Lender attitudes toward the firm and the industry.

PROBLEMS

19-1.   A firm has a debt ratio of 75 percent. If it has total assets of $200 million, how much can these assets drop in value before creditors are unprotected?

Solution: (amounts in millions)

$200 Total assets
−150 Debt (.75 × $200)
$ 50 Equity

The $50 million representing owners' equity is the dollar amount that assets could drop before creditors would begin to lose protection.

19-2.   The leverage factors of firms A and B are 67 percent and 33 percent respectively. Each firm has $300 million assets and each pays a 6 percent interest rate on debt. Firm A earns 10 percent on assets before interest and taxes; what does it earn on common stock after taxes? What rate of return (before interest and taxes) must firm B earn on its assets if it earns the same rate on common stock after taxes as A? (Assume a 50 percent corporate tax rate.)

Solution (dollar amounts in millions):

	Firm A		Firm B	
Debt	0.67	$200	0.33	$100
Equity	0.33	100	0.67	200
Assets	1.00	$300	1.00	$300

A earns $300 (0.10)	= $30
Less: Debt $200 (0.06)	= 12
Taxable income	= 18
Less: Taxes	= 9
Net income	= $ 9
Rate of return to common stock	= $9/$100 = 9%.

B's net income $200 (0.09)	= $18
Plus: Taxes (0.50)	= 18
Taxable income	= 36
Plus: Debt $100 (0.06)	= 6
	$42
Rate of return to assets	= $42/$300 = 14%.

19-3. One useful test or guide for evaluating a firm's financial structure in relation to its industry is by comparison with financial ratio composites for its industry. A new firm or one contemplating entering a new industry may use such industry composites as a guide to what its financial position is likely to approximate after the initial settling-down period.

Denmark Furniture estimates its sales during 1977 as $1,400,000. The following data represent the ratios for the furniture manufacturing industry for 1977:

Sales to net worth	5 times
Current debt to net worth	55%
Total debt to net worth	75%
Current ratio	2.5 times
Net sales to inventory	10 times
Average collection period	42 days
Fixed assets to net worth	37.5%

Denmark Furniture, *Pro Forma* Balance Sheet, 1977

Cash	$_____	Current debt	$_____
Accounts receivable	_____	Long-term debt	_____
Inventory	_____	Total debt	_____
Current assets	_____	Net worth	_____
Fixed assets	_____		
Total assets	$_____	Total claims	$_____

Complete the above *pro forma* balance sheet. (Round to nearest thousands).

Solution:

1. Net worth = sales ÷ net worth turnover = $\dfrac{\$1,400,000}{5}$ = $280,000.

2. Total debt = 75% of net worth = $280,000 x 75% = $210,000.

3. Current debt = 55% of net worth $280,000 x 55% = $154,000.

4. Long-term debt = total debt — current debt = $210,000 — $154,000 = $56,000.

5. Total claims on assets = net worth + total debt = $280,000 + $210,000 = $490,000.

6. Current assets = current debt x current ratio = $154,000 x 2.5 = $385,000.

7. Inventory = sales ÷ inventory turnover = $\dfrac{\$1,400,000}{10}$ = $140,000.

8. Accounts receivable = average collection period x sales per day = $\dfrac{1,400,000}{360} \times \dfrac{42}{1}$ = $163,000.

9. Cash = current assets — (receivables + inventory) = $385,000 — ($163,000 + $140,000) = $82,000.

10. Fixed assets = net worth x 37.5% = $280,000 x 37.5% = $105,000.
11. Total assets = current assets + fixed assets = $385,000 + $105,000 = $490,000.

Denmark Furniture, *Pro Forma* Balance Sheet, 1977

Cash	$ 82,000	Current debt	$154,000
Accounts receivable	163,000	Long-term debt	56,000
Inventory	140,000		
Total current assets	$385,000	Total debt	$210,000
Fixed assets	105,000	Net worth	280,000
Total assets	$490,000	Total claims	$490,000

19-4. The McElroy Company seeks to increase its current capacity by 50 percent in anticipation of increasing market demand. New financing alternatives are:

a. Common stock to net $25 per share. (The price-earnings ratio will be 12 times if stock financing is used.)

b. Straight 8 percent debt. (The price-earnings ratio will be 10 times if debt financing is used.)

Current Balance Sheet

		Debt (6%)	60,000
		Common stock ($10 par)	60,000
		Retained earnings	80,000
Total assets	$200,000	Total claims	$200,000

Assume that income, before interest and taxes, is 12 percent of anticipated sales and that the tax rate is 50 percent.

a. What are the expected market prices at sales assumptions of $100,000, $500,000, and $1,000,000 under the two financing alternatives?

b. Make break-even charts for earnings per share and market value per share for the company under the two financing alternatives.

c. At sales volume of $500,000 find (1) the degree of operating leverage, (2) the degree of financial leverage, and (3) the degree of combined leverage effect, under the following three alternatives:

a. No additional financing.

b. Debt financing.

c. Common stock financing.

Assume the following relationships hold at this sales volume:

Average sales price per unit of output	= P =	$10.00
Variable cost per unit of output	= V =	$4.00
Total fixed costs	= F =	$240,000.00
Units of output	= Q =	50,000

Solution:

a.

Debt Financing

Sales	$100,000	$500,000	$1,000,000
Income before interest			
and taxes (12% x sales)	12,000	60,000	120,000
Interest (6% x $60,000)			
(8% x $100,000)	11,600	11,600	11,600
Taxable income	$ 400	$ 48,400	$ 108,400
Less: Income tax (50%)	200	24,200	54,200
Net profit after taxes	200	$ 24,200	$ 54,200
Earnings per share			
(6,000 shares outstanding)	$ 0.03	$ 4.03	$ 9.03
Market price†	$ 0.33	40.33	90.33

Common Stock Financing

Sales	$100,000	$500,000	$1,000,000
Income before interest			
and taxes	12,000	60,000	120,000
Interest (6% x $60,000)	3,600	3,600	3,600
Taxable income	$ 8,400	$ 56,400	$ 116,400
Less: Income tax (50%)	4,200	28,200	58,200
Net profit after taxes	$ 4,200	$ 28,200	$ 58,200
Earnings per share			
6,000			
+4,000			
10,000 shares outstanding	$ 0.42	$ 2.82	$ 5.82
Market price†	$ 5.04	$ 33.84	$ 69.84

†Market price = Earnings per share x (price-earnings ratio).

b. Break-even chart for financing alternatives.

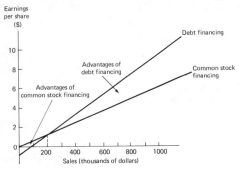

Figure 19-2. Earnings per Share Break-even Analysis for Alternative Methods of Financing

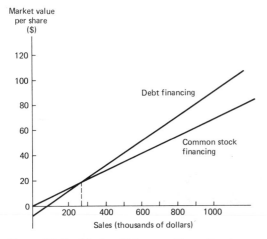

Figure 19-3. Market Value per Share Break-even Analysis for Alternative Methods of Financing

c. 1. Degree of operating leverage at point of $500,000 sales volume =

$$\frac{Q(P-V)}{Q(P-V)-F} = \frac{50,000\ (\$6.00)}{50,000\ (\$6.00) - \$240,000} = \frac{\$300,000}{\$60,000} = 5.00$$

2. Degree of financial leverage $= \dfrac{Q(P-V)-F}{Q(P-V)-F-I} = \dfrac{EBIT}{EBIT-I}$

At $500,000 sales volume:

a) No additional financing $= \dfrac{\$60,000}{\$60,000 - \$3,600} = \dfrac{\$60,000}{\$56,400} = 1.06$

b) Debt financing $= \dfrac{\$60,000}{\$60,000 - \$11,600} = \dfrac{\$60,000}{\$48,400} = 1.24$

c) Common stock financing $= \dfrac{\$60,000}{\$60,000 - \$3,600} = \dfrac{\$60,000}{\$56,400} = 1.06$

3. Combined leverage effect $= \dfrac{Q(P-V)}{Q(P-V)-F-I}$

At $500,000 sales volume:

a) No additional financing $= \dfrac{\$300,000}{\$300,000 - \$240,000 - \$3,600} =$

$\dfrac{\$300,000}{\$56,400} = 5.32$

b) Debt financing $= \dfrac{\$300,000}{\$300,000 - \$240,000 - \$11,600} =$

$\dfrac{\$300,000}{\$48,400} = 6.20$

c) Common stock financing $= \dfrac{\$300,000}{\$300,000 - \$240,000 - \$3,600} =$

$\dfrac{\$300,000}{\$56,400} = 5.32$

The Cost of Capital

20

THEME

Valuation concepts are applied to develop a weighted cost of capital for the firm.

I. Basic definitions—the capital structure components and their component costs are identified by the following symbols:

k_d = interest rate on firm's new debt = component cost of debt, before-tax.

$k_d(1 - t)$ = component cost of debt, after-tax, where t = marginal tax rate; $k_d(1 - t)$ is the debt cost used to calculate the marginal cost of capital.

k_p = component cost of preferred stock.

k_r = component cost of retained earnings (or internal equity). k_r is identical to k_s, the required rate of return on common equity as developed in Chapter 18. Here we distinguish between equity obtained from retained earnings versus selling new stock, hence the distinction between k_r and k_s.

k_e = component cost of new issues of common stock (or external equity).

k_a = a weighted average, or "composite," cost of capital. If a firm raises $1 of new capital to finance asset expansion, and if it is to keep its capital structure in balance (that is, if it is to keep the same percentage of debt, preferred, and equity), then it will raise part of the dollar as debt, part as preferred, and part as common equity (with equity coming either as retained earnings or from the sale of new common stock). k_a is also a *marginal cost:* there is a value of k_a for each dollar of new capital the firm raises.

II. Costs of the individual components of the firm's capital structure.

   A. The *cost of debt* is defined as the interest rate that must be paid on new increments of debt capital, less the tax reduction effect.

      1. Therefore, the cost of debt capital is calculated as follows:

$$k_d(1-t) = \text{after-tax cost of debt}$$
$$= \text{(before-tax cost)} \times (1.0 - \text{tax rate}). \qquad (20\text{-}1)$$

      Whenever the composite, or average cost of capital (k_a) is calculated, $k_d(1-t)$ and not k_d is used.

      2. Taxes have an influence.

         a. Interest payments on debt are deductible; preferred and common stock dividends are not deductible for tax purposes.

         b. Adjust by putting all costs on an after-tax basis.

   B. The cost of *preferred stock* is the effective yield as measured by the annual preferred dividend, divided by the net price the company receives when it sells new preferred stock.

      1. Assuming a preferred issue is a perpetuity that sells for $100 a share and pays an $8 annual dividend, its yield is calculated as follows:

$$\text{Preferred yield} = \frac{\text{preferred dividend}}{\text{price of preferred stock}} = \frac{D_p}{P_p} = \frac{\$8}{\$100} = 8\%. \qquad (20\text{-}2)$$

      2. If the firm receives less than the market price of preferred stock when it sells new preferred, P_p in the denominator of Equation 20-2 should be the net price received by the firm. Suppose, for example, the firm must incur a selling or *flotation* cost of $4 a share.

$$k_p = \text{cost of preferred} = \frac{D_p}{P_{pn}} = \frac{\$8}{\$96} = 8.33\%. \qquad (20\text{-}2a)$$

   C. *Cost of equity.*

      1. *Retained earnings.*

         a. The cost of retained earnings is the minimum rate of return that must be earned on equity-financed investments to keep unchanged the value of the existing common stock.

         b. This minimum rate of return is that return which investors expect to receive on the company's common stock.

         c. Investors' expectations are greatly influenced by returns they have received in the past.

         d. The cost of retained earnings can be estimated by the formula

$$k_r = \frac{D_1}{P_0} + \text{expected } g. \qquad (20\text{-}3)$$

2. To find the cost of new outside equity, one must consider flotation costs. The following formula may be used if growth is assumed constant.

$$k_e = \frac{D_1}{P_0(1-F)} + g = \frac{D_1}{P_n} + g = \frac{\text{dividend yield}}{(1-\text{flotation percentage})} + \text{growth.} \quad (20\text{-}4)$$

Here F is the percentage cost of selling the issue, so $P_0(1-F) = P_n$ is the net price received by the firm. For example, if $P_0 = \$10$ and $F = 10$ percent, then the firm receives \$9 for each new share sold; hence $P_n = \$9$.

3. How is the basic required rate of return on common equity estimated?

Although one *can* use very involved, highly complicated procedures for making this estimation, satisfactory estimates may be obtained in one of three ways:

a. Estimate the capital market line (CML) as described in Chapter 18; estimate the relative riskiness of the firm in question; and then use these estimates to obtain the required rate of return on the firm's stock:

$$k_s = k_r = R_F + p.$$

Under this procedure, the estimated cost of equity (k_r) will move up or down with changes in interest rates and with changes in "investor psychology."

b. An alternative procedure, the use of which is recommended in conjunction with the one described above, is to estimate the basic required rate of return as follows:

1) Assume that investors expect the past-realized rate of return on the stock, $\bar{k}_r$, to be earned in the future, so the expected rate of return $\hat{k}_r$, is equal to $\bar{k}_r$.

2) Assume that the stock is in equilibrium, with $k_r = \hat{k}_r$.

3) Under these assumptions, the required rate of return may be estimated as equal to the past realized rate of return:

$$k_r = \hat{k}_r = \bar{k}_r = \frac{D_1}{P_0} + \text{past growth rate.}$$

c. For "normal" companies in "normal" times, past growth rates may be projected into the future, and the second method will give satisfactory results. *However, if the company's growth has been abnormally high or low, either because of its own unique situation or because of general economic conditions, then investors will not project the past growth rate into the future, so method 2 will not yield a good estimate of k_r.* In this case, g must be estimated in some other manner.

D. Leverage affects the cost of equity.

1. The more debt a given company employs, other things held constant, the higher its required rate of return on equity capital.

2. The required rate of return, k_r, consists of three elements.
   a. A riskless rate of return, R_F.
   b. A premium for business risk, ρ_1.
   c. A premium required to compensate investors for additional risk brought on by financial leverage, ρ_2.

$$k_r = R_F + \rho_1 + \rho_2.$$

The riskless rate of return, R_F, is a function of general economic conditions, Federal Reserve policy, and the like. The premium for business risk, ρ_1, is a function of the nature of the firm's industry, its degree of operating leverage, its diversification, and so on. Financial risk, ρ_2, depends upon the degree of financial leverage employed. See Figure 20-1.

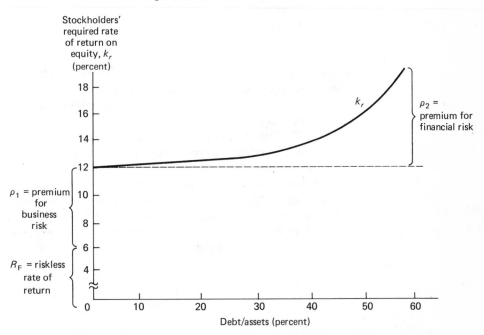

Figure 20-1. Relationship between Cost of Equity and Financial Leverage

E. Leverage also affects the cost of debt.
   1. The higher the leverage ratio, the higher the cost of debt.
   2. The cost of debt will rise at an increasing rate with increasing leverage.
      a. The initial amount of debt issued, which could be covered upon liquidation by a sale of assets, would be considered virtually riskless.
      b. Increases in debt increase interest requirements, as well as the probability that earnings, EBIT, will not be sufficient to cover these charges. Creditors, seeing the increased risk, will charge some risk premium, causing the interest rate to rise.

    c. As a firm uses up its limit of funds from one source and proceeds to borrow from another source, increased interest rates will probably be charged.

III. By combining debt and equity, one can find a weighted cost of capital.

  A. The first steps.

    1. Determine the costs of individual capital components.

    2. Determine the proper set of weights to use in the calculation process.

  B. The optimum capital structure is determined.

    1. This varies from industry to industry.

    2. Management's existing choice of capital structure may be used as a starting point.

  C. Should book weights or market weights be used?

    1. Theoretically, market yields and the market value capital structure should be employed.

    2. For marginal increments of capital, book and market values should not differ greatly.

IV. The marginal cost of capital schedule.

  A. The marginal cost of capital schedule shows the relationship between the weighted cost of each dollar raised (k_a) and the total amount of capital raised during the year, other things, such as the riskiness of the assets acquired, held constant.

    1. The MCC schedule increases at the point where retained earnings are exhausted and a firm begins to use more expensive new common stock.

    2. Any time any component cost rises, a similar break will occur.

    3. In general, breaks in the MCC schedule will occur whenever any component cost increases as a result of the amount of funds raised.

    4. It is necessary to calculate a different MCC = k_a for the interval between each of the breaks in the MCC schedule. The values of k_a for each interval are plotted as the step-function MCC schedule shown in Figure 20-2(a).

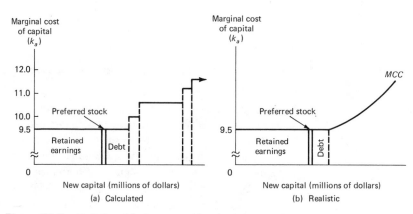

Figure 20-2. Relationship between Marginal Cost and Amount of Funds Raised

5. This graph is highly idealized; in fact, the actual MCC curve looks much more like that shown in Figure 20-2(b). Here we see that the curve is first flat, then turns up gradually and continues rising. The curve will continue to rise, because, as more and more of its securities are put on the market during a fairly short period, it will experience more and more difficulty in getting the market to absorb the new securities.

V. Combining the MCC and the investment opportunity schedules.
   A. Procedure.
      Step 1. Calculate and plot the MCC schedule as shown in Figure 20-2, panel (b).
      Step 2. Ask the operating personnel to estimate the dollar volume of acceptable projects at a range of discount rates, say 14, 13, 12, 11, 10, and 9 percent.
      Step 3. Plot the k_a, capital budget points as determined in Step 2 on the same graph as the MCC; this plot is labeled IRR in Figure 20-3.

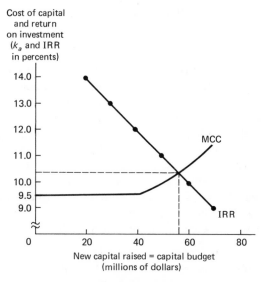

Figure 20-3.   Interfacing the MCC and IRR Curves to Determine the Capital Budget

      Step 4. The correct MCC for use in capital budgeting—assuming both the MCC and IRR curves are developed correctly—is the value at the intersection of the two curves. This is the capital budget that will maximize the value of the firm.
   B. In practice, both the IRR and MCC schedules are developed on an *ex ante* basis; that is, the schedules are estimated during the planning or budgeting process, when the firm is planning its operations for the coming period or periods.

VI. Illustrations of calculations.

A. This is the initial set of relations.

The Burly Company has total net assets of $75 million. It plans to increase net assets to $105 million during the year. Its present capital structure, considered to be optimal, is shown below:

Debt (6% coupons bonds)	$25,000,000	33 1/3%
Preferred stock (8%)	25,000,000	33 1/3%
Equity (k = 10%)	25,000,000	33 1/3%
	$75,000,000	100%

B. Weighted average cost of capital for initial conditions before addition to capital:

Item	Amount	Cost	Cost Amount
Debt	25,000,000 x 0.03 =		750,000
Preferred stock	25,000,000 x 0.08 =		2,000,000
Common stock	25,000,000 x 0.10 =		2,500,000
			5,250,000 ÷ 75,000,000 = 7.00%.

C. Financing the additional $30,000,000 creates the following situation:

1. Assume that new bonds will have a 7 percent coupon and will sell at par. $100 par value preferred will have a coupon rate of 9 percent and will net Burly $90 per share after flotation costs. Common stock, currently selling at $50 a share, can be sold to net the company $45 a share after flotation costs. Stockholders' required rate of return is estimated to be 10 percent. It also is estimated that retained earnings will be $10 million, which will be available and used to meet part of the financing required. The same capital structure will be maintained. The marginal corporate tax rate is 50 percent.

2. Calculations of component costs are as follows:

Cost of debt = (coupon rate) x (1 − tax rate) = .07 x .50 = 3.5%
Cost of preferred stock = 0.09/(1 − .1) = 10.0%
Cost of retained earnings = 10.0%
Cost of new outside equity = .10/(1 − .1) = 11.1%

3. The average cost of capital for the new financing:

	Cost	Weight	Product
Debt	0.035 x	0.333 =	0.0117
Preferred	0.100 x	0.333 =	0.0333
Common	0.100 x	0.333 =	0.0333
			0.0783 = 7.83% weighted, marginal cost of capital.

4. Here is an alternative calculation of weighted marginal cost of capital:

Total cost of financing after $30,000,000 addition: $7,600,000
Total cost of financing before $30,000,000 addition: 5,250,000
Increment in the total cost of financing: $2,350,000

$$\frac{\text{Incremental cost}}{\text{Incremental funds}} = \frac{\$2,350,000}{\$30,000,000} = 7.83\%$$

D. The weighted cost of new capital if retained earnings had been only $6 million instead of $10 million is shown.

1. Cost of equity:

Retained earnings = 10.0%
External equity   = 0.110 = .10/(1 − .1) = 11.1%.

2. Calculations:

		Weight		Cost		Product
Debt	10	0.333	x	0.035	=	0.0117
Preferred	10	0.333	x	0.100	=	0.0333
Retained earnings	6	0.200	x	0.100	=	0.0200
External equity	4	0.133	x	0.111	=	0.0148
	30					0.0798 = 7.98%.

3. This again represents the marginal (weighted) cost of new capital. The higher cost of the segment of equity funds raised externally causes the weighted marginal average cost of new capital to rise from 7.83 percent to 7.98 percent.

VII. Large firms versus small firms.

A. Significant differences in capital costs exist between large and small firms.

B. It is difficult to arrive at reasonable estimates of equity capital costs for small firms.

C. Tax considerations for privately owned firms may cause the effective after-tax cost of retained earnings to be considerably lower than the after-tax cost of new outside equity.

D. Flotation costs for new security issues are much higher for small than for large firms.

E. These considerations cause the marginal cost curves for small businesses to rise rapidly after retained earnings have been exhausted.

PROBLEMS

20-1. Magie Machines, Inc., is currently earning $4 a share, paying a $3.40 dividend, and selling at $42 a share. The company's earnings, dividends, and stock price have all been growing at about 2½ percent a year, and this growth rate is expected to continue indefinitely. According to the firm's investment bankers, a new common stock issue at this time could be sold to net $40.40.

a. Using one of the equations given in the text, calculate Magie's cost of retained earnings (as its required rate of return).

Solution:

$$k_r = D_1/P_0 + g$$
$$= \$3.40/\$42 + 0.025$$
$$= 0.08905 + 0.02500$$
$$= 0.10595$$
$$= 10.595\%.$$

Alternative Solution:

$$P = \frac{D_1}{1 + k_r} + \frac{P_1}{1 + k_r}$$

$$\$42 = \frac{\$3.40}{1 + k_r} + \frac{42(1.025)}{1 + k_r}$$

$$1 + k_r = \frac{\$3.40}{42} + \frac{42(1.025)}{42}$$

$$1 + k_r = 0.08095 + 1.02500$$
$$= 1.10595 - 1.0$$
$$= 10.595\%.$$

b. Using one of the equations given in the text, calculate the price of the stock at the end of one year if the firm's retained earnings are reinvested to yield 2¼ percent rather than the cost of capital. (Assume this new growth rate is expected to be permanent.)

Solution:

1. Calculate the new EPS:

$4.00 − $3.40 = $0.60 retained EPS
$0.60 x 0.0225 = $0.014 incremental EPS

4.00
+0.014
$4.014 new EPS.

2. Calculate the actual growth rate:

$$\frac{\$4.014}{4.000} = 1.0035; g = 1.0035 - 1.0000 = 0.0035 = .35\%.$$

3. Use either formula to obtain the new price:

a) $P = \dfrac{D}{k_r - g} = \dfrac{\$3.40}{.10595 - .0035}$

$$= \frac{\$3.40}{0.10245} = \$33.19.$$

b) $P = \dfrac{D}{1 + k_r} + \dfrac{P(1 + g)}{1 + k_r}$

$$P = \frac{3.40}{1.10595} + \frac{P(1.0035)}{1.10595}$$

$P = \$33.19.$

Notice the big decline in stock price, from $42 to $33.19, caused by the reduced rate of growth.

c. If, when it learned of the reduced return on reinvested earnings, the firm had retained *none* of its earnings (had paid a $4 dividend) and hence had a zero rate of growth, what rate of return would stockholders receive? (Use the original stock price in your calculation.)

Solution:

$$k_r = D/P + g = \$4/42 + 0 = 0.0952 = 9.52\%.$$

d. What is the percentage cost of Universal's newly issued common stock? (Use the required rate of return as calculated in a.)

Solution:

1. $k_e = \dfrac{D_1}{P_0 (1 - F)} + g.$

2. % flotation costs $= \dfrac{\$1.60}{\$42.00} = 0.03809 = 3.809\%.$

3. $k_e = \dfrac{\$3.40}{\$42.00 \, (1 - .03809)} + 2.5$

$= \dfrac{\$3.40}{\$40.40} + 2.5 = 8.42 + 2.5 = 10.92\%.$

20-2. Boston Enterprises has total net assets of $75 million. It plans to increase net assets to $105 million during the year. Its present capital structure, considered to be optimal, is

Debt (3% coupon bonds)	$25,000,000	33 1/3%
Preferred stock	25,000,000	33 1/3%
Net worth	25,000,000	33 1/3%
	$75,000,000	100%

New bonds will have a 6 percent coupon rate and will sell at par. $100 par value preferred will have a 7 percent rate and will also be sold at par. Common stock, currently selling at $50 a share with a dividend of $1, can be sold to net the company $45 a share after flotation costs. Stockholders' required rate of return is estimated to be 10 percent. It is estimated that retained earnings will be $4 million. The marginal corporate tax rate is 50 percent.

a. To maintain the present capital structure, how much of the capital budget must be financed by common equity?

Solution:

1. $\dfrac{\$25,000,000}{\$75,000,000 \text{ total liabilities and capital}} = 1/3.$

2. $30,000,000 capital budget x 1/3 = $10,000,000 new equity needed

b. How much of the new equity funds must be generated externally?

Solution:

$10,000,000 net equity needed
$\underline{-4,000,000}$ retained earnings
$\underline{\$ 6,000,000}$ external equity needed

c. Calculate the cost of retained earnings and new (external) equity.

Solution:

Cost of retained earnings = k_r = 10%.

Step 1: Calculate the growth rate.

$$g = k_r - \frac{D_1}{P_0} = .10 - \frac{\$1.00}{\$50.00} = .10 - .02 = .08 = 8\%.$$

Step 2: Calculate the cost of new equity.

$$k_e = \frac{D_1}{P_0 \, (1 - F)} + g = \frac{D_1}{P_N} + g = \frac{\$1.00}{\$45.00} + g$$

$$= .0222 + .08 = .1022 = 10.22\%.$$

d. Compute the marginal cost of capital for Boston Enterprises.

Solution:

	Percent ×	After tax cost =	Product
Debt	33 1/3	3.00%	0.00999
Preferred stock	33 1/3	7.00%	0.02333
New common stock (k_e)	33 1/3	10.22%	0.03406
	100		
Marginal cost of capital			0.06738 = 6.738%.

20-3. The Davis Manufacturing Company has the following capital structure as of December 31, 1974:

Debt (7%)		$ 40,000,000
Preferred stock (8%)		20,000,000
Common stock	$15,000,000	
Retained earnings	25,000,000	
Equity		40,000,000
Total capitalization		$100,000,000

Earnings per share have grown steadily from $1.52 in 1967 to $2.60 estimated for 1974. The investment community, expecting this growth to continue, applies a price-earnings ratio of 25 to yield a current market price of $65.00. Davis is paying a current annual dividend of $2.60, and it expects the dividend to grow at the same rate as earnings. The addition to retained earnings for 1974 is projected at $4 million; these funds will be available during the next budget year. Assume a 50 percent corporate tax rate.

Assuming that the capital structure relations set out above are maintained, new securities can be sold at the following costs:

Bonds:	Up to and including $4.0 million of new bonds	— 8% yield to investor.
	From $4.01 to $12 million of new bonds	— 9% yield to investor.
	Over $12 million of new bonds	—10% yield to investor.
Preferred:	Up to and including $2.0 million of pref. stock	— 9% yield to investor.
	From $2.01 to $6 million of preferred stock	—10% yield to investor.
	Over $6 million of preferred stock	—11% yield to investor.
Common:	Up to $8 million of new outside common stock	
	flotation cost per share = $65 — $60 = $5	
	Over $8 million of new outside common stock	
	flotation cost per share = $65 — $55 = $10	

a. Compute the (weighted) and marginal costs of new capital for asset expansion levels of (a) $10 million, (b) $20 million, and (c) $50 million.
b. Graph the (weighted) marginal costs of capital.

Solution:

a. *Step 1.* Calculation of weights:

	Amount	% of Total
Debt	$ 40,000,000	.40
Preferred	20,000,000	.20
Equity	40,000,000	.40
	$100,000,000	1.00

Step 2. Calculation of component cost of capital:

a) Component cost of debt:

Up to $4.0 million:	$k_d = .08 \times (1 - .50) = .040.$
$4.01 million to $12 million:	$k_d = .09 \times (1 - .50) = .045.$
Over $12 million:	$k_d = .10 \times (1 - .50) = .050.$

b) Component cost of preferred stock:

Up to $2.0 million:	$k_p = .090.$
$2.01 million to $6 million:	$k_p = .100.$
Over $6 million:	$k_p = .110.$

c) Component cost of common stock:

$$\frac{\text{EPS (1974)}}{\text{EPS (1967)}} = \frac{\$2.60}{\$1.52} = 1.711.$$

In the table of compound sums (Appendix table A-1), the factor 1.711 (approximately) appears in the row for seven years in the 8 percent column—this implies an 8 percent growth rate.

Stockholders' approximate required rate of return:

$$k_r = \frac{D_1}{P_0} + g = \frac{\$2.60}{\$65.00} + 0.08 = 0.04 + 0.08 = \underline{\underline{0.12}} = \underline{\underline{12\%}}.$$

Up to $8 million new outside equity,

$$k_e = \frac{\$2.60}{\$65\,(1-F)} + .08 = \frac{\$2.60}{\$60} + .08$$

$$k_e = .0433 + .08 - 12.33\%.$$

Over $8 million new outside equity,

$$k_e = \frac{\$2.60}{\$65\,(1-F)} + .08 = \frac{\$2.60}{\$55} + .08$$

$$k_e = .0473 + .08 = 12.73\%.$$

Step 3. Calculations of (weighted) marginal cost of capital at various asset expansion levels: Use Table on page 210.

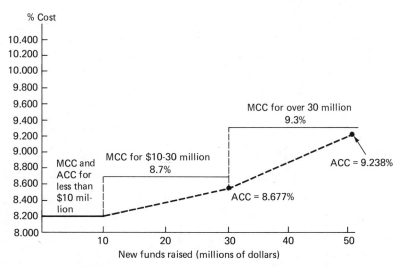

Figure 20-4. **Influence of Amount of Funds Raised on the Marginal and Average Cost of Capital**

a.

$10,000,000

	$ Amt.	Weight	×	Cost	=	Product
Debt	$4.0	.400	×	.040	=	0.01600
Preferred	2.0	.200	×	.090	=	0.01800
Equity	4.0					
Retained earnings	$4.0	.400	×	.120	=	0.04800
New common stock	—0—					
Average cost of new capital						0.08200
						8.200%

	Weight	×	Marginal cost	=	Product
Debt	.40	×	.0400	=	0.01600
Preferred	.20	×	.0900	=	0.01800
Equity	.40	×	.1200	=	0.04800
Weighted marginal cost of new capital					0.08200
					8.200%

$30,000,000

	$ Amt.	Weight	×	Cost	=	Product
Debt	$12.0	.400	×	.045	=	0.01800
Preferred	$ 6.0	.200	×	.100	=	0.02000
Equity	12.0					
Retained earnings	$ 4.0	.133	×	.120	=	0.01596
New common stock	8.0	.266	×	.1233	=	0.03279
Average cost of new capital						0.08675
						8.675%

	Weight	×	Marginal cost	=	Product
Debt	.40	×	.0450	=	0.01800
Preferred	.20	×	.1000	=	0.02000
Equity	.40	×	.1233	=	0.04932
Weighted marginal cost of new capital					0.08732
					8.732%

$50,000,000

	$ Amt.	Weight	×	Cost	=	Product
Debt	$20.0	.400	×	.0500	=	0.02000
Preferred	10.0	.200	×	.1100	=	0.02200
Equity	20.0					
Retained earnings	$ 4.0	.080	×	.1200	=	0.00960
New common stock	16.0	.320	×	.1273	=	0.04073
Average cost of new capital						0.09233
						9.233%

	Weight	×	Marginal cost	=	Product
Debt	.40	×	.0500	=	0.02000
Preferred	.20	×	.1100	=	0.02200
Equity	.40	×	.1273	=	0.05092
Weighted marginal cost of new capital					0.09292
					9.292%

Dividend Policy and Internal Financing

21

THEME

Dividend policy affects the financial structure, the flow of funds, corporate liquidity, and investor attitudes. Thus, it is one of the central financial decision areas related to policies seeking to maximize the value of the firm's common stock.

I. These are legal rules influencing dividend policy.
   A. The *net profits rule* states that dividends must be paid from present and/or past retained earnings.
   B. The *capital impairment rule* states that dividends cannot be paid out of invested capital.
   C. The *insolvency rule* states that no dividends can be paid during insolvency.

II. Business factors affect dividend policy.
   A. The cash or *liquidity position* of a firm influences its ability to pay dividends.
   B. Its *need to repay debt* also influences the availability of cash flow to pay dividends.
   C. *Restrictions in debt contracts* may specify that dividends may be paid
      (1) only out of earnings generated after signing the loan agreement and
      (2) only when net working capital is above a specified amount.
   D. A *high rate of asset expansion* creates a need to retain funds rather than to pay dividends.
   E. A *high rate of profit* on net worth makes it desirable to retain earnings rather than to pay them out if the investor will earn less on them.
   F. *Stability of earnings* will allow a high payout ratio which can be maintained even during difficult economic times.

G. *Age and size of firm* influence the ease of access to capital markets.

H. *Control considerations* may influence dividend policy, since additional external financing is influenced by the dividend payout.

I. The *tax position of stockholders* also affects dividend policy. Corporations owned largely by taxpayers in high income tax brackets tend toward lower dividend payouts. Corporations owned by small investors tend toward higher dividend payouts. However, if a firm's growth possibilities suggest a low payout, there will be a tendency for it to attract stockholders who do not want current dividends.

J. In addition, the *tax position of the corporation* affects its dividend policies. Possible penalties for excess accumulation of retained earnings may cause dividend payouts to be higher than financial considerations alone would indicate.

K. Maintenance of a *target dividend* will lead to low payouts when profits are temporarily high and to high payouts when profits are temporarily depressed. This will cause dividend growth to lag profit growth.

III. Alternative dividend policies.

A. *Stable dollar amount per share.* This is the policy followed by most firms.

B. *Constant payout ratio.* A few firms pay out a constant percentage of earnings.

C. *Low regular dividend plus extras.* A compromise policy between the first two, giving a little more flexibility to the firm.

IV. Residual theory of dividends.

A. The theory is based on the premise that investors prefer to have the firm retain and reinvest earnings rather than pay them out in dividends if the return on reinvested earnings exceeds the rate of return the investor could, himself, obtain on other investments of comparable risk.

   1. The cost of equity capital obtained from retained earnings is an opportunity cost which is lower than the cost of new outside equity because the costs of floating a stock issue are avoided.

   2. Proper balance within the capital structure will minimize the marginal cost of capital. The more internally generated capital available, the lower this marginal cost will be.

B. A very important consideration is the investment opportunities available to the firm.

   1. An investment opportunity schedule, or internal rate of return schedule, can be drawn to rank the available projects.

C. Comparing the investment opportunity schedule with the marginal cost of capital curve shows the proper level of investment to be at the point where the two curves intersect.

   1. This point of intersection will help a firm determine the amount of earnings that should be retained to finance the specified project(s).

D. The above framework can be reconciled to the concept of a target dividend payout ratio.

1. A firm may utilize debt over a short period of time to take advantage of good investment opportunities without having to adjust dividend payouts annually.

V. There is a theoretical dispute regarding dividend policy. The dispute centers upon the psychology of the investor in relation to the choice of whether earnings should be taken as capital gains or as dividend payments. Dividends are probably less risky than capital gains. However, dividends are taxed at a higher rate than capital gains.

A. Gordon, Lintner, and others have suggested that cash flows from a firm with a low payout ratio will be capitalized at higher rates than those of a high payout firm, because investors think that capital gains resulting from earnings retention are more risky than are dividend payments.

B. The approach typified by Miller and Modigliani holds that a change in dividends affects the price of a firm's stock primarily because it provides information about expected future earnings. Miller and Modigliani believe that investors, on balance, are indifferent between returns coming in the form of dividends or capital gains.

C. A third approach, favored by the authors of this text, is that neither set of generalizations hold. Rather, the optimum dividend policy varies from firm to firm depending upon the following:

1. The tax status and current income needs of the stockholders.
2. The firm's internal investment opportunities.
3. Other conditions of the firm in question, including its long-run plans and objectives.

VI. Patterns in dividend payouts.

A. Dividends are more stable than earnings.

1. Studies have indicated a tendency toward a stable dollar dividend.
2. Advantages of a stable dividend policy.

   a. The more certain the dividends are, the lower the capitalization rate, and, therefore, the higher the market price of the stock.
   b. Stockholders who live on income received in the form of dividends seek a relatively assured minimum dollar dividend.
   c. If stable dividends cause a lower payout ratio and if the firm's rate of return is greater than the market rate, a higher market price should result.
   d. Qualification for legal lists (that is, listing of securities in which institutions of a fiduciary nature are allowed to invest) requires a stable and uninterrupted dividend history. Placement on legal lists increases the breadth of the market and the potential demand for the firm's securities.

B. Between 1870 and 1939 NYSE corporations paid out approximately two-thirds of earnings in the form of dividends.

C. The dividend payout rate has varied.

1. In the early post-war period it dropped below 40 percent.

      2. During the decade of the fifties it rose to 45 percent.

      3. In the early sixties it rose to 50 percent, while investment opportunities were still limited.

      4. With an increase in the growth rate in the economy and increased investment opportunities, as well as tight money, payout ratios dropped again in the late 1960s.

VII. Dividend payout patterns among industries.

    A. Low dividend payout patterns have been used by firms in industries with low favorable investment opportunities and rapid growth rates.

      1. Electronics.

      2. Office equipment.

      3. Color television.

    B. Slow growth industries have had higher dividend payouts.

      1. Cigarette manufacturing.

      2. Textiles.

      3. Coal mining.

    C. Industries growing at about the same rate as the general economy have an average dividend payout.

      1. Oil.

      2. Steel.

      3. Banking.

    D. The above patterns fit into the theory of dividend payouts which relates the firm's investment opportunities to its cost of capital.

VIII. Dividend payments.

    A. Management generally tries to convey to investors certain ideas:

      1. The regular dividend will be maintained.

      2. Earnings will be sufficient to maintain dividends.

    B. In order to attain these goals, what may firms with volatile cash flows and investment needs do?

      1. They will set a lower regular dividend rate than firms with the same average earnings but less volatility.

      2. They may also declare extra dividends in years when earnings are high and funds are available.

IX. The payment procedure.

    A. Directors declare the dividend and the payment date.

    B. On the *holder of record* date the stock transfer books are closed.

    C. The right to the dividend expires on the *ex-dividend* date, 4 days prior to the holder of record date.

    D. The company mails checks to the holders of record on the payment date.

X. Stock dividends and stock splits are discussed.

    A. There are some distinctions between them.

      1. A stock dividend is a transfer of earned surplus to the capital stock account and a concomitant pro-rata distribution of stock to the owners.

      2. A stock split simply increases the number of shares outstanding.

B. There are also some similarities.
   1. No cash is distributed in either case.
   2. Both result in a larger number of shares outstanding.
   3. Total net worth remains unchanged.
   4. In a practical sense, there is no difference between the two. The NYSE recognizes this by defining a stock dividend as a stock distribution up to 24 percent of the outstanding stock of the firm, and a stock split as any distribution of 25 percent or more.
C. Identifying characteristics.
   1. A split does not affect the capital accounts, whereas a stock dividend increases the capital stock account and reduces earned surplus.
   2. A split may result in change of the par or stated value, but a stock dividend does not.
D. Some effects of stock splits or stock dividends.
   1. Effect on the market price of the stock depends on prospective changes in underlying earning power reflected in current or announced changes in dividend payouts.
   2. Cash conservation is accomplished to a degree. However, the total amounts paid out for dividends will increase if the effective dividend rate is increased for the larger number of shares.
   3. Tax benefit accrues to stockholders in payment of capital gains tax rather than income taxes on cash dividends.
   4. Number of shareholders is increased by reducing the unit price of stock to a more popular trading range.
XI. Stock repurchases as an alternative to dividends.
   A. Stock repurchased by the issuing firm is called treasury stock.
   B. Acquisition of treasury stock is an alternative to dividend payments.
      1. Fewer shares remaining increase EPS.
      2. Increased EPS should increase the market price of the stock.
   C. Repurchases on a regular basis do not appear feasible due to various uncertainties.
   D. Occasional repurchases do offer some significant advantages over dividends.

PROBLEMS

21-1.   A firm plans a $30 million expansion in net assets during the coming year. Given a debt-assets ratio of 40 percent (considered to be optimal), earnings after taxes of $60 million, and a dividend payout policy of 80 percent, how much external equity must the firm seek?

Solution:

$60,000,000 earnings

x _____ 0.8 payout rate

$48,000,000 dividends

$60,000,000 earnings

−48,000,000 dividends

$12,000,000 retained earnings

$30,000,000 capital budget (net assets added)

x _____ 0.6 1.0 − (debt-assets ratio), or % of total to be financed

_____ with equity = 1.0 − 0.4 = 0.6

$18,000,000 new equity needed

$18,000,000 new equity needed

−12,000,000 retained earnings

$ 6,000,000 external equity needed

21-2. An increase in which of the following is likely to *decrease* a firm's ability or willingness to pay dividends?

a. Current ratio.

b. Target growth rate in assets.

c. Debt ratio.

d. Rate of return on assets.

e. b and c.

f. c and d.

Solution:

e.

21-3. A decrease in which of the following is likely to *decrease* a firm's willingness to pay dividends?

a. Earnings stability.

b. Access to capital market.

c. Investment opportunities.

d. Net worth/total assets ratio.

e. a, c, and d.

f. a, b, and d.

g. c and d.

Solution:

f.

21-4. What does the residual theory of dividend policy assert?

Solution:

Dividends are paid out of the residual remaining after internal investments by the firm.

21-5. On February 1, the directors of Missouri Corporation met and declared the regular quarterly dividend of $2.50 per share to holders of record on March 15, payment to be made April 1. You own 400 shares of Missouri stock, 100 shares purchased on each of the following dates: February 15, March 1, March 10, and March 15. What total dividends will you receive? (The stock goes ex-dividends four days prior to the date of record.)

Solution:

February 15: 100 shares
March 1:   100 shares
March 10:   100 shares
              300 shares

$ 2.50 dividend per share
    x300 shares
$750.00 total dividends received

21-6. The Ohio Corporation has retained earnings of $600,000, capital stock of $300,000, and capital surplus of $80,000. Its common stock is selling for $50 per share. 100,000 shares are currently outstanding. If the firm now declares and distributes a 5 percent stock dividend, what balances will the capital stock, capital surplus, and retained earnings accounts show?

Solution:

Step 1: $\dfrac{\$300{,}000 \text{ capital stock}}{100{,}000 \text{ shares outstanding}}$ = $3.00 par value.

Therefore the amount that will be added to the capital stock account is (5,000 x $3.00 par value) = $15,000.

Step 2:   100,000 shares outstanding

   <u>x5% %stock dividend</u>

   5,000 shares issued in stock dividend

   5,000 shares x $50 market value = $250,000

   transferred from retained earnings, with $15,000 to capital stock and $235,000 to capital surplus.

Step 3:   Capital stock ($300,000 + $15,000) = <u>$315,000.</u>

   Capital surplus ($80,000 + $235,000) = <u>$315,000.</u>

   Retained earnings ($600,000 − $250,000) = <u>$350,000.</u>

21-7.   What is the effect of a stock dividend on book value per share?

Solution:

It will tend to decrease book value per share.

21-8.   The market price of Middleton Corporation's stock was $45 per share prior to splitting 3-for-1 last month. The firm's $2.00 dividend on the new (split) shares is an increase of 5 percent over the previous dividend on the pre-split stock. What was the pre-split dividend per share?

Solution:

$2.00 post-split dividend

<u>   x3   </u>

$6.00 equivalent pre-split dividend

$6.00 = 1.05X

X = $5.71 = previous pre-split dividend.

21-9.   The Williams Minicomputer Company perceives some new expected growth opportunities. The Company estimates that an investment of $30 to $35 million will be required, yielding a return of approximately 20 percent. Current earnings are $20 million with a probable sustained growth of 10 percent per year if the new opportunities are undertaken. The current dividend payout is $1 per share on 8 million shares outstanding. The market value of the stock is $50.

   The cost of new debt for the Williams Company is 10 percent, the net yield from an issue of new common is expected to be $45 per share, and the tax rate is 50 percent. Assume that the total debt to total asset ratio of 40 percent is a target that will be maintained.

a. What levels of total financing are available with the $1 dividend and with no dividend?
b. What are the associated marginal costs of capital in financing the project if the $1 per share dividend is maintained compared with eliminating the cash dividend?
c. Should the $1 dividend be eliminated or maintained and perhaps increased?

Solution:

a. Financing requirement effects of alternative dividend policies:

		$1 dividend	*No dividend*	
1.	Net Income	$20 million	$20 million	
2.	Less Dividend ($1/share x 8M shares)	8 million	0	
3.	Retained Earnings	$12 million	$20 million	(internal financing)
4.	$(3) \div (1-.4)$	20	33.3	(total financing—
5.	Debt (4–3)	$ 8 million	$13.3 million	(external financing)

Over 50 percent greater total financing capability is available if no dividends are paid.

b. Marginal costs of capital if the $1 dividend is maintained:

Up to $20 million (limit of retained earnings):

Cost of retained earnings =

$$k = \frac{D_1}{P} + g = \frac{\$1}{\$50} + .10 = .12$$

Weighted cost of retained earnings = rate of return (k) x retained earnings =
.12 x $12 M = $1.44M

Weighted cost of debt = cost of new debt x (1 — tax rate) x debt =
.10(1 — .5) x $ 8M = 0.40M
totals   20M $1.84M

Marginal cost of capital = $\dfrac{\$1.84M}{20M}$ = .092 = 9.2%

From $20M to $33.3M (requires outside equity financing):

Cost of new equity issue =

$$k_e = \frac{D_1}{P} + g = \frac{D_1}{P_{\text{Net}}} + g = \frac{\$2}{\$45} + .10 = .122$$

Weighted cost of new equity = cost of new equity capital (k_e) x percent
equity = .122 x .6 = .073

Weighted cost of debt = cost of new debt x (1 − tax rate) x percent debt
= .10(1 −.5) x $\frac{.4}{1.0}$ = $\frac{.020}{0.93}$
totals   1.0   0.93

Marginal cost of capital = $\frac{.093}{1.0}$ = .093 = 9.3%

The above calculations show that when no dividends are paid and all
internal financing is used for the equity growth, the cost of equity would
be 12 percent and the marginal cost of capital would be 9.2 percent.
This cost of 9.2 percent is the cost of the first $12 million of financing
(from retained earnings) when the $1 dividend is maintained as well as
to the $20 million of financing from retained earnings when no dividend
is paid. However, if the $1 dividend were maintained, to raise the same
$33.3 millions of financing would require the sale of $13.3 million new
outside equity. If the combination of price pressure and flotation costs
caused the market price of the stock to fall to $45 per share, the cost
of the outside equity would rise to 12.2 percent and the new marginal
cost of financing would be 9.3 percent.

c. The decision with regard to dividend policy would take the following
possibilities into account. If the dividend is reduced, investors who
bought the stock for income would be disappointed (*adverse clientele
effect*). Also some investors might regard the reduced dividend as a
signal that the future prospects of the company have deteriorated (*information effect*). However, this might be offset by publicity on the
new growth opportunities of the company.

If outside equity financing is required, more price pressure might
develop because of the increased supply of equity shares put into the
market (the *dilution effect*). The price might drop further to $40,
resulting in a new cost of external equity of 12.5 percent and a new
marginal cost of financing of 9.5 percent. But the prospective marginal
cost of financing will be well below the expected 20 percent return from
the new program.

The present $1 dividend on $2.50 per share earnings represents a 40
percent dividend payout. As the earnings per share grow from the increased earnings brought in by the new program, the dividend payout is
automatically decreased. We would reason that the small rise in the
costs of financing resulting from increased external equity financing is
small in relation to the risks of decreasing the $1 dividend. We would
recommend maintaining the $1 cash dividend and initiating a program
of stock dividends as the earnings of the company increase from the
new growth program.

Integrated Topics in Financial Management

Part Seven

The Timing of Financial Policy

22

THEME

The financial manager is not only concerned with how to finance, but he is also vitally concerned with when to finance. Since good financial timing is a result of sound judgment, it is essential that the financial manager understand the variables involved.

I. Impact of interest rates.
   A. A differential impact of rates on different types of investment must be recognized.
   B. The heavy, long-term investments in certain areas cause the impact of interest rates on profitability to be especially significant.
      1. Business.
         a. Heavy industry versus light industry.
         b. Inventories versus plant and equipment.
         c. Small firms versus large.
      2. State and local governments.
      3. Housing and construction activity.
   C. Large interest rate fluctuations, especially short-term rates, make capital costs one of the most volatile of input costs.
   D. The greatest influence of interest rates lies in their role as an index of the availability of financing. Especially for small and medium-sized firms, a period of rising interest rates may indicate increasing difficulty in obtaining financing.
II. Characteristic patterns in the cost of money.

A. Short-term interest rates show the widest amplitude of swings and move more quickly than long-term rates.

B. Long-term rates are not as volatile as short-term rates. In part, long-term rates are an average of expected short-term rates over the life of the security.

C. Under certain conditions, there is a greater risk to holding long-term securities than short-term securities. Furthermore, the prices of long-term bonds are much more volatile than those of short-term bonds when interest rates change.

D. The spread between long-term and short-term rates typically grows larger during a period of low growth and tends to narrow during a business up-swing.

E. The cost of debt money tends generally to coincide with movements in general business conditions, both at the peak and the trough.

F. The cost of equity money exhibits wide fluctuations. It tends to rise in the later stages of the business cycle.

III. Money and capital market behavior.

A. Federal Reserve policy tools.

 1. Changes in reserve requirements.

 2. Open market policy.

 3. Discount rates.

 4. Selective controls, for example, over margin requirements and consumer credit.

B. Fiscal policy.

 1. A cash budget deficit stimulates the economy.

 2. A surplus has a restraining influence.

 3. The extent of the influence depends on how the deficit is financed or the way the surplus is used.

C. The growth rates of GNP, the monetary stock, and government expenditures tend to move together. Inflationary expectations developed in the period since 1968, resulting in the controls over wages and prices in August 1971.

IV. Forcasting interest rate patterns.

A. Demand and supply factors.

 1. The main task is to assess the future behavior of the major supply and demand factors. By projecting the sources and uses of funds in detailed individual categories, the direction of the pressure on interest rates may be estimated.

 2. For example, if the forecasted quantity demanded exceeds the indicated supply of funds (when the sum of demands and the sum of supplies are totaled at existing interest structure), interest rates are likely to go up.

 3. Most longer-term predictions for the financial market call for continued price level increases and high interest rates. This has a number of effects on corporate financial policy.

B. Future movements in price levels significantly affect interest rates. This occurs in two ways:
   1. Nominal interest rates reflect expectations of future price level behavior.
   2. The outlook for inflation influences government monetary policy, which in turn affects interest rates.
C. Sources and uses of corporate funds.
   1. Significant changes in the proportions of internal and external financing occurred in the late 1960s. Internal financing, especially that from retained earnings, declined, while dependence on external long-term financing through stocks and bonds increased.
   2. A changing pattern of long-term financing emerged as interest rates rose in the 1960s. The level of stock financing grew significantly and the importance of bond financing dropped. Hybrid forms of financing— debt with equity participation such as convertibles or warrants—were used more in response to the increased uncertainties about the rate of inflation and the increased difficulties in forecasting interest rate patterns.
   3. Both of these trends have slowed down or reversed themselves as interest rates began to decline in the early 1970s.
   4. However, the broad package of economic controls initially introduced in August 1971, and later modified, could radically alter future interest rate patterns. If interest rates rise and remain high, and fluctuations continue, a shift to medium-term and floating rate long-term securities can be anticipated.
V. Implications of fluctuations in the cost and availability of funds include the following:
A. During a period of relatively slow growth in the economy:
   1. Short-term rates are lower than long-term rates.
   2. Long-term rates, however, are low in relation to the average level.
   3. Earnings-price ratios on common stocks are relatively high (P/E ratios are low).
   4. Qualitative terms of debt financing will be favorable at this stage of the business cycle.
   5. Therefore, long-term debt should be used to finance growth when the economy is in a slump.
B. During a period of high economic growth or strong inflationary pressures, the following can be expected:
   1. Short-term rates are high—perhaps higher than long-term rates—but both long and short-term rates are high.
   2. Availability of debt funds may be limited.
   3. Terms of credit may be relatively onerous.
   4. Earnings-price ratios are relatively low (if profit prospects have not deteriorated).
   5. A tendency to sell equity, maybe even to refund longer-term debt.

This reduces debt and builds equity base, facilitating the use of more debt at the beginning of the next upswing.

VI. Important changes in financing that seem to occur during a prolonged period of inflation.
   A. Internal sources become less able to finance growth.
   B. An increase occurs in long-term relative to short-term financing.
   C. An increase occurs in public flotations of equity issues to balance to some extent the debt increases.
   D. Debt ratios rise despite equity sales.
   E. An increase occurs in the use of convertibles and warrants.
   F. Insurance companies and other institutional lenders virtually cease to provide credit to small and medium-sized borrowers on a straight debt basis.
   G. An increase occurs in the wholesaling of credit by large firms to smaller firms through trade credit.

PROBLEMS

22-1. Past experience indicated that when interest rates reach high levels smaller firms:
   a. Become quite insensitive to the interest rate.
   b. Often find funds are not available to them.
   c. Switch to commercial paper financing.
   d. Rely on their investment banking ties to fill their funds requirements.

Solution:

   b. The process is often called credit rationing.

22-2. Fill in the blanks with either *short-term* or *long-term* to best complete the sentences about interest rates.
   a. _____ rates fluctuate less than _____ rates.
   b. _____ rates reflect current supply and demand conditions for funds.
   c. _____ rates reflect future expectations about the availability of funds.
   d. _____ rates are (1) more volatile and (2) more sensitive to general business conditions than _____ rates.

Solution:

   a. Long-term, short-term.
   b. Short-term.
   c. Long-term.
   d. Short-term, long-term.

22-3. True or false? Firms generally wait too long into an expansionary period to raise long-term debt.

Solution:

True.

22-4. After several years of excellent performance, in mid-1958, the Eaten Company made a reappraisal of its sales budgets for the next one, two, and five years. The picture looked dim for existing products, so the company initiated a product development program scheduled to run for at least the next five years. The officers decided that an annual sales growth of only 2 to 4 percent (on a compound basis) could be expected during the developing program, but an increased rate of growth would occur thereafter.

The Eaten Company had total assets of $20 million, and its debt ratio was 60 percent at the time. Since the company planned to spend heavily on research and development during the five-year period, its profits would be depressed and the stock would be unfavorably regarded by investors. The company learned that it could borrow on a short-term basis at 2.5 percent, sell some common stock, or float nonconvertible long-term bonds at 4 percent. Eaten financed by selling $4 million of nonconvertible long-term bonds, with terms requiring strong a current ratio and limitations on fixed assets purchases.

In early 1960 investment bankers informed the company that further bond sales were not feasible because of the high level of fixed charges. However, additional financing was required for the research and development program. At this point Eaten reluctantly sold $6 million of common stock at a price of $40, down from a 1958 high of $97.

Evaluate the timing of the selections of forms of financing by the Eaten Company.

Solution:

Eaten should have financed by common stock in mid-1958 because of the already high debt ratio (60 percent); the expected decline in the growth of sales and profits, which tends to limit the ability of the company to secure the heavy fixed charges; and the then-high price of the stock. Another unfavorable factor is that Eaten may find future expansion handicapped by the requirements of the debt agreement. The above situation limits the firm's use of debt financing after five years, when the development program came to fruition.

Eaten sold common stock too late. In mid-1958 the market price of the stock was near its peak, and the firm should have taken advantage of this fact.

In conclusion, it would have been better to have sold common stock before the decline in the growth of sales and profits, and to have built a base for later financing by long-term debt.

22-5. In the autumn of 1974 money market conditions were very tight. The prime rate had reached 12 percent. The stock market was depressed so that the prices of the common stock of many companies was selling at no more than five times the current level of (depressed) earnings. The Barten Corporation was considering adding to its capacity by building another plant in anticipation of increased sales which its generally favorable growth experience indicated might take place after the future revival of the economy. Some members of the Board of Directors urged that the company sell $20 million of 10 percent notes since this would represent a money cost below the current prime rate on short-term commercial bank loans. Other members of the Board felt that a common stock sale was safer because the company's operations inherently involved a high degree of operating leverage which made its earnings highly sensitive to fluctuations in sales. Still another group on the Board of Directors argued for using interim short-term financing until capital market conditions improved, at which time the firm could choose between 10-year notes, 20-year bonds, or the sale of common stock when equity market conditions were favorable.

Which point of view represents the best timing of financing?

Solution:

Even in the fall of 1974 it was generally recognized that the money and capital markets were experiencing a severe "crunch." The high level of the prime rate was clearly unusual and represented very tight money conditions, reflecting efforts to tighten the growth in the money supply to deal with the inflation problem that the United States had been experiencing. Yet many of the causes of inflation appeared to be temporary. The doubling of the price of oil by OPEC in the autumn of 1973 was still working its way through the economy. Downward devaluation of the American dollar was increasing the prices of imports. Foreign grain sales were increasing the prices of foodstuffs.

By 1976, the prime rate had dropped to 6.5 percent. Long-term notes and bonds for corporations of the bond-rating category of Barten Corporation were selling to yield below 9 percent. Price earnings ratios on stocks had more than doubled as the Dow Jones Industrial Average rose above the 1,000 level by March 1976.

Thus, the point of view which argued for using interim short-term financing until money and capital markets conditions improved was correct. Money and capital market conditions had improved substantially by mid-

1975. Many corporations entered both the equity and long-term debt markets during 1975 and 1976.

22-6. The Inland Steel Company is the sixth largest steel producer in the United States whose raw steel production in 1975 was 7.3 million tons. The total production of steel in the United States in 1973 and 1974 represented capacity utilization approaching 100 percent. After the cyclical decline of 1975, the worldwide demand for steel was expected to continue to grow. The company has planned the largest capital expansion in its history to increase steel capacity by 1.8 million tons. On March 29, 1976, the company sold 1.5 million shares of common stock at a price of $49.375 to net additional equity funds of $71,437,500. Table 22-1 provides some general financial background materials. Table 22-2 summarizes trends in leverage ratios. Discuss the timing and form of financing utilized by the Inland Steel Company.

Table 22-1. Selected Financial Statistics, Inland Steel Company, 1966-1975

Year	Gross Revs. ($ Mill.)	Oper. Profit Margin %	Net Income ($ 000)	Earn Per Sh. $	Div. Per Sh. $	Div. Pay. %	Price Range	Avg. Price x Earn.	Avg. Yield %
66	1,054.5	12.1	65,801	3.60	2.00	56	45^3—29^5	10.4	5.3
67	991.9	9.1	54,017	2.95	2.00	68	39^7—30^5	11.9	5.7
68	1,073.7	14.1	75,820	4.17	2.00	48	40^6—30^6	8.6	5.6
69	1,216.4	9.1	58,662	3.05	2.00	66	42^5—25^6	11.2	5.8
70	1,195.1	8.0	52,300	2.69	2.00	74	29^2—22^6	9.7	7.7
71	1,253.6	8.3	47,779	2.44	2.00	82	34^2—26^2	12.3	6.6
72	1,469.8	9.1	65,913	3.43	2.00	58	37 —30	9.8	6.0
73	1,829.0	10.5	83,129	4.39	2.16	49	34^6—25^1	6.8	7.2
74	2,450.3	11.5	148,009	7.96	2.70	34	36 —28^3	4.0	8.4
75	2,107.4		83,350	4.43	2.40	54	45 —32^2	8.7	6.2

Source: Moody's Handbook of Common Stocks, Spring 1976.

Table 22-2. Inland Steel Company, Trends in Leverage Ratios, 1968-1975 (in millions of dollars)

	1968	1969	1970	1971	1972	1973	1974	1975 Before Financing	1975 After Financing
Total assets	$1,175	$1,305	$1,363	$1,376	$1,473	$1,559	$1,760	$1,867	$1,938
Stockholders' equity	$ 744	775	782	787	811	849	939	971	1,041
Total debt	$ 431	530	581	589	662	710	821	896	896
Long-term debt	$ 196	240	335	327	330	347	390	507	507
Total debt to equity (%)	57.9%	68.4%	74.3%	74.8%	81.6%	83.6%	87.4%	92.3%	86.1%
Long-term debt to equity (%)	26.3%	31.0%	42.9%	41.6%	40.7%	40.9%	41.5%	52.2%	48.7%

Solution:

The steel industry is subject to wide swings in sales, and, with heavy fixed costs it has high operating leverage, so that its fluctuations in sales result in even wider swings in earnings per share. From the data of Table 22-1, it can be determined that the 34 percent increase in sales in 1974 over 1973 resulted in an 81 percent increase in earnings per share. The 14 percent decline in sales between 1974 and 1975 resulted in a 43 percent decrease in earnings per share. This high volatility in earnings inherent in the nature of the steel industry has argued for moderation in the use of financial leverage.

The data in Table 22-2 show that Inland Steel's ratio of long-term debt to equity had risen from 26 percent in 1968 to 52 percent in 1975. For many years a ratio of long-term debt to equity of 30 percent was regarded as the norm for the steel industry. This norm was raised to 40 percent as the levels of long-term debt increased for most large steel companies. The continued rise in the ratio of long-term debt to equity to over 50 percent carries risks of downgrading the ratings of its bonds. Before the mid-1960s the ratio of total debt to equity for most steel companies was around 50 percent. In Table 22-2 we note a rise from 58 percent toward 100 percent for Inland by 1975. These leverage trends indicated the use of common stock to moderate the rising debt ratios.

The timing of the common stock financing appears to have been sound. The selling price of just under $50 is the highest price at which the Inland Steel common stock had sold during the decade covered by Table 22-1. Yet the prospects of higher future sales plus operating leverage provided the possibility of further increases in the future price of its common stock.

External Growth: Mergers and Holding Companies

23

THEME

Mergers and holding company formations have played important roles in the growth of firms. Since financial managers are required to participate in appraising the desirability of a prospective merger and in the evaluation of companies involved in the merger, these materials are a necessary part of their background.

I.   Definitions.
   A. *Merger* — When firm A acquires firm B and firm B entirely disappears. In general usage, "merger" means any combination that forms one economic unit from two or more previous ones.
   B. *Combination* or *consolidation* — When firms A and B join to form firm C.
   C. *Purchase* — An accounting term indicating acquisition by large company of small company and complete absorption of small company.
   D. *Pooling* — An accounting term indicating a combination of companies of about equal size in which the once separate managements and firms continue to carry on important functions.
II. Reasons for seeking growth.
   A. Research — Certain types of research can be performed best by large firms.
   B. Top management skills — Skilled executives are an extremely scarce commodity, and it is often economical to spread their talents over a relatively large enterprise.
   C. Operating economies — For some types of production, the average cost per unit of output is lower when large-scale plants and distribution systems are used.

    D. Risk reduction — Risk is reduced by diversification in large enterprises. Tax considerations add to the importance of this factor.

    E. Market capitalization rates — Market capitalization rates are lower for large firms, giving them a lower cost of capital.

III.   Advantages of use of mergers versus internal growth.

    A. Speed — New facilities acquired more quickly.

    B. Cost — Purchase of existing facilities may cost less.

      1. Securities of a desired firm may be selling for less than cost of building similar facilities outright.

      2. May obtain desired personnel through merger where direct hiring might have failed.

    C. Financing — Sometimes acquisitions can be financed when it is not possible to finance internal growth.

    D. Risk — New product, process, organization, and so on, may be developed with less uncertainty.

      1. In the acquisition of a going concern, the revenue-yielding ability of facilities may have already been demonstrated.

      2. New process or new product acquired may have also demonstrated revenue capability.

    E. Mergers may be the best method of obtaining stability at certain stages of industrial growth.

    F. Taxes and their effect on mergers.

      1. High level of taxes since World War II had effect of increasing merger movement.

      2. Inheritance taxes precipitated a number of these sales.

      3. The fact that any tax loss from a merger can be offset against future taxable income provides the incentive to purchase companies with tax losses.

    G. Competitive advantages to merger.

      1. Acquisition of a company already in a desired market may cut down cost of entrance and of battling competition to gain a foothold.

      2. However, mergers may bring about market control.

        a. Such actions may bring federal intervention.

        b. Manager must therefore consider effects as well as objectives in a proposed merger.

IV.   Arriving at the terms of a merger.

    A. Quantitative factors to be considered on the basis of their trends and variability.

      1. *Present earnings* and *expected future earnings* after the merger, which are reflected in expectations about the effects of the merger on the surviving firm's *growth rate*, are perhaps the most important determinants of the price that will be paid for a firm that is being acquired.

      2. *Dividends* paid are likely to have little influence on the market price of companies with a record of high growth and profitability.

3. *Market prices* clearly influence the price that must be paid in an acquisition, but the acquisition price is likely to exceed the current market price because:
   a. A low current market price may be reflective of industry-wide conditions rather than of the true value of the firm.
   b. The acquired company may be worth more to an informed purchaser than it is in the general market.
   c. Higher prices will be offered to current stockholders as an inducement to sell.
4. *Book value.* Depending on whether or not asset values are indicative of the approximate value of the merged firm, book values may exert an important influence on the terms of the merger.
5. *Net current assets.* Net current assets are an indication of the amount of liquidity being purchased; this can be an important factor in the merger.
   a. Acquiring a company with high net current assets may leave the acquiring company in a position for further mergers.
   b. If it is debt free, the acquired firm's assets and earning power may be used as security for the purchase loan.
B. Qualitative factors to be considered.
   1. Management experience.
   2. Technical competence of its staff.
   3. Abilities of the sales organization.
   4. Possible economies through cost saving.
   5. Degree to which one firm complements the operations of the other.
   6. Synergistic, or 2 + 2 = 5, effects represent reinforcement of capabilities in a very broad sense.
V. Effects of mergers on earnings per share.
   A. Illustrative examples.
      1. Assume the following facts for two companies:

	Company A	Company B
Total earnings	$20,000	$50,000
Number of shares of common stock	5,000	10,000
Earnings per share of stock	$ 4.00	$ 5.00
Price-earnings ratio per share	15X	12X
Market price per share	$ 60.00	$ 60.00

2. The firms agree to merge, with B, the surviving firm, acquiring the shares of A by a one-for-one exchange of stock. The exchange ratio here is based on their respective market prices.
3. Assuming no immediate increase in earnings, the effects on earnings per share are shown in the following tabulation.

	Shares of Company B Owned After Merger	Earnings per Share Before Merger	Earnings per Share After Merger
A stockholders	5,000	$4	$4.67
B stockholders	10,000	5	4.67
Total	15,000		

4. Earnings will *increase* by 67 cents for A's stockholders, but they will *decline* by 33 cents for B's.
5. The effects on market value are less certain: Will A's or B's P/E ratio prevail after the merger?
6. If the merger takes place on the basis of earnings rather than market prices, neither earnings dilution nor earnings appreciation will take place.

	Shares of Company B Owned After Merger	Earnings per Old Share Before Merger	Earnings per Old Share After Merger
A shareholders	4,000	$4	$4
B shareholders	10,000	5	5
Total	14,000		

B. Generalizations on initial effects on earnings per share.
   1. If the exchange terms are based on market prices and the prevailing price-earnings ratios differ, the company with the higher P/E ratio will attain initial earnings accretion while the company with lower P/E ratio will suffer initial earnings dilution.
   2. If the merger takes place on the basis of earnings, no earnings accretion or dilution will occur.
   3. Any initial earnings dilution or accretion may be offset by resulting growth rates of the company as compared with what the growth rates of the individual companies would have been.
   4. If synergy is present in a merger, future earnings per share for stockholders of both companies may be greater than earnings per share would have been for the companies without the merger.
VI. Accounting policies in mergers†—Guidelines of the APB of the AICPA, in APB 16 and APB 17, effective October 31, 1970.
   A. Pooling of interests.
      1. Six conditions—if met, pooling of interest *must* be used.

---

†The material in this section is rather technical and is generally covered in accounting courses. The section may be omitted and the reader may skip to the section on holding companies without loss of continuity.

     a. Acquired firm's stockholders continue ownership.

     b. Basis for accounting for the assets of acquired entity is unchanged.

     c. Each entity had been autonomous; no more than 10 percent common ownership before the merger.

     d. Single transactions; contingent payouts not permitted in poolings, but may be used in purchases.

     e. Payment by acquiring company in common stock for substantially all of the voting common stock of company acquired; substantially defined at 90 percent.

     f. No intention to dispose of a significant portion of the assets within two years after the merger.

  2. Accounting treatment.

     a. The total assets of the surviving firm are equal to the sum of the assets of the two independent companies.

     b. No goodwill is involved.

     c. The excess of market value paid over book value is charged first against capital surplus and then against retained earnings.

B. Purchase.

  1. Involves:

     a. New owners.

     b. New basis for accounting for assets of the acquired entity.

     c. Possibility of consideration paid not equal to book value of entity acquired.

  2. Accounting treatment.

     a. When payment is greater than acquired net worth, the excess is associated with either tangible depreciable assets or with goodwill.

     b. Asset write-offs are tax deductible.

     c. Goodwill is depreciable over a reasonable period no longer than 40 years but it is not tax deductible.

     d. Total assets after the purchase may thus exceed the sum of the total assets of the individual companies.

VII. A holding company is formed for the purpose of owning the stock of other companies, which operate as separate legal entities.

A. Advantages of holding companies.

  1. In general, advantages of the holding company may include any which accrue to large scale operations.

  2. Advantages specific to the holding company form.

     a. Control with fractional ownership is possible with widely distributed stock.

       1) A firm in secular decline may use funds to buy a position in a growth industry.

       2) Greater leverage is obtainable through fractional ownership.

     b. Isolation or risks — Each firm in a holding company is a separate legal identity, and the obligations of any one unit are largely separate from the obligations of the other units.

    c. Approval not required — Stockholder approval is required before a merger can take place. This is not necessary if a holding company purchases the securities of another firm. This feature is, however, somewhat limited by SEC actions in 1974 and 1975.

B. Disadvantages of holding companies.

    1. *Partial multiple taxation* — If the holding company owns less than 80 percent of the subsidiary's stock, returns may not be consolidated. However, it is taxable on only 15 percent of the dividends received from the subsidiary.

    2. *Risks from excessive pyramiding* — The leverage effects possible in holding companies can subject them to risks involved for any fluctuation in sales or earnings. This results in magnification of both potential profits as well as losses.

    3. *Ease of dissolution* — The Antitrust Division of the Department of Justice can much more easily force the breakup of a holding company than it can the dissolution of two completely merged firms.

VIII.   Tender offers.

A. Definition.

    1. A group seeking a controlling interest in another corporation invites the stockholders of the firm it is seeking to control to submit, or tender, their shares in exchange for a specified price.

    2. A tender is a direct appeal to stockholders, so it is not necessary to receive approval of the management of the acquired firm.

B. Advantages.

    1. No prior approval is required.

    2. The percentage of shares to be acquired can be specified in advance.

C. Disadvantages.

    1. Conflict and dissension between firms that are joined.

    2. Legislative controls enacted July 29, 1968:

        a. The acquiring firm must give 30 days' notice both to management of the acquired firm and to the Securities and Exchange Commission.

        b. When substantial blocks of stocks are purchased through tender offers, the beneficial owner must be disclosed as well as the party providing the funds.

PROBLEMS

23-1.   Companies A and B have the following financial data:

	Company A	Company B
Total earnings	$50,000	$80,000
Number of shares of stock outstanding	15,000	20,000
Earnings per share of stock	$ 3.33	$ 4.00
Price-earnings ratio per share	12X	9X
Market price per share	$ 39.93	$ 36.00

a. A and B have agreed to merge. B, the surviving firm, is to acquire the shares of A by a one-for-one exchange of stock. Assuming no increase in total earnings, what will be the effect on EPS for B's stockholders?

Solution:

1. $ 80,000
   50,000
   $130,000 total earnings of A and B

2. $\dfrac{\$130,000}{35,000 \text{ shares}}$ = $3.71 EPS after merger.

3. $4.00
   3.71
   $0.29 decline

b. If the merger of A and B is based on earnings per share instead of relative market prices, what will be the change in earnings after the merger for a holder of 100 shares of company A stock?

Solution:

No change.

$\dfrac{EPS\ A}{EPS\ B} = \dfrac{\$3.33}{\$4.00}$ = 0.8325 number of shares of B
   for each share of A.

   100
   x0.8325
   83.25 shares of B after merger

   83.25
   x $4
   $333.00 total earnings after merger

$$\begin{array}{r} 100 \\ \times\ \$3.33 \\ \hline \end{array}$$

$333.00 total earnings before merger; therefore, no change.

c. What is the new expected growth rate of the merged firm if, prior to the merger, A is expected to grow at 10 percent and B at 6 percent? Assume no synergistic effects occur in the merger.

Solution:

Total earnings:
    Company A = $50,000
    Company B = $80,000
      A + B = $130,000

Expected growth rate $g = \dfrac{\$50,000}{\$130,000} \times 0.10 + \dfrac{\$80,000}{\$130,000} \times 0.06 =$ 0.0754 = 7.54%.

d. Which of the following is *not* typically considered a disadvantage in a holding company situation?
    1. Pyramiding.
    2. Partial multiple taxation.
    3. Risk reduction from diversification.
    4. Legal vulnerability.
    5. None of above.

Solution:

3.

e. Circle the criteria that suggest using a purchase rather than a pooling of interest for two firms that are about to merge.
    1. Small/large size differential between the firms.
    2. Ownership interest of the acquired firm is/is not substantially reduced.
    3. The purchased assets of the acquired company are/are not sold off.
    4. The management of the acquired company is/is not retained.

Solution:

1. large.
2. is.
3. are.
4. is not.

23-2. Given the following balance sheets:

The Holden Company—Consolidated Balance Sheet (in thousands of dollars)

Cash	$ 700	Borrowings	$ 500
Other current assets	300	Common stock	1,100
Net property	1,000	Surplus	400
Total assets	$2,000	Total claims on assets	$2,000

A Company—Balance Sheet

Current assets	$250	Net worth	$500
Net property	250		
Total assets	$500	Total net worth	$500

a. The Holden Company buys operating Company A with "free cash" of $500. Show the new consolidated balance sheet for Holden after the acquisition.

Solution:

The Holden Company—Consolidated Balance Sheet (in thousands of dollars)

Cash	$ 200	Borrowings	$ 500
Other current assets	550	Common stock	1,100
Net property	1,250	Surplus	400
Total assets	$2,000	Total claims	$2,000

b. Instead of buying A, the Holden Company now buys operating Company B with "free" cash of $700. The balance sheet of B Company follows.

B Company—Balance Sheet

Current assets	$ 300	Borrowings	$ 300
Net property	700	Net worth	700
Total assets	$1,000	Total claims on assets	$1,000

Show the new consolidated balance sheet for Holden after the acquisition.

Solution:

The Holden Company—Consolidated Balance Sheet (in thousands of dollars)

Cash	$ 0	Borrowings	$ 800
Other current assets	600	Common stock	1,100
Net property	1,700	Surplus	400
Total assets	$2,300	Total claims on assets	$2,300

c. What are the implications of your consolidated balance sheets for measuring the growth of firms resulting from acquisitions?

Solution:

When the acquisition is by cash and no debt is assumed, as in Part a, the
total consolidated assets of Holden are not increased by the acquisition.
To measure growth, the composition of Holden's assets before and after
the acquisition must be analyzed.

When the acquisition is by cash and debt is taken over as in Part b, the
total consolidated assets of Holden's increase only by the amount of debt
taken over, not by the full amount of assets acquired. The composition of
Holden's assets would again have to be studied.

Of course, the best indicator of potential growth from the acquisition is
possibly the dollar amount of sales of the firm acquired. The volume of
sales is a better measure of the impact of the firm on the market than are
the total assets since sales to total asset ratios vary according to the line of
business.

23-3. Control Corporation is a holding company owning the entire common
stock of S1 Company and S2 Company. The balance sheet as of December
31, 1976 for each subsidiary is identical with the following one.

Balance Sheet, December 31, 1976

Current assets	$2,400,000	Current liabilities	$ 600,000
Fixed assets, net	3,600,000	First mortgage bonds	
		(4%)	2,000,000
		Preferred stock (5%)	1,000,000
		Common stock	
		(par $10)	2,000,000
		Surplus	400,000
Total assets	$6,000,000	Total claims	$6,000,000

Each subsidiary company earns $660,000 annually before taxes and
before interest and preferred dividends. A 50 percent tax rate is assumed.
a. What is the annual rate of return on each subsidiary company's net
worth (common stock plus surplus)?

Solution:

$660,000 income
  80,000 interest on bonds
$580,000 income before taxes

290,000 income tax
$290,000 income after taxes
  50,000 preferred stock dividends
$240,000 earnings available to common

$$\frac{\$240{,}000 \text{ earnings}}{\$2{,}400{,}000 \text{ net worth}} = 10\%.$$

b. Construct a balance sheet for Control Corporation based on the following assumptions: (1) The only asset of the holding company is the common stock of the two subsidiaries; this stock is carried at par (not book). (2) The holding company has $500,000 of 4 percent coupon debt and $1,000,000 of 6 percent preferred stock.

Solution:

Balance Sheet of Control Corporation

		Debt (4%)	$ 500,000
		Preferred stock (6%)	1,000,000
		Common stock	
		(par $10)	2,500,000
Total assets			
($2,000,000 x 2)	$4,000,000	Total claims	$4,000,000

c. What is the common rate of return on the book value of the holding company's common stock?

Solution:

Since each company earns $240,000 annually after taxes and other deductions, total gross receipts are $480,000 or (2 x $240,000).

Book value = common stock + surplus = $2,500,000 + 0 = $2,500,000.

Interest costs are:
  Debt at 4% of $500,000 = $20,000.

Preferred costs are:
  Preferred at 6% of $1,000,000 = $60,000.

$480,000 income
 −20,000 interest on debt
 460,000 income after interest
 −60,000 preferred stock dividends
$400,000 earnings available to common

Rate of return on book value of Control $= \dfrac{\$400,000}{\$2,500,000} = 16.0\%.$

Note that no income tax is deducted here since the Control Corporation owns 100 percent of its subsidiaries' stock and therefore may deduct all of this income from taxable income.

d. How could the rate of return in part c be increased?

Solution:

More leverage by the subsidiaries and/or the holding company could increase the rate of return.

e. What investment is necessary to control the three companies under the assumptions of the initial conditions?

Solution:

It depends on how widely the holding company's stock is held. For example, a small percentage of the stock in General Motors would permit control. On the other hand, a far greater percentage of Ford stock would be necessary to gain control.

f. If ownership of 30 percent of the holding company's common stock ($2.5 million of common) could control all three firms, what percentage would this be of the total assets?

Solution:

30% of $2.5 million = $750,000

Total assets controlled = 2 x total operating assets of each subsidiary
= 2 x $6,000,000 = $12,000,000.

$\dfrac{\$750,000}{\$12,000,000} = 6.25\%$ of total operating assets will control all three firms.

23-4. You are given the following data on two companies:

Terms of Merger Analysis

	Company A	Company B	Adjustments or Ratio	Consolidated Statement AB
Current assets	$120,000	$120,000		1. _____
Fixed assets	80,000	80,000		2. _____
Total assets	$200,000	$200,000		3. _____
Current liabilities	$ 60,000	$ 60,000		4. _____
Long-term debt	40,000	40,000		5. _____
Total debt,† 5%	$100,000	$100,000		6. _____
Common stock, par value $5	$ 50,000	$ 50,000	1. _____	7. _____
Capital surplus	40,000	40,000	2. _____	8. _____
Earned surplus	10,000	10,000		9. _____
Total claims on assets	$200,000	$200,000		10. _____

Ratios

1. Number of shares of stock	10,000	10,000		1. _____
2. Book value per share	_____	_____	1. _____	2. _____
3. Amount of profit before interest and taxes††	$ 45,000	$ 35,000		3. _____
4. Earnings per share	_____	_____	2. _____	4. _____
5. Price/earnings ratio	30	20		
6. Market price of stock	_____	_____	3. _____	
7. Working capital per share	_____	_____	4. _____	
8. Dividends per share, 50% payout	_____	_____	5. _____	
9. Exchange ratio	_____	_____	6. _____ (A/B)	
10. Equivalent earnings per old share	_____	_____		

†Average rate on interest-bearing and noninterest-bearing debt combined.
††Assume a 50 percent tax rate.

Use the market price of stock relation as the basis for the terms of exchange of stock in the old company for stock in the new company (2 shares of AB for 1 share of A, or 1 share of AB for 1 share of B). Then complete all calculations for filling in all the blank spaces, including the adjustments for making the consolidated statement. Treat this problem as a situation that the SEC and accountants would refer to as a pooling of interests.

Solution:

Terms of Merger Analysis

	Company A	Company B	Adjustments or Ratio	Consolidated Statement AB
Current assets	$120,000	$120,000		1. $240,000
Fixed assets	80,000	80,000		2. 160,000
Total assets	$200,000	$200,000		3. $400,000
Current liabilities	$ 60,000	$ 60,000		4. $120,000
Long-term debt	40,000	40,000		5. 80,000
Total debt†, 5%	$100,000	$100,000		6. $200,000
Common stock, par value $5	$ 50,000	$ 50,000	1.Cr.$50,000‡‡	7. $150,000
Capital surplus	40,000	40,000	2.Dr.$50,000‡‡	8. 30,000
Earned surplus	10,000	10,000		9. 20,000
Total claims on assets	$200,000	$200,000		10. $400,000

Ratios

	Company A	Company B	Adjustments or Ratio	Consolidated Statement AB
1. Number of shares of stock	10,000	10,000		1. 30,000
2. Book value per share	$10.00	$10.00	1.0	2. $6.67
3. Amount of profit before interest and taxes††	$ 45,000	$ 35,000		3. $ 80,000
4. Earnings per share	$ 2.00	$ 1.50	4/3	4. $1.17‡
5. Price-earnings ratio	30	20		
6. Market price of stock per share	$60.00	$30.00	2.0	
7. Working capital per share	$ 6.00	$ 6.00	1.0	
8. Dividends per share, 50% payout	$ 1.00	$ 0.75	4/3	
9. Exchange ratio	2/1	1/1	2/1	
10. Equivalent earning per share	$ 2.33	$ 1.17		

† Average rate on interest-bearing and noninterest-bearing debt combined.

†† Assumes a 50% tax rate.

$$\ddagger \text{New EPS} = \frac{(\text{Earnings} - \text{Interest}) \times (1 - \text{Tax rate})}{\text{Number of shares outstanding}} = \frac{(\$80,000 - \$10,000) \times (1 - 0.50)}{30,000}$$

‡‡ The point in these adjustments is as follows: There are 30,000 shares outstanding after the merger. 30,000 x $5 par value = $150,000 = common stock. To force common stock to equal $150,000, take $50,000 from "capital surplus" and add to "common stock."

failure, Reorganization, and liquidation

24

THEME

The financial manager has double responsibility in relation to financial difficulties. If it is his own firm that has financial problems, the financial manager's ability may make the difference between loss of ownership of the firm and the rehabilitation of the firm as a going enterprise. When other firms fall into financial difficulties, knowledge of the rights of creditors may make the difference between large losses and small or no losses.

I. Financial life cycle.
   A. The life cycle of an industrial firm can be described in four steps:
      1. Experimentation period.
      2. Rapid growth period.
      3. Maturity.
      4. Decline.
   B. Financial readjustment problems appear most often during the declining phase of the industry life cycle.

II. Failure.
   A. Economic — A firm's revenues do not cover costs.
   B. Financial —Financial failure signifies insolvency.
      1. Technical insolvency: A firm cannot meet its current obligations as they come due (even though its total assets may exceed its total liabilities).
      2. In bankruptcy sense, if a firm's total liabilities exceed its total assets, the net worth of the firm is negative.
   C. Cause of failure.

        1. Neglect.

        2. Fraud.

        3. Disaster.

        4. Management incompetence.

    D. Financial problems among large firms may be understated.

        1. Except in cases of fraud, or where the failing company is too large to be absorbed by another firm, mergers or government intervention often are arranged to prevent bankruptcy.

        2. These actions are taken to prevent a loss of public confidence in similar organizations, to maintain a viable supplier, or to avoid disrupting an entire community.

III. Informal reorganization.

    A. The alternatives available to meet insolvency or bankruptcy include:

        1. *Extension* involves the postponement of the due date of an obligation.

        2. *Composition* is a voluntary reduction of creditor claims. A pro rata cash settlement is paid to the creditors.

        3. A *combination settlement* is a mixture of extension and composition.

    B. Advantages:

        1. Bankruptcy costs are avoided.

        2. Debtor is kept in business and avoids stigma of bankruptcy.

        3. Creditors absorb a temporary loss but have better chance of greater recovery.

    C. Procedure for settlement.

        1. An adjustment bureau normally arranges and conducts meetings between the debtor and his creditors.

        2. The creditors are represented by a committee composed of the largest four or five creditors and one or two representatives of the smaller creditors.

        3. The bureau receives the facts of the case and sends investigators to examine the firm.

        4. The bureau and the creditors' committee prepare an adjustment plan.

        5. Meetings are held between the debtor and the creditors' committee to reach a final agreement. An agreement is feasible under the following conditions.

           a. Debtor is a good moral risk.

           b. Debtor has the ability to recover.

           c. General business conditions are favorable.

    D. Appraisal of voluntary settlements.

        1. Advantages include its simplicity, minimum costs, and maximum benefits to creditors.

        2. Disadvantages include the fact that control of the business stays with the debtor. Also, one has to contend with the nuisance of small creditors who demand full payment.

        3. An extension is preferred by creditors because it provides payment in full.

IV. Formal reorganization.
   A. A firm is reorganized if it is determined that the net value of the rehabilitated firm will be greater than the value of the sum of the parts if dismembered.
   B. Formal reorganization may take several forms, all of which have these features in common:
      1. The firm is either insolvent or bankrupt.
      2. New funds are needed for working capital or property improvement.
      3. Management must be improved.
   C. A sound reorganization plan meets the tests of fairness and feasibility.
      1. The basic doctrine of *fairness* is met if claims are scaled down in order of their contractual priority and if junior claimants are included only when they make an additional cash contribution to the firm.
      2. A reorganization plan is *feasible* if it will not result in subsequent default. Necessary steps to prevent another default:
         a. Improve management.
         b. Reduce inventories.
         c. Modernize plant and equipment.
         d. Improve operations in the sales and finance areas.
         e. Revamp product policies.
   D. Both the courts and the SEC review reorganization plans to determine their fairness and feasibility.
V. Liquidation procedures.
   A. Liquidation of a business occurs when it is estimated that the value of the firm is greater "dead than alive."
   B. Assignment: A liquidation procedure that does not have to go through the courts.
      1. Common law assignment: A trustee is selected to liquidate the assets and distribute the proceeds among creditors on a pro rata basis.
      2. Statutory assignment: Court appoints an assignee who administers the liquidation and distribution proceedings.
      3. Assignment plus settlement: Creditors agree beforehand that assignment will represent complete discharge of the obligation.
   C. Bankruptcy: Federal Bankruptcy Acts provide safeguards against frauds and provide for an equitable distribution of debtor's assets. Insolvent debtors may discharge obligations and start new businesses unhampered by prior debt.
      1. Acts of Bankruptcy.
         a. Concealment or fraudulent conveyance.
         b. Preferential transfer.
         c. Legal lien or distraint.
         d. Assignment.
         e. Appointment of receiver or trustee.
         f. Admission in writing.
      2. Petition for bankruptcy can be initiated voluntarily by the debtor or

involuntarily by the creditors.

3. Bankruptcy case procedure.

    a. In succession, the petition is filed; the debtor is subpoenaed; the court adjudges him bankrupt if there is no contest; a referee is appointed to act in place of the judge.

    b. A receiver may be appointed as property custodian until the creditors appoint a trustee at their first meeting.

    c. The court appoints property appraisers.

    d. The trustee converts the assets to cash. He cannot sell assets at less than 75 percent of appraised value without consent of the court.

    e. Proceeds minus liquidation costs are then paid out to claimants.

    f. The trustee makes an accounting to the creditors and the referee.

    g. The U.S. Attorney General examines the case for possibility of fraud, and, if necessary, initiates criminal proceedings.

    h. If no criminal proceedings are initiated, the debtor is discharged of his obligations and may begin business again.

4. Certain payments are made before general creditors receive any funds.

    a. Costs of administering and operating the bankrupt estate.

    b. Accrued wages.

    c. Accrued taxes.

    d. Secured creditors are paid with the proceeds from the sale of the specific property pledged.

5. The priority of claims of general creditors is scaled down as follows:

    a. The ratio of available funds to creditors' claims is calculated.

    b. The ratio is applied to the amounts claimed.

    c. Allocations to subordinated creditors are transferred to senior creditors until their claims are satisfied.

    d. The balance, if any, is allocated to the stockholders.

6. Weaknesses in bankruptcy proceedings.

    a. An involuntary bankruptcy case will be dismissed if the bankrupt proves himself solvent. The creditors must bear the court costs.

    b. Proceedings are cumbersome and costly. In approximately two-thirds of the cases there are no assets to liquidate.

    c. The trustee may be unfamiliar with the business, and, therefore, management of the properties during receivership may be inefficient.

    d. Creditors should be alert to potential fraud through the sale of assets at lower than market value.

    e. Creditors often lack interest in the proceedings and fail to press their claims vigorously.

PROBLEMS

24-1. True or false: You would expect a creditor of an insolvent firm to prefer composition over assignment if he had immediate, highly profitable investments available to him.

Solution:

True.

24-2. True or false: Reorganization is an informal equivalent to bankruptcy.

Solution:

False. Assignment is an informal equivalent to bankruptcy.

24-3. Which of the following has the lowest priority of claims in the distribution of proceeds from a bankruptcy liquidation?
a. Taxes due all governmental agencies.
b. Cost of administering the bankrupt estate.
c. Secured creditors.
d. Unsecured creditors.
e. Preferred stockholders.

Solution:

e.

24-4. The financial statements of the System Electronics Company for 1976 were as follows:

System Electronics Company—Balance Sheet, December 31, 1976
(in millions of dollars)

Current assets	$50	Current liabilities	$ 25
Investments	20	Advance payments for subscriptions	35
Net fixed assets	65	Reserves	5
Goodwill	15	$6 preferred stock, $60 par,	
		1,000,000 shares	60
		$8 preferred stock, no par, 100,000 shares,	
		callable at $100 (but fair price $50)	5
		Common stock, 1 million shares at	
		par value of $5	5
		Retained earnings	15
Total assets	$150	Total claims	$150

A recapitalization plan is proposed in which each share of the $6.00 preferred will be exchanged for one share of $1.50 preferred (stated value, $15) plus one 6 percent subordinated income debenture (stated principal, $45).

Note: The $8 preferred stock is fully paid off by drawing down the cash account of current assets (from $50 to $45 million). Notice that the trustees have decided that $50 per share is a fair price rather than the call price of $100.

a. Show the *pro forma* balance sheet giving effect to the recapitalization, showing the new preferred at its stated value and the common stock at its par value.

Solution:

System Electronics Company—*Pro Forma* Balance Sheet
(in millions of dollars)

Current assets	$ 45	Current liabilities	$ 25
Investments	20	Advance payments for subscriptions	35
Net fixed assets	65	Reserves	5
Goodwill	15	6% subordinated income-debentures, 1,000,000 at $45	45
		$1.50 preferred stock, 1,000,000 at $15	15
		Common stock outstanding, 5 million shares at $1 par	5
		Retained earnings	15
Total assets	$145		$145

b. Adjust the income statement below to a *pro forma* income statement (in millions of dollars carried to two decimal places).

System Electronics Company—Consolidated Statement of Income and Expense for Year Ended December 31, 1976 (in millions of dollars)

Operating income		$200.0
Operating expense		175.0
Net operating income		25.0
Other income		3.0
Other expense		0.0
Earnings before income tax		28.0
Income tax at 50%		14.0
Income after taxes		14.0
Dividends on $6.00 preferred stock	$6.0	
Dividends on $8.00 preferred stock	0.8	6.8
Income available to common stock		7.2

Solution:

System Electronics Company (in millions of dollars)

Net operating income		$25.00
Other income	$3.00	
Interest expense (0.06 x 45)	2.70	0.30
Earnings before income tax		25.30
Income tax, 50%		12.65
Income after taxes		12.65
Dividends on preferred stock (1.5 x 1)		1.50
Income available to common stock		$11.15

c. How much does the firm increase income available to common stock by the recapitalization?

Solution:

Income available to common stock increased by (11.15 − 7.2) = 3.95 or $3,950,000.

d. How much less is the required pre-tax earnings after the recapitalization compared to those before the change? "Required earnings" is that amount which is just enough to meet fixed charges, debenture interest, and/or preferred dividends.

Solution:

Preferred dividends were $6.8 million. To pay these, the firm had to earn double that amount—$13.6 million. After recapitalization, it need earn only the debenture expense of $2.7 million plus double the preferred dividends of $1.5 million, a total of $5.7 million, representing a reduction of $7.9 million in required earnings before interest and taxes.

Multinational Business Finance

25

THEME

Basic financial concepts remain the same, but the multinational financial manager must make his decisions within the framework of the international environment, as well as the environment of the countries where his firm is operating.

I. Trend toward international operations.
   A. Since World War II, international operations of U.S. businesses have increased markedly.
   B. Export of goods manufactured in the U. S. has declined in importance relative to overseas operations.
   C. There is a concurrent increase in foreign investment into the U. S.
II. The evolving structure of multinational business.
   A. Initial entry into international merchandising is often through specialized export brokers and international bankers.
   B. Expanding foreign sales generally cause many firms to concentrate expertise in an international sales department.
   C. Increasing pressures from competition and danger of import restrictions provide the incentive to locate production "on site."
   D. A subsidiary corporation managing international operations may be the most efficient method of profitably controlling operations in many countries.
III. Advantages of overseas production and service units.
   A. Marketing advantages.
      1. Elimination of import quota restrictions.

      2. Lower transportation costs.

      3. Lower inventory requirements.

  B. Production advantages.

      1. Lower labor costs.

      2. Ease of meeting local engineering standards.

  C. Financial advantage.

      1. Tax advantages.

      2. Access to local capital.

      3. Flexibility to move assets across national boundaries.

  D. Management advantages.

      1. Increased earnings prospects as markets and production facilities are diversified.

      2. Improved relations with customers and governments.

      3. Easier access to foreign technology.

      4. Conformity of administrative practices to local customs.

IV. Evaluation of entry into overseas facilities.

  A. Initial screening process.

      1. Points out general economic and political conditions in the country being considered.

      2. Examines present and potential local market.

  B. International environment screening.

      1. Inquiries about the company's experience to handle the project are made.

      2. Potential product mix of the firm is considered.

      3. Alternative proposals are evaluated.

      4. Regulatory factors concerning the project must be examined.

  C. Financial analysis.

      1. The cash flow is evaluated to determine the risk adjusted present value.

      2. Factors affecting the cash flows.

         a. Demand forecast.

         b. Duties and taxes.

         c. Applicable exchange rates.

         d. Reinvestment and restrictions on repatriation of profit.

      3. Two sets of cash flow data must be analyzed.

         a. Cash flows within the overseas project.

         b. Cash flows from the overseas project to the parent company.

V. Problems faced by multinational firms.

  A. Nationalization.

      1. To minimize this danger, the firm should make net contributions to the host country's economy.

      2. The firm should be assured of adequate compensation when nationalization occurs.

  B. Devaluation.

      1. Possibility must be continuously monitored.

      2. Defensive measures can be taken to provide some protection.

        a. Accelerate funds flow to parent.

        b. Increase debt in country in danger of devaluation.

        c. Hedge currency transactions in the futures market.

        d. Maintain low balances in local currency.

VI. Financing the project.

    A. Parent company.

      1. Amount of financing is limited by U.S. regulations on direct foreign investments.

      2. Loans.

      3. Equity.

    B. U.S. bank loans guaranteed by the parent company.

    C. Foreign central bank loans.

    D. Local capital.

    E. Eurodollar loans (short-term).

    F. Eurobonds (long-term).

PROBLEMS

25-1. World Industries has a textile subsidiary, Continental Fabrics, in Kowlum, a large island off the coast of Africa. Kowlum has been losing foreign capital since nationalizing American and British oil refineries. The rumor has spread that a devaluation is fairly probable. The textile subsidiary's balance sheet is given below:

Continental Fabrics—Balance Sheet (in U.S. Dollars)

Cash	$ 112,000	Accounts payable	$ 140,000
Accounts receivable	210,000	Notes payable	70,000
Inventory	280,000	Other liabilities	70,000
Investment in mar-		Long-term dollar	
ketable securities	140,000	liabilities	280,000
Fixed assets	420,000	Equity	602,000
	$1,162,000		$1,162,000

    a. Normally the assets and liabilities of Continental Fabrics are simply added to those of the parent and the other subsidiaries to develop the consolidated balance sheet. If Kowlum devalues by 40 percent as is expected, what adjustments will have to be made to the dollar value of the accounts when the consolidated statement is made? (Note: the value of the long-term liability will not have to be changed as it is a dollar liability.)

    b. From a above, what can be done with current assets and liabilities to reduce the effects of the evaluation?

Solution:

a. The 40 percent devaluation will reduce the value of all of Continental Fabrics' assets and all of its liabilities except dollar obligations. The firm's new balance sheet becomes:

Continental Fabrics—Balance Sheet

Cash	$ 67,200	Accounts payable	$ 84,000
Accounts receivable	126,000	Notes payable	42,000
Inventory	168,000	Other liabilities	42,000
Investment in mar-		Long-term dollar	
ketable securities	84,000	liabilities	280,000
Fixed assets	252,000	Equity	249,200
	$679,200		$679,200

Notice that equity was decreased by 58.6 percent rather than 40 percent due to the fixed dollar obligation.

Reported profits would be decreased by $352,800, the equity loss.

b. If a firm has some prior indication of a devaluation, it can convert excess cash to a stronger currency. Accounts receivable would be held to a minimum. Accounts payable could be allowed to build up. Debt payable in Kowlum currency should be increased as much as possible.

The treasurer of today's multinational firm must keep abreast of local currency conditions as he has the ability to save the firm millions through this type of financial maneuver.

25-2. How does the multinational company assess proposed entry into a foreign country or market in which it is not allowed majority ownership or control?

Solution:

A. It may still be able to service the market by utilizing one of the following:
1. Exportation to the market.
2. A licensing agreement with a local manufacturer.
3. A joint venture with local partners.
4. A management contract.
   Consider General Motors' purchase of 30 percent of a Japanese auto company. GM had always operated previously with 100 percent ownership.

B. Disadvantages of having a minority position.
1. May disagree on policies.
2. May be "frozen out."
3. May give up some know-how.

    4. No independent decisions on dividend policy, profit reinvestment, or transfer payment policy.

C. Advantages of being in the market with a local partner.
    1. May be the only method available to enter the market.
    2. May learn from local partners (patents, licenses, local marketing techniques).
    3. May sell domestically produced materials and parts to the foreign joint venture.
    4. May also be permitted to sell some domestic final product.
    5. May thereby avoid trade barriers (tariffs, quotas).

25-3. What discount rate should be used for evaluating projected overseas investments?

a. Does the possibility of added risk change the rate to be used?

b. Is it possible for the overseas investment to lower the corporate business risk?

c. Does this have any effect on the corporation's financial structure? (How might this happen?)

Solution:

a. The appropriate discount rate to use for evaluating foreign investments should be the same base discount rate that would be applied to a similar project (with a particular risk class) undertaken in the headquarter's country (which may be different than the firm's prior project's risk class), plus a risk differential for the "special risks of the internationality" of the project.

b. It is possible for an overseas project to lower a firm's risk class—if not offset by the internationality premium. An example might be if Baskin-Robbins moved into the Australian market. That is, if the seasonality attributable to operating in the Northern Hemisphere were offset by the seasonality of operating in the Southern Hemisphere, the overall variability of earnings might lessen (lowering uncertainty, and therefore risk).

c. This perceived reduced risk might contribute to lowering the firm's weighted average cost of capital, and finally to increasing the wealth of its stockholders or perhaps to the use of more leverage.

Financial Management in the Small Firm

26

THEME

Although the same general principles apply in the financial management of both large and small firms, the small firm faces a somewhat different set of problems, has a different goal orientation, and has access to different financial sources and means than a large firm.

I.   The role of small business in the economy.
   A. Of about 8.5 million firms in the U.S. about 8 million are defined as "small."
   B. Small firms often serve as the vehicle for the development of new products and services.
   C. They represent a valuable competitive force.
II. Alternative forms of business organization.
   A. Sole proprietorship.
      1. Formation.
         a. A person merely begins business operations.
         b. City or state licenses may be required for the particular business operation.
      2. Advantages for small operations.
         a. Easily and inexpensively formed.
         b. Subject to few government regulations.
         c. Pay no corporate income taxes.
      3. Limitations.
         a. The small firm is unable to obtain large sums of capital.

  b. The proprietor has unlimited personal liability for his business debts.

  c. Proprietorship is limited to the life of the individual who created it.

B. Partnership.

 1. Definition.

  a. Two or more persons associated to conduct a business operation.

  b. May be an informal understanding or a written partnership agreement.

 2. Advantages.

  a. Ease in economy of formation.

  b. Freedom from special government regulations.

  c. Partnership profits are taxed as personal income in proportion to partners' claims.

  d. Pooling of particular skills or contacts.

 3. Drawbacks.

  a. Impermanence—death or withdrawal of any one of the partners dissolves the partnership.

  b. Difficulties of transferring ownership.

  c. Unlimited liability—partners risk their personal assets as well as their investments in the business (jointly and separately liable for business debts).

  d. Partnership profits are taxed as personal income whether distributed or not.

  e. To avoid financial pressures caused by the death of one of the partners, life insurance may be carried naming the remaining partners as beneficiaries.

C. Corporation.

 1. Definition.

  a. A legal entity created by the state.

  b. An entity distinct from its owners and managers.

 2. Advantages.

  a. It has an unlimited life not related to the life of its owners or managers.

  b. Limited liability—stockholders are not personally liable for the debt of the firm.

  c. Easy transferability of ownership interest—usually expressed as shares of stock which are bought and sold in the open market.

 3. The process of forming a corporation.

  a. A certificate of incorporation is drawn up, including the following information:

   1) name of proposed corporation.

   2) purposes.

   3) amount of capital stock.

   4) number of directors.

   5) names and addresses of directors.

   6) duration of life.

    b. Certificate is notarized and sent to the Secretary of the state in which the business seeks to incorporate.

    c. If approved by Secretary of State the certificate is filed and applicant is notified.

  4. Operations of a corporation are governed by special documents.

    a. Charter.

     1) Certificate of incorporation.

     2) General corporation laws of the state.

    b. By-laws represent a set of rules for internal management of the company including:

     1) Election of directors.

     2) Whether cumulative voting.

     3) Whether the preemptive right is granted to existing stockholders.

     4) Provision for management committees and their duties.

     5) Procedures for changing the by-laws themselves.

III. Economic aspects of firm size.

  A. Some firms are small because the nature of the industry (for example, personal services activities such as barber shops) dictates that small scale operations are more efficient than large ones. (Traditional small firms.)

  B. Other firms are small because they are new companies in established industries or they are in industries that are new and the firms have not yet had time to grow and reach their optimal size. (Small firms with growth potential.)

IV. Traditional small firms.

  A. Characteristics:

   1. A localized market.

   2. Low capital requirements.

   3. Relatively simple technology.

   4. One man entrepreneurial leadership. This often leads to problems of inadequate breadth of managerial skills and resources critical to the continued success and expansion of the firm.

  B. Although profitability outlook has been quite discouraging, incentives to operate own businesses still exist. These include:

   1. Freedom to make own decisions.

   2. Challenge of building own business.

   3. Continued hope of success.

  C. Financing considerations.

   1. The proprietor of the traditional small business must rely on internal financing (retained earnings) to a greater extent than that of a large firm.

   2. Working capital management is critical to the small entrepreneur whose funds are limited.

   3. Financial ratio analysis made on a regular basis for control purposes is essential to the long-run survival of the traditional small firm.

     D. Use of franchise arrangements.
       1. Frequently used by small firms.
       2. Training and experience programs required for a particular line of business are sold to the proprietor on a rental contract basis.
       3. Sometimes the franchise includes a valuable trademark or the supply of some key item.
       4. The franchiser may provide the franchisee with the benefits of bulk buying as well.
       5. The owner of the franchised operation must compare prices paid for the trademark, especially inputs and supplies, or managerial advice with the value received.

V.   Overview of stages and related financing sources.
     A. Introduction period.
       1. Sales and profits grow slowly following the introduction of a new product.
       2. Financing mainly from personal savings, trade credit, and government agencies.
     B. Rapid growth period.
       1. The firm experiences a rapid growth of sales, high profitability, and acceptance of the product.
       2. Financing is mainly internal or from trade credit, short-term bank credit, and venture capital.
     C. Maturity.
       1. The rate of growth of sales begins to slow down since growth is dependent in large part upon replacement demand.
       2. At this stage the firm may go public and thus draw upon the money and capital markets generally.
     D. Decline.
       1. Substitute products cause sales to decline.
       2. Financing decisions include internal financing, share repurchase, diversification, and mergers.

VI. The small firm with growth potential—early stages.
     A. Formation period.
       1. Typically, the firm has developed a new product or an innovative way of providing an old service.
       2. Sales and profits grow slowly as the firm is trying to establish itself in the market.
       3. Personal savings, trade credit, and government agencies provide the main sources of financing.
       4. Planning for growth is especially important at this stage.
       5. Financial planning and control processes are also important.
     B. Exploitation and rapid growth period.
       1. The firm enjoys rapid growth of sales, high profitability, and acceptance of the product.

    2. Cash flows and working capital management become increasingly important here.

    3. At this stage, the firm has an extraordinary need for additional outside financing. This need is directly proportional to the rate of growth experienced.

    4. Reluctance to share control by the original owners is a deterrant to seeking additional outside equity money for financing purposes.

    5. Excessive debt financing through trade credit and short-term bank credit increases the risk potential of the small growth firm.

    6. Because of the greater risks facing the small growth firm, special types of financing are required.

  C. Specialized venture capital financing sources.

    1. Venture capital companies can be organized either as partnerships or as formal companies called *investment development companies.*

    2. Venture capital companies generally take an equity position in the firms they finance, but they may also provide debt capital.

    3. Typically, they do not require voting control, but do try to maintain continuous contact, provide management counsel, and monitor the progress of their investment.

    4. Since venture capital firms are largely owned by wealthy individuals who favor receiving income in the form of capital gains, they are in a position to take larger risks.

    5. There is an increasing interest in venture capital investments by large established business firms in recent years.

VII. The Small Business Administration.

  A. The business loan program.

    1. Provides funds for construction, machinery, equipment, and working capital.

    2. Two types.

      a. Direct loans—the SBA simply makes a loan to a small business borrower.

      b. Participation loans.

        1) The SBA lends part of the funds, while a bank or other private lending institution advances the balance.

        2) Under a participation loan a portion of the funds advanced by the private source may be guaranteed by the SBA.

        3) The maximum amount of loan or guarantee is $350,000.

  B. Small business investment companies (SBICs).

    1. Formation.

      a. Act of 1958 enables the SBA to license and regulate SBICs and to provide them with financial assistance.

      b. A minimum of $150,000 in private capital is required for the licensing of an SBIC.

      c. SBICs can sell an equal amount of subordinated debentures directly to the SBA.

  2. Policies—similar to other venture capital companies.

    a. Their investments in other small businesses are generally made by purchase of convertible securities or bonds with warrants.

    b. SBICs emphasize management counsel for which a fee is charged.

  3. Performance.

    a. SBICs benefit from the aura of government sponsorship.

    b. One highly successful investment can make an SBIC profitable.

    c. Financing other small businesses involves considerable risk because a small firm must develop strong management to achieve solid growth.

    d. There has been good but not spectacular progress by the SBICs since the mid-1960s.

VIII. The going public phase.

  A. Growth to maturity—increasing financing requirements during the rapid growth period puts pressure on the firm to raise capital from the public equity markets.

  B. The decision to "go public" represents a fundamental change to the firm in four respects:

    1. The firm moves from informal, personal control to formal controls.

    2. Information must be reported on a timely basis to the outside investors.

    3. Breadth of management is required to operate effectively the expanded business.

    4. A board of directors helps formulate sound plans and policies.

  C. In the valuation process, it should be noted that:

    1. It is difficult to obtain reasonable estimates of the cost of equity capital for small privately owned firms.

    2. The required rate of return for small firms tends to be high because of the risks involved.

    3. Depending on the tax bracket of the owner-managers, the after-tax cost of retained earnings may be lower than the after-tax cost of new outside equity.

    4. Flotation costs for new security issues are much higher for small than for large firms.

  D. The timing of the decision to go public is especially important because small firms are more affected by variations in money market conditions than are larger firms.

IX. Maturity and industry decline.

  A. Sales growth of the firm may slow down for a number of reasons.

    1. The appearance of substitute products.

    2. Technological and managerial obsolescence.

    3. Saturation of demand for its goods.

  B. Financial decisions at this stage include:

    1. Financing mostly from internal sources.

    2. Mergers to reduce costs or to enter product markets with new growth potentials.

3. Share repurchases.

C. The best time to formulate plans for diversification and other long-term strategies is while the firm has high price-earnings ratios and a favorable growth momentum.

PROBLEMS

26-1. The current financial position of the Medtronics Company and the Nutrition Company are very similar. In fact, the following figures may be taken as defining the present financial position of both companies.

	(in thousands of dollars) Year 1
Current assets (30%)†	$150
Fixed assets (20%)	100
Total assets	250
Accounts payable (10%)	50
Notes payable	20
Other accruals (5%)	25
Current liabilities	95
Financing requirements	0
Common stock	100
Retained earnings	55
Net worth	155
Total claims	250

†Percentage of sales.

Sales are $500,000 for the year for both companies. The relationship of of the balance sheet items to sales is given by the percentages in parentheses. The after-tax profit on sales is 6 percent.

The Medtronics Company, operating in a high growth industry, will double its sales in one year. The Nutrition Company on the other hand, grows at a moderate 10 percent over a four-year period. Also, common stock remains unchanged over the relevant period for each company and retained earnings consists entirely of accumulated profits. (No dividend payouts are assumed initially.)

a. Project the balance sheet position for the Medtronics Company to Year 2 and the Nutrition Company to Year 4. Use the item "Financing requirements" as the balancing figure on an interim worksheet. Then, in the balance sheet assume that any financing required will be covered by an increase in notes payable and that any excess funds will be used first to pay off notes payable. After notes payable are completely paid off, any remaining excess funds are used to invest in marketable securities on the final balance sheet.

b. Calculate the following key ratios:

1. Current ratio.
2. Debt ratio (total debt to net worth).
3. Sales to total assets.
4. Sales to net worth.
5. Net income after taxes (profit) to sales.
6. Net income after taxes (profit) to net worth.

c. Using the ratios calculated above, compare the effects of rapid and moderate growth on the financial position and related financial policies of the two firms.

Solution:

a.

Worksheet—Medtronics Company (in thousands of dollars)

	Year 1	Year 2
Sales	$500	$1,000
Current assets (30%)	150	300
Fixed assets (20%)	100	200
Total assets	250	500
Accounts payable (10%)	50	100
Notes payable	20	20
Other accruals (5%)	25	50
Current liabilities	95	170
Financing requirements	0	115
Common stock	100	100
Retained earnings	55	115
Net worth	155	215
Total claims	250	500

Worksheet—Nutrition Company (in thousands of dollars)

	Year 1	2	3	4
Sales	$500	$550	$605	$666
Current assets (30%)	150	165	182	200
Fixed assets (20%)	100	110	121	133
Total assets	250	275	303	333
Accounts payable (10%)	50	55	61	67
Notes payable	20	20	20	20
Other accruals (5%)	25	28	30	33
Current liabilities	95	103	111	120
Financing requirements	0	(16)	(32)	(51)
Common stock	100	100	100	100
Retained earnings	55	88	124	164
Net worth	155	188	224	264
Total claims	250	275	303	333

Note that "financing requirements" is used as the balancing figure on the worksheet. Any effect on notes payable and marketable securities will be shown in the following balance sheets.

Balance Sheet—Medtronics Company (in thousands of dollars)

	Year 1	Year 2
Current assets (30%)	$150	$300
Fixed assets (20%)	100	200
Total assets	250	500
Accounts payable (10%)	50	100
Notes payable	20	135
Other accruals (5%)	25	50
Current liabilities	95	285
Common stock	100	100
Retained earnings	55	115
Net worth	155	215
Total claims	250	500

Balance Sheet—Nutrition Company (in thousands of dollars)

	Year 1	2	3	4
Current assets (30%)	$150	$165	$182	$200
Other current assets:				
Marketable securities	0	0	12	31
Fixed assets (20%)	100	110	121	133
Total assets	250	275	315	364
Accounts payable (10%)	50	55	61	67
Notes payable	20	4	0	0
Other accruals (5%)	25	28	30	33
Current liabilities	95	87	91	100
Common stock	100	100	100	100
Retained earnings	55	88	124	164
Net worth	155	188	224	264
Total claims	250	275	315	364

The $115,000 financing requirement for Medtronics in Year 2 (see worksheet) increases its notes payable account to $135,000 on the balance sheet. Since both are liability accounts, they cancel out and thus do not affect the value of total claims or total assets of the company.

The Nutrition Company, on the other hand, consistently shows negative financing requirements over the four-year period (see worksheet). This excess of funds is used first to pay off notes payable, after which it is used to invest in marketable securities (see Balance Sheet). Thus, notes payable decreased by the amount of excess funds ($16,000) in Year 2. In Year 3, there is still $12,000 left over after paying off the remaining notes payable. This amount is used to invest in marketable securities which is separately categorized here under Other Current Assets. A similar reasoning is applied to Year 4. Note that the value of total assets is affected for Year 3 and Year 4 because both asset and liability accounts are affected.

b. Key ratios.

Medtronics Company

	Year 1	Year 2
1. Current ratio	1.6x	1.1x
2. Debt ratio (total debt to net worth)	61%	133%
3. Sales to total assets	2x	2x
4. Sales to net worth	3.23x	4.65x
5. Net income to sales	6%	6%
6. Net income to net worth	19%	28%

Nutrition Company

	Year 1	2	3	4
1. Current ratio	1.6x	1.9x	2.1x	2.3x
2. Debt ratio (total debt to net worth)	61%	46%	41%	38%
3. Sales to total assets	2x	2x	1.9x	1.8x
4. Sales to net worth	3.23x	2.93x	2.7x	2.52x
5. Net income to sales	6%	6%	6%	6%
6. Net income to net worth	19%	18%	16%	15%

It should be noted first of all that the two firms started out with the same financial ratios. Note also that their net income (or profit) to sales ratio is the same at 6 percent. Because of the faster growth rate for Medtronics, its liquidity ratio deteriorates. It moves from 1.6 in the initial period to 1.1 at the end of Period 2. In contrast, Nutrition improves from 1.6 to 1.9 by the end of Period 2. By the end of Period 4 it is up to 2.3.

We define the *debt ratio* as the ratio of total debt to net worth since as a consequence of increased financial requirements or increased liquidity, the debt maturity policy of the firm may be altered. There may be some shift between current debt and long-term debt. But by calculating the ratio of total debt to net worth, we can encompass either form of debt. The total debt to net worth ratio for Medtronics more than doubles between Period 1 and Period 2. It goes from 61 percent to 133 percent. In contrast, for Nutrition, the debt ratio drops sharply from 61 percent to 46 percent between Period 1 and Period 2 because the financing available is used to pay off the notes payable. Subsequent thereto, the negative excess financing or increase in liquidity available is used to increase marketable securities. Thus, debt remains the same but net worth is increased by any retained earnings and, as a consequence, the debt ratio continues to fall but not as rapidly as when debt is paid off. By the end of Period 4 Nutrition has a debt ratio which is only 38 percent.

The sales to total asset ratio for Medtronics remains at two times because, as sales increase, all of the asset accounts increase by a constant percentage of sales. So, the sales to total asset ratio remains the same. The reason that the sales to total asset ratio for Nutrition declines is that total assets begin to increase by the increase in marketable securities. The inclusion of this item, which is not related to sales, causes the sales to total asset ratio to decline. As a general point, when the sales to total asset ratio of a firm declines, this may be a signal that its investment and marketable securities has increased.

Since the debt ratio of Medtronics has increased and its sales to total asset ratio has remained unchanged, we can expect that the sales to net worth ratio will have increased. We find that this is actually what happened. Its sales to net worth ratio rises from slightly over 3 to 4.65. In contrast, for Nutrition, starting out with the same sales to net worth ratio of 3.23, its sales to net worth ratio declines rather than increases. It declines because net worth becomes an increasing proportion of total assets and the sales to total asset ratio is actually declining slightly. We see next that, as assumed, the net income to sales ratio for both Medtronics and Nutrition remain the same over all the time periods. Given a constant net income to sales ratio for each firm and given that the sales to net worth ratio rises for Medtronics, we can predict that the ratio of net income to net worth will rise for Medtronics and decline for Nutrition. Indeed, this turns out to be the case. The net income to net worth ratio of Medtronics rises from 19 percent to 28 percent. Thus, the increased profitability as measured by net income to net worth for Medtronics has come about not because the inherent profitability of Medtronics has increased but because its net income to sales has remained the same. But it has benefited from an increase in leverage. Profit to net worth rises to 28 percent. (The actual percentage might be somewhat lower because we have not taken the increased interest on the increased debt into account.) We will do this in the modification of the problem set forth in Problem 26-2.

General Comments on Financial Policy

Medtronics now has a debt ratio at which the creditors of the firm have invested $133 for every $100 invested by the owners of the firm. This results in a very high profit ratio as measured by the return on net worth, but it is a high profit ratio associated with the risks of the high leverage ratio. The creditors, of course, are incurring high risks without benefiting from the increased profitability of Medtronics. Undoubtedly commercial banks would be unwilling to increase short-term notes payable to the degree indicated in the final balance sheet. Medtronics would have to sell additional equity or a form of debt with a convertible or warrant "sweetener." In this way the creditors would be able to participate in the increased value of the firm that is likely to result from its increase in return on net worth and growth in earnings per share.

With regard to dividend policy, Nutrition Company would probably have a pretty liberal dividend payout since the alternative is piling up the funds in marketable securities. Medtronics has had a substantial increase in its debt ratio. It needs to add to its net worth ratio as much as possible. Therefore, as a high growth company, it will undoubtedly have a zero dividend payout for the time being.

26-2. In the formulation of Problem 26-1, to focus on the main relationships without getting into too much detail, we ignored taxes and variations in interest costs as the leverage ratios of the firms changed. We will take them explicitly into account for the Medtronics Company now. All of the facts are assumed to be the same as in Problem 26-1 except that instead of the profit ratio to sales being 6 percent after taxes, it is now 12 percent before taxes. We define profits in terms of net operating income before taxes. Interest on notes payable is assumed to be 10 percent. The applicable corporate tax rate is 40 percent. The par value of the capital stock is $1. The dividend policy of Medtronics is to have a zero payout.

a. Show for Medtronics its balance sheets and income statements for the two periods involved.

b. Recalculate ratios 1 to 6 and also show earnings per share for the two periods for Medtronics.

c. Compare the results with Problem 26-1.

Solution:

a.

Balance Sheet—Medtronics Company (in thousands of dollars)

	Year 1	Year 2
Current assets (30%)	$150	$300
Fixed assets (20%)	100	200
Total assets	$250	$500
Accounts payable (10%)	50	100
Notes payable	20	127
Other accruals (5%)	25	50
Current liabilities	95	277
Common stock (par $1)	100	100
Retained earnings	55	123
Net worth	155	223
Total claims	$250	$500

Income Statement—Medtronics Company (in thousands of dollars)

	Year 1	Year 2
Sales	$500	$1,000.00
Net operating income†(12%)	60	120.00
Interest††(10%)	2	7.35
Profit before taxes	58	112.65
Taxes at 40%	23	45.06
Profit after taxes	$ 35	$ 67.59
Earnings per share	$ 0.35	$ 0.68
Dividends	$ 0	$ 0

†Percent of sales.
††On previous year-end notes payable plus one-half (the average) the increase
in notes payable after the first year. Interest for Year 2 is thus computed as
$(.10)[($20) + 1/2($127 − $20)] = 7.35. This is simply the interest on the average
amount of notes payable outstanding for the year.

The key to completing the balance sheet and income statement of
Medtronics for Year 2 is to solve for the amount of increase in notes
payable. This gives the value of the interest expense needed to determine
net income for the year which is in turn added to retained earnings on
the balance sheet. An exact formulation to obtain the amount of increase in notes payable for the problem is given below:

$$.5\Delta S - .15\Delta S = \left[.12S - .10(NP_{t-1} + \frac{\Delta NP}{2}) \right] (1 - t) + \Delta NP$$

where ΔS = change in sales
ΔNP = amount of increase in notes payable
NP_{t-1} = amount of notes payable in the previous period

The logic of the formulation simply rests on the basic accounting equation: Assets = Liabilities + Net Worth. A statement of the formulation
goes as follows:

A 50 percent spontaneous increase in sales representing the
total value of the increase in total assets (assumed as 30 percent
for current assets and 20 percent for fixed assets) less a 15 percent
increase due to accounts payable and other accruals equals the
after-tax net profit plus the amount of increase in notes payable.

The after-tax net profit consists of the 12 percent pre-tax profit margin on sales less the 10 percent interest expense on average notes payable
outstanding. Also, both sales and notes payable of the previous period
are known variables, so that the only unknown left is the increase in
notes payable (ΔNP),

The earnings per share (EPS) value is calculated by dividing profit after taxes by the number of common shares outstanding. The $1 par value on common stock of $100,000 gives 100,000 shares. The result is an EPS of $0.35 and $0.68 for the two periods respectively.

b.

Medtronics Company

	Year 1	Year 2
1. Current ratio	1.6x	1.1x
2. Debt ratio	61%	124%
3. Sales to total assets	2x	2x
4. Sales to net worth	3.23x	4.48x
5. Net income to sales	7%	6.8%
6. Net income to net worth	22.6%	30.5%
7. EPS	$0.35	$0.68

c. The financial ratios calculated here are based on our modified assumptions which include the effect of taxes and interest cost on the company.

First it should be noted that the Year 1 profit ratio (after tax) of the firm increases slightly from 6 percent in Problem 26-1 to about 7 percent here because of our assumption of a 40-percent tax rate on a 12-percent before-tax profit margin. The higher initial profitability of the firm results in a lesser need for debt financing. Consequently, Medtronics' debt ratio rose to 124 percent in Year 2 versus 133 percent for Problem 26-1. Sales to total assets remain unaffected. However, with a smaller need for debt, sales to net worth can be expected to increase but not as much as in Problem 26-1. The sales to net worth increases to 4.48x versus 4.65x in Problem 26-1. Although sales to net worth did not increase as much, the increase in after-tax profit on sales was more than enough to result in a higher net income to net worth for both periods. Thus, net income to net worth rose from 22.6 percent to 30.5 percent compared to 19 percent and 28 percent in Problem 26-1.

26-3. Starting with the situation as of the end of Problem 26-2, we observe that Medtronics had a very high debt ratio, all in current debt. Let us assume that in order to sustain such a high debt ratio, Medtronics finds that it cannot obtain short-term debt financing so is forced to do long-term debt financing. Medtronics sells $100,000 of convertible debentures paying an interest rate of 5 percent and convertible into common stock at a common stock price of $12.50. Assume that total assets remain unchanged for Year 2 and that notes payable account for the difference.

a. Present the balance sheet showing the shift from notes payable to the convertible debentures. Next assume that all of the debentures are converted into common stock and present the new balance sheet in period 2 after conversion takes place.

b. Present the income statement for Medtronics before and after the conversion of the debentures.

c. Recalculate the previous seven financial ratios for Medtronics adding an eighth ratio, the market value of its common stock assuming a multiplier of 15.

Solution:

a.

Balance Sheet—Medtronics Company (in thousands of dollars)

| | Year 2 | |
	Before Conversion	After Conversion
Current assets (30%)	$300	$300
Fixed assets (20%)	200	200
Total assets	500	500
Accounts payable (10%)	100	100
Notes payable	27	27
Other accruals (5%)	50	50
Current liabilities	177	177
Convertible debentures	100	—
Common stock (par $1)	100	108
Paid-in capital	—	92
Retained earnings	123	123
Net worth	$223	$323
Total claims	500	500

In the balance sheet before conversion, notes payable are reduced by $100,000 and convertible debentures are increased by $100,000.

In the balance sheet after conversion the $100,000 of convertible debentures becomes common stock and paid-in-capital. A $1,000 debenture convertible at $12.50 is convertible into $1,000/$12.50 equals 80 shares of common stock. This results in an addition of $8,000 (80 shares times 100 convertible debentures times $1 par value) to the common stock and $92,000 ($100,000 minus $8,000) to paid-in-capital.

b. Income Statement—Medtronics Company (in thousands of dollars)

		Year 2	
		Before Conversion	After Conversion
Sales		$1,000	
Net operating income		120	120
Interest†:			
Notes payable (10%)	2.35		2.35
Debentures (5%)	2.50	4.85 —	2.35
Profit before taxes		115.15	117.65
Taxes at 40%		46.06	47.06
Profit after taxes		69.09	70.59
Number of shares of common			
stock (in thousands)		100	108
Earnings per share		$ 0.69	$ 0.65

†Calculated as $.10 \ [\frac{20 + 27}{2}] + .05 \ [\frac{0 + 100}{2}] = .10(23.5) + .05(50) =$ $4.85 before conversion and likewise after conversion.

As compared with the income statement in the previous problem, the amount of interest is reduced from $7,350 to $4,850. This results from the lower rate of interest on the debentures as compared with the straight short-term debt in the form of notes payable. Since their debentures provide the holder with a claim on a possible increase in the market price of common stock, the interest rate that is required to be paid is reduced. Earnings per share as a consequence rise slightly to $0.69 per share.

After conversion of the debentures, interest cost falls to $2,350 because of the elimination of the debenture interest. However, the number of shares of common stock increases by 8,000. Hence, earnings per share are "diluted" by the conversion and fall to $0.65.

c.

	Before Conversion	After Conversion
1. Current ratio	1.7x	1.7x
2. Debt ratio	124%	54.8%
3. Sales to total assets	2x	2x
4. Sales to net worth	4.48x	3.1x
5. Net income to sales	6.9%	7.1%
6. Net income to net worth	31%	21.9%
7. Earnings per share	$0.69	$0.65
8. Market price of stock @15	$10.35	$9.75

The financial ratios are based on the balance sheet and income statements before and after conversion respectively. As a consequence of shifting $100,000 of notes payable, a form of short-term debt, into convertible debentures, a form of long-term debt, current liabilities are reduced to $177,000. Hence, the current ratio is greatly improved from 1.1 in the previous problem to 1.7. All of the other ratios remain about the same. The new item, line 8, the market price of stock, is $10.35.

The conversion of the debentures into common stock greatly reduces the total debt ratio. Hence, after conversion, the current ratio remains high, the debt ratio as measured by the ratio of debt to net worth drops from 124 percent to 54.8 percent, representing a substantial improvement. Because net worth is increased, the sales to net worth ratio drops. The increase in net worth causes the net income to net worth ratio to drop also from 31 percent to 22 percent. With the increased number of shares, the earnings per share drop slightly to $0.65. After conversion, therefore, other things being equal, the market price of the stock would also drop slightly if the multiplier remained the same. However, the financial ratios have been greatly strengthened by replacing short-term notes payable with convertible long-term debt that is converted into net worth.

26-4. Janet Lindholm decided to leave school to open a shop that specializes in indoor potted green plants. Janet had received an allowance from her parents for some years and was able to save a little over $1,000. After making some inquiries Janet recognized that she must consider such things as location, potential flow of customer traffic, and present and potential competition. Also, she realized that she must analyze the alternatives to buying a building or renting a store and buying or renting the equipment and fixtures she will need—counters, shelving, cash register, and the like. The store space she had in mind had not been occupied by a greenery shop before, so it lacked shelves and counters.

a. Should Janet buy or rent the store facilities?

b. How should Janet acquire the equipment and fixtures?

c. What kinds of questions is she likely to face with regard to choice of product line?

d. For planning purposes, assume sales per day of $100, $500, and $800, and a "normal" profit ratio of net income after taxes to sales of 5 percent. What are her earnings per hour before taxes, assuming that she works 10 hours per day, 7 days a week, for 50 weeks per year?

e. With a sales to net worth ratio of 20 times, what investment on her part is indicated at each level of sales? Comment on how she may raise the funds to reach the various likely levels of sales, and also comment upon the implications of her taking withdrawals from the business.

f. What additional questions must Janet face if she sells on credit?

g. What problems are likely to be faced if sales start at $800 per day?

Solution:

a. Janet Lindholm should rent the store facilities. This will minimize her investment requirements and minimize her risks.

b. Janet should check around at used furniture and used equipment fixture stores to buy or rent used equipment to the extent possible. In addition, for some of the shelving she could try a wrecking company where used lumber may be available. After buying the used lumber, she, with the help of some friends, could build shelves and build some reasonable counters which they could then paint. All of this is to minimize her investment requirements.

c. A fundamental question is how broad a merchandise line she should carry. What kind of indoor potted green plants should she carry? Should she sell roses and other types of flowers at all? What other related materials and accessories such as seedlings, fertilizers, and gardening tools should she consider? In addition, she has to determine where to get her supply of plants and/or fresh flowers. Or should she just buy the seedlings and pots and grow them herself? She also has to determine how to keep the plants and the flowers in top condition in the shop. These questions indicate that, even in a relatively simple retail trade operation, some broader experience than her own personal purchase experience is required.

d.

	Sales Daily		
	$100	$500	$800
(1) Sales annually (daily x 7 days a week x 50 weeks)	$35,000	$175,000	$280,000
(2) Before tax profits (5%)	$ 1,750	$ 8,750	$ 14,000
(3) Earnings per hour at 10 hours per day [(line 2) ÷ 3,500 hours]	$ .50	$ 2.50	$ 4.00

It will be observed from the above that Janet's earnings per hour after taxes will be very low until she reaches a very large level of sales per day. This indicates the importance of very close control over·costs if she is to realize something approximating even a minimum wage for the two lower likely levels of volume.

e.

	$100	$500	$800
Sales	$35,000	$175,000	$280,000
Indicated "worth" requirement (sales ÷ 20)	$ 1,750	$ 8,750	$ 14,000

As can be seen from the above, even a level of sales that would result in before-tax earnings of only $.50 an hour would require an indicated investment on her part of $1,750. Although she possesses only slightly over $1,000, which is barely sufficient for even the lowest indicated level of sales, she could initially maximize the use of her funds by slowing down payment of her bills. Obviously, she should keep her withdrawals from the business to a minimum as the growing business needs as much funds as she can leave in it.

f. If the greenery shop sells on credit, a number of additional questions will arise. How will she evaluate the credit-worthiness of her customers? Some small shops have a policy that they will not extend credit except to regular customers who have established a good credit record with the shop. In addition, sometimes higher prices are charged to customers who buy on credit. Janet will also have to consider how she will make collections if people buy on credit and then do not pay. This is important as she could lose not only the receivables but also sales if the customer decides to buy elsewhere to avoid the embarrassment of being "dunned" into paying the outstanding bill.

g. If sales should reach as much as $800 per day, which is indicative of a fairly substantial business operation, it will then be very important that Janet develop sufficient accounting records to know how she is utilizing the funds. With this volume it may be necessary for her to have one or two part-time helpers for the peak hours. She will then have to maintain control over the cash register and guard against pilferage both by her customers and her part-time employees.

Another important problem that Janet may face is that with a cash flow of around $800 a day, she may get a sense of affluence. Yet she will be lucky if she is making $4.00 per hour; hence, she must refrain from purchasing heavily for herself and from making loans and gifts to friends at this point. The growing business will require all the funds she can leave in the business since the indicated net worth requirement is almost $14,000.

Appendix
Compound Interest Tables

27

Table A-1. Compound sum of $1 (CVIF)

$$S_n = P(1 + r)^n$$

Year	1%	2%	3%	4%	5%	6%	7%	8%	9%	10%	11%	12%	13%	14%	15%	16%
1	1.010	1.020	1.030	1.040	1.050	1.060	1.070	1.080	1.090	1.100	1.110	1.120	1.130	1.140	1.150	1.160
2	1.020	1.040	1.061	1.082	1.102	1.124	1.145	1.166	1.188	1.210	1.232	1.254	1.277	1.300	1.322	1.346
3	1.030	1.061	1.093	1.125	1.158	1.191	1.225	1.260	1.295	1.331	1.368	1.405	1.443	1.482	1.521	1.561
4	1.041	1.082	1.126	1.170	1.216	1.262	1.311	1.360	1.412	1.464	1.518	1.574	1.631	1.689	1.749	1.811
5	1.051	1.104	1.159	1.217	1.276	1.338	1.403	1.469	1.539	1.611	1.685	1.762	1.842	1.925	2.011	2.100
6	1.062	1.126	1.194	1.265	1.340	1.419	1.501	1.587	1.677	1.772	1.870	1.974	2.082	2.195	2.313	2.436
7	1.072	1.149	1.230	1.316	1.407	1.504	1.606	1.714	1.828	1.949	2.076	2.211	2.353	2.502	2.660	2.826
8	1.083	1.172	1.267	1.369	1.477	1.594	1.718	1.851	1.993	2.144	2.305	2.476	2.658	2.853	3.059	3.278
9	1.094	1.195	1.305	1.423	1.551	1.689	1.838	1.999	2.172	2.358	2.558	2.773	3.004	3.252	3.518	3.803
10	1.105	1.219	1.344	1.480	1.629	1.791	1.967	2.159	2.367	2.594	2.839	3.106	3.395	3.707	4.046	4.411
11	1.116	1.243	1.384	1.539	1.710	1.898	2.105	2.332	2.580	2.853	3.152	3.479	3.836	4.226	4.652	5.117
12	1.127	1.268	1.246	1.601	1.796	2.012	2.252	2.518	2.813	3.138	3.499	3.896	4.335	4.818	5.350	5.936
13	1.138	1.294	1.469	1.665	1.886	2.133	2.410	2.720	3.066	3.452	3.883	4.363	4.898	5.492	6.153	6.886
14	1.149	1.319	1.513	1.732	1.980	2.261	2.579	2.937	3.342	3.797	4.310	4.887	5.535	6.261	7.076	7.988
15	1.161	1.346	1.558	1.801	2.079	2.397	2.759	3.172	3.642	4.177	4.785	5.474	6.254	7.138	8.137	9.266
16	1.173	1.373	1.605	1.873	2.183	2.540	2.952	3.426	3.970	4.595	5.311	6.130	7.067	8.137	9.358	10.748
17	1.184	1.400	1.653	1.948	2.292	2.693	3.159	3.700	4.328	5.054	5.895	6.866	7.986	9.276	10.761	12.468
18	1.196	1.428	1.702	2.026	2.407	2.854	3.380	3.996	4.717	5.560	6.544	7.690	9.024	10.575	12.375	14.463
19	1.208	1.457	1.754	2.107	2.527	3.026	3.617	4.316	5.142	6.116	7.263	8.613	10.197	12.056	14.232	16.777
20	1.220	1.486	1.806	2.191	2.653	3.207	3.870	4.661	5.604	6.728	8.062	9.646	11.523	13.743	16.367	19.461

Table A-2. Present value of $1 (PVIF)

$$P = S_n(1+r)^{-n}$$

Years Hence	1%	2%	4%	6%	8%	10%	12%	14%	15%	16%	18%	20%	22%	24%	25%	26%	28%	30%	35%	40%	45%	50%
1	0.990	0.980	0.962	0.943	0.926	0.909	0.893	0.877	0.870	0.862	0.847	0.833	0.820	0.806	0.800	0.794	0.781	0.769	0.741	0.714	0.690	0.667
2	0.980	0.961	0.925	0.890	0.857	0.826	0.797	0.769	0.756	0.743	0.718	0.694	0.672	0.650	0.640	0.630	0.610	0.592	0.549	0.510	0.476	0.444
3	0.971	0.942	0.889	0.840	0.794	0.751	0.712	0.675	0.658	0.641	0.609	0.579	0.551	0.524	0.512	0.500	0.477	0.455	0.406	0.364	0.328	0.296
4	0.961	0.924	0.855	0.792	0.735	0.683	0.636	0.592	0.572	0.552	0.516	0.482	0.451	0.423	0.410	0.397	0.373	0.350	0.301	0.260	0.226	0.198
5	0.951	0.906	0.822	0.747	0.681	0.621	0.567	0.519	0.497	0.476	0.437	0.402	0.370	0.341	0.328	0.315	0.291	0.269	0.223	0.186	0.156	0.132
6	0.942	0.888	0.790	0.705	0.630	0.564	0.507	0.456	0.432	0.410	0.370	0.335	0.303	0.275	0.262	0.250	0.227	0.207	0.165	0.133	0.108	0.088
7	0.933	0.871	0.760	0.665	0.583	0.513	0.452	0.400	0.376	0.354	0.314	0.279	0.249	0.222	0.210	0.198	0.178	0.159	0.122	0.095	0.074	0.059
8	0.923	0.853	0.731	0.627	0.540	0.467	0.404	0.351	0.327	0.305	0.266	0.233	0.204	0.179	0.168	0.157	0.139	0.123	0.091	0.068	0.051	0.039
9	0.914	0.837	0.703	0.592	0.500	0.424	0.361	0.308	0.284	0.263	0.225	0.194	0.167	0.144	0.134	0.125	0.108	0.094	0.067	0.048	0.035	0.026
10	0.905	0.820	0.676	0.558	0.463	0.386	0.322	0.270	0.247	0.227	0.191	0.162	0.137	0.116	0.107	0.099	0.085	0.073	0.050	0.035	0.024	0.017
11	0.896	0.804	0.650	0.527	0.429	0.350	0.287	0.237	0.215	0.195	0.162	0.135	0.112	0.094	0.086	0.079	0.066	0.056	0.037	0.025	0.017	0.012
12	0.887	0.788	0.625	0.497	0.397	0.319	0.257	0.208	0.187	0.168	0.137	0.112	0.092	0.076	0.069	0.062	0.052	0.043	0.027	0.018	0.012	0.008
13	0.879	0.773	0.601	0.469	0.368	0.290	0.229	0.182	0.163	0.145	0.116	0.093	0.075	0.061	0.055	0.050	0.040	0.033	0.020	0.013	0.008	0.005
14	0.870	0.758	0.577	0.442	0.340	0.263	0.205	0.160	0.141	0.125	0.099	0.078	0.062	0.049	0.044	0.039	0.032	0.025	0.015	0.009	0.006	0.003
15	0.861	0.743	0.555	0.417	0.315	0.239	0.183	0.140	0.123	0.108	0.084	0.065	0.051	0.040	0.035	0.031	0.025	0.020	0.011	0.006	0.004	0.002
16	0.853	0.728	0.534	0.394	0.292	0.218	0.163	0.123	0.107	0.093	0.071	0.054	0.042	0.032	0.028	0.025	0.019	0.015	0.008	0.005	0.003	0.002
17	0.844	0.714	0.513	0.371	0.270	0.198	0.146	0.108	0.093	0.080	0.060	0.045	0.034	0.026	0.023	0.020	0.015	0.012	0.006	0.003	0.002	0.001
18	0.836	0.700	0.494	0.350	0.250	0.180	0.130	0.095	0.081	0.069	0.051	0.038	0.028	0.021	0.018	0.016	0.012	0.009	0.005	0.002	0.001	0.001
19	0.828	0.686	0.475	0.331	0.232	0.164	0.116	0.083	0.070	0.060	0.043	0.031	0.023	0.017	0.014	0.012	0.009	0.007	0.003	0.002	0.001	
20	0.820	0.673	0.456	0.312	0.215	0.149	0.104	0.073	0.061	0.051	0.037	0.026	0.019	0.014	0.012	0.010	0.007	0.005	0.002	0.001	0.001	
21	0.811	0.660	0.439	0.294	0.199	0.135	0.093	0.064	0.053	0.044	0.031	0.022	0.015	0.011	0.009	0.008	0.006	0.004	0.002	0.001		
22	0.803	0.647	0.422	0.278	0.184	0.123	0.083	0.056	0.046	0.038	0.026	0.018	0.013	0.009	0.007	0.006	0.004	0.003	0.001	0.001		
23	0.795	0.634	0.406	0.262	0.170	0.112	0.074	0.049	0.040	0.033	0.022	0.015	0.010	0.007	0.006	0.005	0.003	0.002	0.001			
24	0.788	0.622	0.390	0.247	0.158	0.102	0.066	0.043	0.035	0.028	0.019	0.013	0.008	0.005	0.005	0.004	0.003	0.002	0.001			
25	0.780	0.610	0.375	0.233	0.146	0.092	0.059	0.038	0.030	0.024	0.016	0.010	0.007	0.004	0.004	0.003	0.002	0.001	0.001			
26	0.772	0.598	0.361	0.220	0.135	0.084	0.053	0.033	0.026	0.021	0.014	0.009	0.006	0.004	0.003	0.002	0.002	0.001				
27	0.764	0.586	0.347	0.207	0.125	0.076	0.047	0.029	0.023	0.018	0.011	0.007	0.005	0.003	0.002	0.002	0.001	0.001				
28	0.757	0.574	0.333	0.196	0.116	0.069	0.042	0.026	0.020	0.016	0.010	0.006	0.004	0.002	0.002	0.002	0.001	0.001				
29	0.749	0.563	0.321	0.185	0.107	0.063	0.037	0.022	0.017	0.014	0.008	0.005	0.003	0.002	0.002	0.001	0.001	0.001				
30	0.742	0.552	0.308	0.174	0.099	0.057	0.033	0.020	0.015	0.012	0.007	0.004	0.003	0.002	0.001	0.001	0.001	0.001				
40	0.672	0.453	0.208	0.097	0.046	0.022	0.011	0.005	0.004	0.003	0.001	0.001										
50	0.608	0.372	0.141	0.054	0.021	0.0091	0.003	0.001	0.001	0.001												

Table A-3. Sum of an annuity for $1 for n years (CVIF$_a$)

$$S_{n,r} = \$1\left[\frac{(1+r)^n - 1}{r}\right] = \$1C_{n,r}$$

Year	1%	2%	3%	4%	5%	6%	7%	8%	9%	10%	11%	12%	13%	14%	15%	16%
1	1.000	1.000	1.000	1.000	1.000	1.000	1.000	1.000	1.000	1.000	1.000	1.000	1.000	1.000	1.000	1.000
2	2.010	2.020	2.030	2.040	2.050	2.060	2.070	2.080	2.090	2.100	2.110	2.120	2.130	2.140	2.150	2.160
3	3.030	3.060	3.091	3.122	3.152	3.184	3.215	3.246	3.278	3.310	3.342	3.374	3.407	3.440	3.473	3.506
4	4.060	4.122	4.184	4.246	4.310	4.375	4.440	4.506	4.573	4.641	4.710	4.779	4.850	4.921	4.993	5.066
5	5.010	5.204	5.309	5.416	5.526	5.637	5.751	5.867	5.985	6.105	6.228	6.353	6.480	6.610	6.742	6.877
6	6.152	6.308	6.468	6.633	6.802	6.975	7.153	7.336	7.523	7.716	7.913	8.115	8.323	8.536	8.754	8.977
7	7.214	7.434	7.662	7.898	8.142	8.384	8.654	8.923	9.200	9.487	9.783	10.089	10.405	10.730	11.067	11.414
8	8.286	8.583	8.892	9.214	9.549	9.897	10.260	10.637	11.028	11.436	11.859	12.300	12.757	13.233	13.727	14.240
9	9.369	9.755	10.159	10.583	11.027	11.491	11.978	12.488	13.021	13.579	14.164	14.776	15.416	16.085	16.786	17.518
10	10.462	10.950	11.464	12.006	12.578	13.181	13.816	14.487	15.193	15.937	16.722	17.549	18.420	19.337	20.304	21.321
11	11.567	12.169	12.808	13.486	14.207	14.972	15.784	16.645	17.560	18.531	19.561	20.655	21.814	23.044	24.349	25.733
12	12.683	13.412	14.192	15.026	15.917	16.870	17.888	18.977	20.141	21.384	22.713	24.133	25.650	27.271	29.002	30.850
13	13.809	14.860	15.618	16.627	17.713	18.882	20.141	21.495	22.953	24.523	26.212	28.029	29.985	32.089	34.352	36.786
14	14.947	15.974	17.086	18.292	19.599	21.051	22.550	24.215	26.019	27.975	30.095	32.393	34.883	37.581	40.505	43.672
15	16.097	17.293	18.599	20.024	21.579	23.276	25.129	27.152	29.361	31.772	34.405	37.280	40.417	43.842	47.580	51.659

APPENDIX—COMPOUND INTEREST TABLES

Table A-4. Present value of $1 received annually (PVIF$_a$)

$$A_{n,r} = \$1\left[\frac{1-(1+r)^{-n}}{r}\right] = \$1\,P_{n,r}$$

Periods to Be Paid	1%	2%	2½%	3%	4%	5%	6%	8%	10%	12%	14%	15%	16%	18%	20%	22%	24%	25%	26%	30%	40%	50%
1	0.990	0.980	0.976	0.971	0.962	0.952	0.943	0.926	0.909	0.893	0.877	0.870	0.862	0.847	0.833	0.820	0.806	0.800	0.794	0.769	0.714	0.667
2	1.970	1.942	1.927	1.914	1.886	1.859	1.833	1.783	1.736	1.690	1.647	1.626	1.605	1.566	1.528	1.492	1.457	1.440	1.424	1.361	1.224	1.111
3	2.941	2.884	2.856	2.829	2.775	2.723	2.673	2.577	2.487	2.402	2.322	2.283	2.246	2.174	2.106	2.042	1.981	1.952	1.923	1.816	1.589	1.407
4	3.902	3.808	3.762	3.717	3.630	3.546	3.465	3.312	3.170	3.037	2.914	2.855	2.798	2.690	2.589	2.494	2.404	2.362	2.320	2.166	1.849	1.605
5	4.853	4.713	4.646	4.580	4.452	4.330	4.212	3.993	3.791	3.605	3.433	3.352	3.274	3.127	2.991	2.864	2.745	2.689	2.635	2.436	2.035	1.737
6	5.795	5.601	5.508	5.417	5.242	5.076	4.917	4.623	4.355	4.111	3.889	3.784	3.685	3.498	3.326	3.167	3.020	2.951	2.885	2.643	2.168	1.824
7	6.728	6.472	6.349	6.230	6.002	5.786	5.582	5.206	4.868	4.564	4.288	4.160	4.039	3.812	3.605	3.416	3.242	3.161	3.083	2.802	2.263	1.883
8	7.652	7.325	7.170	7.020	6.733	6.463	6.210	5.747	5.335	4.968	4.639	4.487	4.344	4.078	3.837	3.619	3.421	3.329	3.241	2.925	2.331	1.922
9	8.566	8.162	7.971	7.786	7.435	7.108	6.802	6.247	5.759	5.328	4.946	4.772	4.607	4.303	4.031	3.786	3.566	3.463	3.366	3.019	2.379	1.948
10	9.471	8.983	8.752	8.530	8.111	7.722	7.360	6.710	6.145	5.650	5.216	5.019	4.833	4.494	4.192	3.923	3.682	3.571	3.465	3.092	2.414	1.965
11	10.368	9.787	9.514	9.253	8.760	8.306	7.887	7.139	6.495	5.938	5.453	5.234	5.029	4.656	4.327	4.035	3.776	3.656	3.544	3.147	2.438	1.977
12	11.255	10.575	10.258	9.954	9.385	8.863	8.384	7.536	6.814	6.194	5.660	5.421	5.197	4.793	4.439	4.127	3.851	3.725	3.606	3.190	2.456	1.985
13	12.134	11.348	10.983	10.635	9.986	9.394	8.853	7.904	7.103	6.424	5.842	5.583	5.342	4.901	4.533	4.203	3.912	3.780	3.656	3.223	2.468	1.990
14	13.004	12.106	11.691	11.296	10.563	9.899	9.295	8.244	7.367	6.628	6.002	5.724	5.468	5.008	4.611	4.265	3.962	3.824	3.695	3.249	2.478	1.993
15	13.865	12.849	12.381	11.938	11.118	10.380	9.712	8.559	7.606	6.811	6.142	5.847	5.576	5.092	4.676	4.315	4.001	3.859	3.726	3.268	2.484	1.995
16	14.718	13.578	13.055	12.561	11.652	10.838	10.106	8.851	7.824	6.974	6.265	5.954	5.668	5.162	4.730	4.357	4.033	3.887	3.751	3.283	2.488	1.997
17	15.562	14.292	13.712	13.166	12.166	11.274	10.477	9.122	8.022	7.120	6.373	6.047	5.749	5.222	4.775	4.391	4.059	3.910	3.771	3.295	2.492	1.998
18	16.398	14.992	14.353	13.754	12.659	11.690	10.828	9.372	8.201	7.250	6.467	6.128	5.818	5.273	4.812	4.419	4.080	3.928	3.786	3.304	2.494	1.999
19	17.226	15.678	14.979	14.324	13.134	12.085	11.158	9.604	8.365	7.366	6.550	6.198	5.878	5.316	4.844	4.442	4.097	3.942	3.799	3.311	2.496	1.999
20	18.046	16.351	15.589	14.877	13.590	12.462	11.470	9.818	8.514	7.469	6.623	6.259	5.929	5.353	4.870	4.460	4.110	3.954	3.808	3.316	2.497	1.999
21	18.857	17.011	16.185	15.415	14.029	12.821	11.764	10.017	8.649	7.562	6.687	6.312	5.973	5.384	4.891	4.476	4.121	3.963	3.816	3.320	2.498	2.000
22	19.660	17.658	16.765	15.937	14.451	13.163	12.042	10.201	8.772	7.645	6.743	6.359	6.011	5.410	4.909	4.488	4.130	3.970	3.822	3.323	2.498	2.000
23	20.456	18.292	17.332	16.444	14.857	13.489	12.303	10.371	8.883	7.718	6.792	6.399	6.044	5.432	4.924	4.499	4.137	3.976	3.827	3.325	2.499	2.000
24	21.243	18.914	17.885	16.936	15.247	13.799	12.550	10.529	8.985	7.784	6.835	6.434	6.073	5.451	4.937	4.507	4.143	3.981	3.831	3.327	2.499	2.000
25	22.023	19.523	18.424	17.413	15.622	14.094	12.783	10.675	9.077	7.843	6.873	6.464	6.097	5.467	4.948	4.514	4.147	3.985	3.834	3.329	2.499	2.000
26	22.795	20.121	18.951	17.877	15.983	14.375	13.003	10.810	9.161	7.896	6.906	6.491	6.118	5.480	4.956	4.520	4.151	3.988	3.837	3.330	2.500	2.000
27	23.560	20.707	19.464	18.327	16.330	14.643	13.211	10.935	9.237	7.943	6.935	6.514	6.136	5.492	4.964	4.524	4.154	3.990	3.839	3.331	2.500	2.000
28	24.316	21.281	19.965	18.764	16.663	14.898	13.406	11.051	9.307	7.984	6.961	6.534	6.152	5.502	4.970	4.528	4.157	3.992	3.840	3.331	2.500	2.000
29	25.066	21.844	20.454	19.188	16.984	15.141	13.591	11.158	9.370	8.022	6.983	6.551	6.166	5.510	4.975	4.531	4.159	3.994	3.841	3.332	2.500	2.000
30	25.808	22.396	20.930	19.600	17.292	15.372	13.765	11.258	9.427	8.055	7.003	6.566	6.177	5.517	4.979	4.534	4.160	3.995	3.842	3.332	2.500	2.000
40	32.835	27.355	25.103	23.115	19.793	17.159	15.046	11.925	9.779	8.244	7.105	6.642	6.234	5.548	4.997	4.544	4.166	3.999	3.846	3.333	2.500	2.000
50	39.196	31.424	28.362	25.730	21.482	18.256	15.762	12.333	9.915	8.304	7.133	6.660	6.246	5.554	4.999	4.545	4.167	4.000	3.846	3.333	2.500	2.000